The Russians
& Their Favorite Books

Klaus Mehnert

& The Russians
Their Favorite Books

Hoover Institution Press
Stanford University, Stanford, California

Hoover Press Publication 282
Copyright 1983 Deutsche Verlags-Anstalt GmbH, Stuttgart
All rights reserved. No part of this publication may be reproduced, stored in a retrieval system, or transmitted in any form or by any means, electronic, mechanical, photocopying, recording, or otherwise, without written permission of the publisher.
First printing, 1983
Manufactured in the United States of America
87 86 85 84 83   9 8 7 6 5 4 3 2 1

Library of Congress Cataloging in Publication Data
Mehnert, Klaus, 1906–
    The Russians & their favorite books.

    Includes index.
    1. Books and reading—Soviet Union. 2. Popular literature—Soviet Union. 3. Russian fiction—20th century—Stories, plots, etc. 4. Authors, Russian—20th century—Biography.
I. Title. II. Title: Russians and their favorite books.
Z1003.5.S62M43 1983   028′.9′0947   83-6108
ISBN 0-8179-7821-6

Design by P. Kelley Baker

Contents

List of Tables

Acknowledgments

My first thanks go to those persons without whose assistance this study could not have been undertaken: to the countless, often anonymous, Russians who allowed me to pester them with questions whenever I had a chance to do so, to those of the 24 writers who generously agreed to meet with me and talk about their work, and to the librarians and bookstore employees who gave me the benefit of their expert knowledge of what the Russians like to read.

Special thanks go to the staff of the Lenin Library in Moscow, the country's largest. Anyone who has entered this huge institution through its main entrance near the west wall of the Kremlin and has seen the many people waiting in line to check their coats must wonder how he would ever be able to work there. But a large, quiet reading room is set aside for foreign scholars and their Russian colleagues, and the service is courteous and efficient. Any book available to the public is quickly brought by friendly library assistants.

Sincere thanks are due to those who contributed their personal efforts to this volume: Anneliese Bonfert, my secretary and assistant for both the German and the English editions; Jane Hedges, the excellent and conscientious editor of the English edition; her husband, Mark Steinberg, who read and reviewed the manuscript; and John Paasche for his helpful advice.

During several months in both 1981 and 1982, I enjoyed the hospitality of the Hoover Institution and the cooperation of its fine staff, including, among many others, associate director and chairman of the Publications Committee Richard T. Burress, archivist and senior fellow Milorad M. Drachkovitch, publications manager Phyllis M. Cairns, director of marketing David L. Fleenor, and head of readers' services David W. Heron. But while I thank all of them, the responsibility for the book is entirely mine.

Introduction

Thousands of specialists throughout the world study the Soviet Union from every conceivable angle and for good reason: the policies of the USSR are among the main factors that will determine mankind's future. Yet we know but little about the Soviet leaders. Can we know more about the Russian people?

For decades the people of the USSR, more precisely the ethnic Russians, have interested me. Much has been written about their character. But without the help of public opinion polls, how does one learn about their mood now, in the 1980s, at a time of serious world tension?

Remembering the old saying, "By knowing what you read, I know what you are," I set out to study the books Russians read. Among Russians today, as among people of all times, fiction is read for entertainment, a word not intended to be pejorative, for fiction includes *Anna Karenina* as well as *The Three Musketeers*. The desire for entertainment is universal, and for the Russians it has always been linked with reading and still is despite the growing role of television. As a result, their reading preferences reveal more about their attitudes than they would in many other Western countries where reading occupies a smaller portion of leisure time.

Best-seller lists are not available in the USSR, and they would not be of much use anyway, for the problem there is not selling books but getting them: the chapter "Too Many Russians Chasing Too Few Books" will make this abundantly clear. In the West, according to the law of supply and demand, the publisher, a businessman, will print as many copies as he can sell. Therefore, sales, as a rule, correspond to the demand, which is in turn, reflected in the best-seller lists. But in the USSR, where political decisions are involved in the allotment of paper as well as in the size of print runs and editions, there is no calculable relationship between the number of books sold and the number of books desired by the readers. Hence I have searched for the "most wanted" or "most popular" books, not for the best-sellers.

"We do not know much of Soviet readers' inclinations," wrote Ronald Hingley in his recent *Russian Writers and Soviet Society* (London, 1979). The book is, as far as I know, the first Western attempt to find out something about these inclinations, to learn about the books *demanded* by Russian readers (instead of those *offered* to them) in order to explore their present attitudes and moods. Rather than ask Soviet publishers and editors—"What do you print?"—I questioned the readers—"What do you want to read?"

What guarantee is there that the Russian respondents did not just rattle off the titles of books they had never read in order to make a good impression on the foreign questioner? This is always a possibility, of course. But whenever time allowed, and it usually did, I discussed the books they mentioned with them, alluding to characters or events described or asking for a brief summary of the plot when I was unfamiliar with the work.

This book deals exclusively with the fiction Russian adults read. The word "Russian" is used in the narrow ethnic sense to denote the group that comprises roughly one-half of the population of the USSR and provides most of its leaders, today as in the days of the tsars. Just like the Russians, I, too, enjoy Russian poetry, especially that which deals with the Russian landscape and its moods, and am an avid theater fan. (During fourteen evenings in Moscow in 1981, I spent ten attending performances of Soviet dramas.) A study of Russians' reactions to the most popular dramas and poems would certainly add some facets to the picture presented here, but it would hardly enlarge it enough to justify such an expansion of the book's scope. Moreover, it is difficult to convey the flavor of poetry adequately through summaries. The reactions Russian youth have to books written especially for them were not considered either; this is a separate subject that merits a study of its own, preferably by a young scholar.

The reader will look in vain in this work for the names of authors who are "dissidents" or for titles published in the *samizdat* underground press. The dissidents cannot be considered among the most popular authors because their works are not available to the average Russian, not even in libraries.

Having spent my childhood in old Russia and frequently stayed in the USSR since then, I have always felt a warm sympathy for the Russian people, though throughout I have been highly critical of the Soviet system. But I started this study with an open mind, without preconceived ideas and without intending to prove anything. My lists of the 24 most popular contemporary Soviet authors and the 24 runners-up do not reflect my own preferences; indeed at the start of my study I knew next to nothing about some of the names I was given by the Russians I questioned. Obviously, it would have been desirable to have a much broader sample and to question not a few hundred people at random and by chance but a few thousand selected by sex, age, profession, and place of residence. However, because the answers I received were similar wherever I went (for reasons I shall explain later), I am confident that my findings reflect general preferences. Anyway, one man could have done no more in three months. To the best of my knowledge, these 24 authors are the present favorites of Russian readers. The focus will be entirely on them, on "our" or "my" authors, as the 24 shall be referred to for the sake of simplicity.

The central library of the USSR, located a few hundred yards from the western wall of the Kremlin and named after Lenin, has published a number of studies, mostly mimeographed and in small editions. These volumes investigate various readerships: the average reader, the reader in small towns, the youthful reader, the village reader. Although these thorough studies with thousands of figures are not quoted in this book, they are recommended to those interested in an in-depth view of these groups of readers. In addition, the Academy of Sciences of the USSR has issued publications on the public's reception of the arts, including literature, and on leisure occupations; one of these is also available in English (Leonid A. Gordon and E. V. Klopov, *Man After Work* [Moscow, 1975]).

While reading the books of our authors, I noticed with surprise— and, I confess, also with pleasure—how much they differed from the earlier Bolshevik literature. The works of the thirties and forties were highly polemic; the character of those popular today will emerge from Part III.

Another surprise was the great difference between the various authors. You can criticize them for this and that, but not for uniformity. Figuratively speaking the literary pot is boiling; the stew has many ingredients and tastes; the lid is not as tight as it was forty or fifty years ago. Only in one aspect are the books alike: they deal almost exclusively with the domestic problems of Soviet society. Except in connection with World War II and some earlier wars, the rest of the world does not figure in these stories.

My study was never intended as an inquiry into Soviet literature as such. I willingly leave the literary evaluation of these novels and short stories to the scholars of contemporary literature. My own judgment, though it comes through here and there, is irrelevant. What is being investigated here is not the standard of Soviet literature but the light its most popular products shed on its readers.

I am conscious of the tense situation in the world today. It is for the reader to judge whether this book lives up to the grave responsibility implicit in a study that deals with the national character of one of the most important nations of our time.

Part I describes my method and explains why my questions were so readily answered: reading is an important aspect of life in the Soviet Union, and Russians enjoy talking about it. Part I continues with a survey of the problems inherent in the access to books in the USSR and with an examination of the paths to success in the literary community.

Part II offers a look at the life and career of each of the 24 authors. In Part III the plot of the 111 most frequently mentioned prose works of our 24 authors is retold. This gives the reader a better chance to form his own opinion than would—necessarily subjective—essays on the entire oeuvre of each writer with only a few lines devoted to each of their many books.

Part IV offers a number of conclusions drawn from the plots and problems, the personages and human interrelationships, described in Part III. These conclusions are obviously the most personal and debatable section of the book.

In the Appendix will be found first the Russian titles of the novels, novellas, and stories mentioned in this book, second the titles of those available in English, third some information on editions and print runs of our authors, and finally an international comparison of paper and book production.

The last paragraphs of the Introduction are addressed to readers in the USSR.

This book describes to Western readers one of the best things you Russians have, your readers and their favorite authors and books. It is written by a man who was born like many of you, though as a German and before most of you, on the banks of the Moskva River and who has loved your literature since his childhood, from Pushkin and Lermontov to Trifonov and Rasputin. Because he is no admirer of the political system under which you live, he is pleased to note that most of your popular literature of today puts far more emphasis on human problems and values than did the agitprop novels he read 30 to 50 years ago. The more realistic and humane the authors and books, the higher he values them. He does not divide people into classes but into nations and individuals. Hence his disinclination to see a dramatic break in the Russian character after 1917. Many factors have affected you since then: revolution and collectivization, urbanization and mechanization, the difficult thirties, the cataclysmic Second World War, and the mass literacy campaign that made you into a nation of readers. In essence, however, you have remained Russians. Other nations have also undergone changes; the Americans, for example, entered world affairs in the same year, 1917, never to be the same again, and the Germans have come from the days of Emperor William II to those of the Bonn republic. Yet in substance they, too, remain Americans and Germans.

From conversations with your countrymen, the author knows that some of you might be irritated that in the summaries of novels in Part III Stalin is given more prominence than in the novels themselves. But throughout the world Stalin is one of the most talked-about leaders of this century, and people are curious to know how the most popular Soviet writers handle this man and his time.

If a Soviet citizen had written this book, it would of course look quite different. But there is no reason why a foreigner should not write it; contrary to institutions that are peculiar to the USSR, such as kolkhozes or soviets, your literature is of interest to more than just Russian readers, in fact, you want it to belong to the world.

The author feels uneasy with emotional declamations about international love and brotherhood because they are so often empty phrases. But he does believe that the danger of a conflict between two neighbors recedes when each is able to put himself into the other's shoes, to understand the other's moods and motives. This book hopes to foster this ability in the West by describing the Russians in one of their most characteristic roles: as readers.

Note on Transliteration

As always with books on the Soviet Union, the awkward problem of transliteration must be dealt with. In the text I generally followed the guidelines suggested by the U.S. Board on Geographic Names, modifying them in some cases in order to approximate the actual pronunciation more closely. For example, the name of the island in V. Rasputin's famous novel has been rendered *Matyora* instead of *Matera*. As no such island exists anyway, I hope the keepers of the U.S. Board on Geographic Names will be lenient with me. In the appendixes, the 24 authors and the titles of their works have been transliterated using the Library of Congress system (without diacritics) since otherwise they cannot be found in library catalogues.

I

On the Trail

1
In Quest of the
Most Wanted Books

When I arrived in Moscow in February 1981, it was cold and the snow was piled in the streets. But the taxi I hired to take me to some friends was pleasantly heated. As I slipped into the front seat, I noticed a book on the low shelf between myself and the driver. We might as well start, I told myself and said, "I have interrupted you in your reading; what is it?"

"Proskurin's *Thy Name*," he answered. "I got it from a friend. I promised to return it in two days, so I have to hurry and finish it."

"I haven't had a chance to read it," I remarked. "What's it all about?"

For the next five minutes, the driver summarized part of the novel. (I shall return to it in the Proskurin chapter in Part III.) Then he said: "And that's as far as I got."

The road was slippery and the traffic slow. I still had time to ask the young man's opinion about the writers on my preliminary list. (Proskurin was not on it yet.) He agreed with most of the names I read to him, especially with Simonov, whom he liked very much. Among those he added was Fyodor Abramov. (There will be one more taxi driver story, but the reader will notice that taxi drivers were not my only source of information.)

At my friends' home I continued my quest. Some other guests also joined us, and after a while they were all puzzling away over my lists, eliminating and adding. By the time I got back to the hotel, I had the first results in my bag. That is how it started.

Pestering People

During three stages of one month each in February 1981, 1982, and 1983, I pestered everyone in sight with my questions. In order to learn the opinions of people in various parts of this vast land, I visited—in addition to Moscow—Kalinin (the former Tver); Yaroslavl; Pskov; Volgograd (formerly Tsaritsyn, and later Stalingrad), on the lower Volga, about one thousand kilometers from the capital; Bratsk in eastern Siberia, almost five thousand kilometers away, as well as villages near these towns.

I encountered no difficulties in getting people to answer my questionnaire. Most of them, it seemed, considered it a kind of game. Once, in a library in Bratsk, four patrons of the library were working simultaneously on my lists and consulting each other, when a woman who had just returned her books asked in a plaintive voice: "Why doesn't anybody want to know *my* opinion about *my* most favorite writers?" I handed her a sheet and she settled down contentedly to make her crosses.

I must explain about the crosses. At first, I asked people to scratch out the names of persons on my lists they did not favor and to add those they especially liked in the space left free. Soon I found that quite a few had qualms about eliminating names, perhaps because they felt badly about removing, with the stroke of a pen, the names of writers. Writers, after all, belong in Russia to a highly respected, almost venerated human species. Then I hit upon the idea of the crosses. "Please make a cross," I said, "next to the names of writers you like." So they did. Some asked: "Am I allowed to make two crosses for the authors I like even more than the others?" I agreed. Eventually a system of one, two or three crosses developed (almost as if it were a list of hotels with one, two, or three stars). The number of crosses soon told me as much about the person who made them as about their tastes. Enthusiasts made nothing but + + or + + +, while cautious souls limited themselves to + and + +. In either case, the preferences were clearly visible. And in the evenings I sat down in my hotel room to count the crosses and watch the ups and downs of my authors on the ladder of popularity.

On the flight to eastern Siberia, we stopped at Omsk to refuel. As we were getting ready to leave the plane, I heard a woman calling: "There must be a foreigner aboard. Who is he?"

Siberians are a lusty folk, and the question was answered by a jocular chorus of voices: "Here! I am the foreigner!"

The woman's voice grew angry. "You are not foreigners," she

shouted, "you are just cheeky Siberians. But where is *my* foreigner?"

She hesitated for a moment when I stepped forward. I did not look very foreign to her in my fur cap and heavy coat. But she believed me when I showed her my papers. We climbed down the ramp into an icy Siberian night—22 degrees below zero Fahrenheit but calm and clear—and she took me to the VIP lounge. Her name was Nadya; she was one of the Intourist guides at Omsk airport.

It was three in the morning Omsk time, and I was the only guest in the lounge. A sleepy waitress served me tea and cookies while I chatted with the equally sleepy Nadya.

"Why are you going to eastern Siberia in the middle of the winter?" she asked. When I explained, she became interested, asked to see my lists, and after another minute began making crosses. The waitress was wide awake by now, and she also wanted a sheet. The two girls were only half through when the loudspeaker called me back to the plane.

"I hope I shall be on duty when you fly back," Nadya said as she accompanied me to the runway, "I want to finish the lists."

As it turned out, she was not; it was her day off. But her friend was on duty and knew all about my questionnaire; she hurried me to the lounge, and this time we finished promptly.

The plane was late in arriving at Moscow's Vnukovo Airport, and, by the time I got to the hotel, it was close to midnight. Just as in my grandfather's days, the "floor ladies" are still present in Soviet hotels to give you the keys and to see what is happening around them. The young woman on duty on my floor seemed pleased when my arrival brought some diversion to her tedious night watch. As she took me to my room, I inquired what she did to while away the long hours.

"Well," she replied, "I read."

And with that we were on my subject. I told her about it, and she asked for my lists. Next morning, when I went to breakfast, she was still on duty. She looked very apologetic when she saw me.

"I feel very bad," she explained. "After I finished answering your questions, the girl from the fourth floor wanted to try it too. Look what she did to your lists!"

Indeed, they were not very tidy, full of crosses and even comments. But that was just fine with me. The girl from the fourth floor, it seems, was quite well read. Among her favorite foreign authors was Thomas Mann. She only slightly misspelled his masterpiece *Die Buddenbrooks* by writing "Bu*tt*enbrooks."

Train rides are especially suited for meeting people. One evening, during my train trip to Volgograd, I stopped by for a chat with the cooks and waitresses after the dining car had closed for the night. They wanted to hear all about Helmut Schmidt and Ronald Reagan, the latter weighing heavily on their minds, and then they told me about their reading.

The retired officer with whom I shared a compartment on that trip had a lady friend on the train who came to visit us. After a discussion of world affairs, we were soon deep in my subject with both of them advising me on their own and their friends' favorite reading.

Restaurants, like trains, are excellent places for conversations. Once I had lunch in the ruble section of Moscow's Hotel National. To its elaborately ornamented turn-of-the-century splendor my grandfather occasionally brought his wife and some of their twelve children in the tsarist days. Most tables were occupied the day I lunched there. Two girls joined me at my table, students as it turned out. I introduced myself and explained my project. One of the girls whose field was mathematics loved the Russian classics, especially Pushkin and Lermontov; the other, a chemist, was a fan of foreign novels, greatly fascinated by Arthur Hailey's fast-paced stories. The trouble, they said, was that—whether classic, foreign, or contemporary Russian works—it was impossible to buy them; one had to borrow from friends and libraries. The girls probably thought I was a teller of tall tales when I mentioned that in the West, even in the small town near the village where I live in the Black Forest, I could get any German book either immediately or within two or three days and books from other Western countries within a fortnight. When we finished our lunches, I had some more lists in my pocket.

Sometimes luck helped me. One evening I went to the theater, to a new Rozov play. The friend I had invited could not join me, so I had one extra ticket. In front of the theater, a dozen or so people waited anxiously, hoping to buy a ticket from someone with a spare one; as usual, the theater was sold out. I gave my extra ticket to a woman who won my attention by telling me imploringly that she was in Moscow for only two days on a *komandirovka* (i.e., sent officially, the Soviet equivalent of our business trip). She was a friendly woman of middle age who thanked me profusely for the ticket. When I asked her about her work, she said: "I am a librarian." Well, I thought, this is my reward for a good deed. Before the curtain rose we were halfway through my list, and we finished the rest during the intermission.

Books of fiction (and poetry) are very hard to come by in the USSR, as the following chapter will tell. Yet some people are known for their private libraries. In one town I spent an evening at a meeting of book lovers held in the local bookstore, listening to their opinions about recent novels. There I met a middle-aged engineer who, I was told, possessed a fabulous private library. When I showed interest, he took me to his home. The two small rooms had shelves to the ceiling that were filled with books, almost two thousand I guessed, mainly, he explained, novels and poetry of the Soviet period but also Russian classics and translations of foreign novels, as well as books on art and technology.

He knew his library well. While his daughter, also an engineer, served us tea, we talked about books. Every so often he took the volumes we were discussing from the shelves, almost without looking. Some of the novels that had only been published in magazines he had neatly bound to form slim brochures. All were stamped with his ex libris, showing his name in the form of a rebus.

"I bought most of my books," he explained, "before 1970. Nowadays it is difficult to get them. But I try to keep up to date. One way is to act immediately, as soon as a new subscription is announced in the paper. Sometimes I get a tip from friends at the bookstore who know my passion. And you need luck, as in everything. This lovely illustrated edition of Grimm's *Fairy Tales* just arrived in the store while I was there and I grabbed it. This very first edition of Shukshin's *Stories* is my pride and joy; I bought it when the author was practically unknown. It cost 90 kopeks; now I would get at least 50 rubles for it."

He mentioned a few more prices connoisseurs would pay for this or that book, and I figured the total value of his library at about twenty thousand rubles. His collection of foreign authors included Thomas Mann's great novels and almost all of Heinrich Böll, whose books he had uniformly bound in gray paper.

"He does not like whodunits and science fiction," his daughter complained, "he says they are only for young people. But I am young!"

In turn I told him about the book trade in the West, the giant annual book fair in Frankfurt, the high price of hardcover books due in part to high wages, and the consequent importance of paperback books. He listened eagerly to all this information.

In another town, the head of a bookstore took me to the homes of two book collectors. The first visit proved a disappointing experience: the young engineer did indeed have a relatively large library (more than one thousand volumes), but his books, especially the various collected works he had bought on subscription, merely sat on the shelves in untouched virginity.

The picture was quite different at the home of a foreman of a machine-tool plant: his books were clearly for reading. He was alone at home—his wife was working—and seemed delighted with the visit of a foreigner. He displayed his treasures even in the bedroom, talked incessantly and intelligently about his favorite books (most recently historical novels), and in addition produced something to eat and drink. When I inquired how he learned about interesting books, he mentioned his colleagues at work and his fellow book lovers. Did he also get his inspiration from reviews (*retsenzii*) in newspapers and magazines? He showed his disdain. "Ya sam sebe retsenzent," he said. (I am my own reviewer.)

Help from Librarians and Booksellers

In addition to pestering individuals, I also adopted a collective approach. Wherever I went, I visited libraries. In a country where books are so hard to buy, libraries play a more important role than in the West. In 1981, in addition to the libraries of universities, institutes, and academies, the Soviet Union had 133 thousand so-called public libraries including 96 thousand village libraries. Together they own close to two billion books. (*Narodnoye khozyaystvo SSSR 1922–1982,* p. 519.)

In the villages usually only one librarian is employed, often a teenager starting her career. In larger libraries in the provincial centers I found up to 200, working in shifts. In a new library I always first introduced myself to the head librarian and explained the purpose of my visit. Then I asked to look around and watch the procedures. The permission was readily granted, often, it seemed to me, with a certain pride in the visit of a foreigner. I was shown the paperwork involved in compiling the daily statistics, for example. All books that are checked out are recorded on the sheets for the various types of literature, so at the end of each day one can see at a glance what kinds of books have been borrowed. The figures are totaled for monthly and yearly reports. After looking at these records compiled by a number of libraries, I found that approximately half of the books that were borrowed belong to the category of belles lettres, mainly fiction, but also poetry; about one-quarter to politics, a very broad term that also includes economics, statistics, social sciences, and law; and the rest to other fields such as science, engineering, or sports.

No objections were voiced when I struck up conversations with the library patrons; this was easy while they waited in line to attend to the formalities associated with returning or checking out books. But even those who had already completed their business did not seem to mind when I approached them.

Only once was I rebuffed during all my visits to libraries. In Moscow I asked an elderly woman with refined features who was standing in line whether I could see which books she wanted to take out. Her eyes flashed me a none-of-your-business look, but she handed me her books. I returned them quickly, without looking at the titles, feeling that I had been indiscreet.

Village libraries, as a rule, are rather modest, with small rooms crammed with shelves of books on agriculture and politics but with empty places where novels should stand. Novels are always *na rukakh* (in hand, meaning "loaned out"). All of my authors' books are in the card catalogues, so are all the Russian classics, of course, but they too are usually *na rukakh*.

The young village librarians I saw were at first overwhelmed by the visit of a "real foreigner," that is, not one from another "socialist country." But once they became accustomed to my presence, they seemed to enjoy being interviewed and showing their treasures and files. The most elegant village library I visited was in a *sovkhoz* in the fertile plains between the Don and the Volga. It occupied the entire upper floor of the House of Culture, one large room with windows to the southwest, comfortable chairs, shelves with easy access, and even some plants.

City libraries are large and well arranged; some have new wings under construction. Factory libraries usually have a room or two in the administration building, but some possess many thousands of books and quite a few of the leading literary reviews. Town libraries have two separate departments. One is the reading room, with its own stack of books that can only be used right there. In addition to reference works, the books most in demand and hence most in danger of disappearing are also kept here. The other department is the *abonement*, literally the "subscription"; people who have a borrower's card, who are its "subscribers," may borrow books here. The *abonement*'s stacks are separate from those of the reading room. In most libraries I visited I found the stacks open to the public, both in the reading room and in the *abonement*. Large libraries may have some closed stacks; I did not ask to see them.

Usually the head librarian took me through the various departments and introduced me to the persons in charge of the *abonement* and the reading room; in some libraries there were extra rooms for fiction and the librarians working there proved especially knowledgeable about the most frequently borrowed novels. In all libraries large and small, the attendants were eager to show me the stacks, and in the fiction section I always saw empty shelves where the books of Aitmatov, Bondarev, Dumas, and others would have stood had they not been *na rukakh*.

In the very first library I visited in Moscow, I had noticed a box on the counter, about the size of a shoe box but somewhat longer and filled with hundreds of postcards with a name and address written on one side and the title of a book and the date on the other. A somewhat taller brown card separated one batch from the next. The brown cards bore inscriptions such as Tolstoy, *Anna Karenina*; Rasputin, *Money for Maria*; or Jack London, *The Seawolf* and thus identified books in great demand. Each time a copy was returned, the next person in line would receive his postcard. I asked one girl whom I saw with such a card in her hand how long she had waited.

"Since April of last year," she replied, showing me her postcard, which bore that date and the title of the book she wanted: Julian Semyonov's detective story, *Petrovka 38*. After that, I always headed straight for these boxes, initially judging the demand for a book by the number of request cards. But some libraries had more than one copy of these most wanted books; their turnover was quicker and the number of request cards correspondingly smaller, even though the demand for them might be greater. Thus, the request cards were not a foolproof indicator, but they did provide some additional help.

According to the acquisitions librarians, new books are ordered from catalogues that the various, of course, not privately owned, publishing houses prepare for the following year. For 1981, of the publishing houses specializing in fiction and poetry, Sovetsky pisatel (Soviet Writer) offered 436 titles on 211 pages, Khudozhestvennaya literatura (Belles lettres) 226 titles on 94 pages, and Sovremennik (The Contemporary) 292 titles on 127 pages, all titles annotated. One librarian showed me a list of her orders for 1982 that she had prepared after listening to the needs of the library's various departments. How many of the ordered books the library actually receives is quite another matter, and the number of books obtained seldom corresponds to the number of books ordered. But it was important for me to see in black and white that from among "my" front-running authors this particular library had ordered, for itself and its many branches in the province, copies of books by Abramov (46), Aitmatov (38), Astafyev (50), Bondarev (110), Bykau (85), Chakovsky (188), Dumbadze (32), Markov (225), Rasputin (105), Semyonov (88), Shukshin (135), Simonov (71), Soloukhin (49), Trifonov (31), and Vasilyev (102). By itself this order list did not, of course, give a conclusive answer to my question, because it included only authors whose new books (or new editions of older books) the publishing houses were offering for 1982. Also, more copies were ordered if an author's books were expected to be available in especially large quantities.

In bookshops I followed similar procedures, also talking to sellers and buyers and looking at the waiting lists that are kept there too. In this respect the long flight to Bratsk in eastern Siberia proved quite rewarding. Not too many foreigners come there, hence those who do receive an especially friendly welcome. I spent hours in the bookstores *Evrika* and *Prometey*. In a place that had been a wilderness twenty years ago, it was strange to find two well-run bookshops sporting ancient Greek names— Archimedes' triumphant *Eureka* (I have found it; also the state motto of California) and the name of the hero who stole fire from the gods for mankind. It was even stranger to see the women working in the book-stores with such Mediterranean names wearing thick fur coats and the biggest fur caps I have ever seen; in fact, the whole town looked like a fur exhibition. And why not? Siberia is, together with Canada, the country of furs.

There are two professions in Russia whose members I especially like: librarians and booksellers. Most of them are women (which may have something to do with my sympathies), and many are true enthusi-asts of their work and want to contribute something to the improvement of their fellow citizens. Watching these librarians and booksellers at work, I noticed that they were familiar with many of their patrons, with their reading interests, and perhaps even with their family situations. Some, it seemed to me, were almost confidants of their clients and the ones to whom these turned with their personal problems. These jobs are among the least controversial in the country; for many women, the library and bookshop offer a relatively quiet haven and a pleasant work atmosphere. It is their privilege all day long to meet people who are as interested in books as they are. Some do more than they are expected to. In one provincial library I found a large card file with information about important reviews of practically all the most wanted books on my lists; these cards had not been supplied by some central organization but were handwritten by the library's staff and most useful for me.

When I returned to the USSR in 1982, I had about four dozen names on my list that I wanted to check once more. The librarians always took my lists with eager curiosity. I urged them to forget their personal evaluation of the authors, literary or otherwise, and, as profes-sionals in the field of books, to focus on the readers' preferences. They read the names half aloud, one by one, while I held another copy in my hand. What followed, went—with some variations— like this: "Abra-mov—yes; Aitmatov—yes, indeed; Alekseyev—well . . .; Ananyev— ye . . . s (with some slight hesitation); Astafyev—yes; Belov—yes; Belyayev—yes, but he is dead; Bogomolov—yes, they read him; Bond-arev—yes, yes, never a copy on the shelf . . ." I made my notes accordingly.

This may not exactly accord with the approved scientific polling methods of Gallup and Kinsey, but I found the spontaneous, though naturally subjective, reaction of these professionals just as revealing and perhaps even more reliable than the methods I used with nonprofessionals. After all, it is by nuances such as "yes," "ye . . . s," "Well . . . yes . . ." and the affirmative or partial nod that the difference between the very great and merely great popularity of an author can be judged.

Wherever I went, I tallied the score of the most wanted fiction—contemporary, classic, and foreign—every two or three days. Although the cities and villages I visited were very different, the results were not. There were some variations, of course (for example, in Siberia an understandable bias in favor of Siberian writers prevailed), but the central core of the authors emerged quickly and was continually reaffirmed.

The trip to Russia in February 1983 served to check the results obtained in 1981 and 1982. I presented my two lists with 24 names each to a number of librarians in Moscow and in the provinces, asking the question: "Are any names of very popular authors missing?"

This time three new names temporarily made an appearance but were, after some thinking, again withdrawn: the two poets Yevgeny Yevtuschenko and Andrey Voznesensky, who had published some prose in 1982 but had still remained poets in the minds of the people, and Ilya Shtemler, whose novel *Univermag* (Department Store), published in *Novy mir* in the fall of 1983 had caused some excitement. (It is a peek behind the scenes of Soviet trade in consumer goods, patterned, it was suggested, somewhat after Arthur Hailey's *Airport*.) Thus the names on the top and on the runners-up lists, which I had worked out during the two previous years, remained unchanged. Naturally, I asked myself whether the librarians refrained from criticizing my lists out of politeness to a foreigner, and I cannot rule out this possibility. But there were other checks available. In some public libraries I saw lists of names of authors who were especially in demand; they had been collected for the libraries' own use, to help them in making up their orders. In one case the readers had been asked which authors the library should order, in another what authors in general they liked to read most; these lists were of unequal length and included poets. The 24 authors that will be examined were all there, though not necessarily in the first 24 positions.

Since Western best-seller lists are controversial even though they are based on widespread and systematic polling, my lists, too, will be called into question. But I feel confident that my final list of 24 authors and their books is sufficiently reliable for the following study. At any rate, one man could do no more in three months in a country in which no recognized and published best-seller lists exist and where they cannot exist because too many Russians are chasing too few books.

2
Too Many Russians
Chasing Too Few Books

In Moscow, you must first find a taxi and then persuade its driver to take you where you want to go. This may occasionally be difficult: it may be getting close to his mealtime, or he may have a reason to head south while your destination is north.

On one afternoon in February, when a taxi finally stopped for me, I opened the door and said, "Kropotkin Street." (This is my second and last taxi driver story.)

"Not my way," he answered gruffly. But before he could slam the door in my face, I offered to pay three times the price on the meter.

Now he showed some interest. "Where to?" he asked.

"To the *Beriozka* bookstore."

His reaction was quick. "I tell you what. You get me a book, and we'll forget the meter."

"Which book?" I enquired as I climbed in.

"*The Three Musketeers* or *The Count of Monte Cristo*, either will do. My son's birthday is coming up soon," he explained, "and he very much wants a Dumas novel. The one possibility of finding it in the whole USSR is the shop I am taking you to." During the rest of the trip I questioned him about his tastes in literature. He too was a Dumas fan, as it turned out.

Every foreign visitor soon learns about Western currency shops in Moscow and in a number of other cities. They are called *Beriozka* (meaning "little birch," the most popular tree in Russia; *Beriozka* is their English spelling) and in exchange for hard currency, such as dollars or German marks, sell goods that the normal ruble shops lack. The *Beriozka* on Kropotkin Street specializes in books in Russian, including translations of foreign titles.

"*The Three Musketeers*, please!" I exclaimed as I rushed into the store, "or *The Count of Monte Cristo!*"

"Both out of stock" was the reply.

I went out and told the driver. Surprisingly he was not too disappointed. "I really did not expect to have that much luck," he said philosophically. "Another book will do just as well."

"Come in with me," I suggested, "and pick one yourself."

But he refused. "I don't want to get into trouble. They might want to know how I obtained the foreign currency. Just buy any book. If my son doesn't like it, he can always trade it for another book or," he added with a smile, "for a pair of foreign shoes." I bought him the Russian version of Stevenson's *Treasure Island* and earned a thankful smile.

For myself I purchased about 65 hardcover books by contemporary Soviet writers for a total of some $230 during my Moscow stay in 1981. Not wishing to take them with me on the plane, I decided to ship them by parcel post. To do this, I had to take them to a post office where they had to be checked. (Since 1982 permission from Moscow's Lenin Library has been needed for every Russian book taken or sent out of the country.) After a clerk packed them in a box, I addressed the carton and paid for packing and postage. Some weeks later the books arrived safely in Germany—all except two, that is, although they were packed together with the others. I will come back to them later.

The Russians, at least those who can read, have always loved books. (There were few who could read prior to the Revolution.) But their present craving for fiction is new. During the early thirties, I worked in the USSR as a foreign correspondent. At that time, it was easy to buy books in the stores, and there were many bookstores in the now defunct Mokhovaya Street, just across from the old Moscow University. I bought books by the hundreds. There were fewer books then but also many fewer readers. Even in the fifties, as a foreign correspondent once again, I spent many pleasant hours in well-stocked Soviet bookshops and sent home boxes and boxes of newly obtained literature.

Only in the seventies did Russians and observers abroad become aware of a new situation. *Literaturnaya gazeta* began to write about a reading boom (using the English expression); others spoke of a reading explosion (*vzryv*). Some authors tried to pinpoint the date the boom began, eventually agreeing on the latter part of the sixties; this coincides with my own observations and with the available statistics (see Table 1).

Table 1

Books, Brochures, and Magazines Published in the USSR, 1940–1981

Books and Brochures in Russian Only		
Years	*Titles*	*Copies*
1940	34,404	345,728,000
1965	57,521	1,038,412,000
1970	60,240	1,086,133,000
1981	64,689	1,565,842,000
Magazines and Journals, All Languages		
Years	*Titles*	*Yearly Copies*
1940	1,822	245,000,000
1965	3,846	1,548,000,000
1970	5,968	2,622,000,000
1981	5,195	3,116,000,000

SOURCE: *Narodnoe khoziaistvo SSSR 1922–1982*, pp. 532–35.

The Reading Boom

Ever since the *Lay of Igor's Campaign* and Nestor's *Primary Chronicle*, the written word has had a special, almost magical quality for the Russians. No one who has seen *Boris Godunov* is likely to forget the scene where the old monk finishes writing the history of his time and thereby makes himself part of history by contributing to the rise of the false Tsar Dimitry and to the Time of Troubles. Precisely because the literate were a minority, books were objects of awe and veneration. In autocratic nineteenth-century Russia, literature played the role of the then nonexistent parliament, poems and novels spoke of liberty for the spirit, demanded justice for the downtrodden, ridiculed stupidity and corruption, pushed for reforms. This aspect of literature is at least as important today as it was a hundred years ago.

"In the beginning was the Word." This extraordinary first sentence in the gospel of John has a special significance for the Russians. Although literacy is now nearly universal thanks to the postrevolutionary effort to "liquidate illiteracy" (*likbez*, for short), respect for books and writers remains undiminished. For example: In February 1981, when I arrived in Bratsk to find out what people were reading in eastern Siberia, I did not know a soul. But I had brought with me three copies of a book by Julian Semyonov, one of the 24 described in this study; all three had his autograph. They proved true open sesames. I gave one to the manager of the local bookstore, two to the directresses of the main libraries—and presto, all doors flew open. A man with signed copies of Julian Semyonov's books must be okay. This was, it seems, the general feeling. Would a German with three signed copies of a book by an American best-selling author find the same open doors in Alaska? I wonder.

Among the reasons for the reading boom is the rapid increase in the number of educated people among the general population. During the first 30 years after the Revolution, 7.5 million people in the USSR graduated from middle school, whereas during the second 30 years (1950–1980) that number grew more than tenfold, to 80 million. At the same time, the graduates' level of education rose because they were required to attend school for ten years, rather than for seven as before.

From grades 4 to 10 a total of 630 hours is allocated to the study of literature and the same number of hours, at least theoretically, to homework on this subject. The program of study is established by the Ministry of Education and is obligatory for all pupils from Leningrad to Vladivostok. From the school program for 1980–81, it appears that the study of literature is rather conservative and traditional. Thirteen of the old and new classic Russian authors mentioned later in this book take up 262 hours, while only Simonov appears from my 24 most popular contemporary writers, and he is given just 2 hours. Only in the "study periods" of grades 8 and 9 and the "summary discussions" of grade 10 do 11 of these 24 merit attention.

The heavy preference for the classics is confirmed by the assigned home reading. The names of 14 old and new classic writers appearing on my lists are recommended, but not a single one of the 24 most popular contemporary authors is. Obviously the government wants young Russians to have a thorough schooling in classic Russian literature, assuming that the influence of parents and friends, in addition to the less formal "study periods" and "summary discussions," will also arouse their interest in contemporary literature.

The impact that literature as taught in school has on one's later life will differ with each student. Some graduates will be led to further studies; others may be sick and tired of the subject. As far as Russians are concerned, I am inclined to believe that the unusually strong interest in literature is attributable to their being exposed to literature. They love spending hours with their classics partly because they carry the reader into spheres of beauty and high spirit, partly because they take him into a world totally different from the one in which he lives. There would not be those millions of Olgas and Tatyanas all over Russia had their parents not loved the two heroines of Pushkin's grand epic *Eugene Onegin*.

The situation is rather different in the West. Although it is not easy to compare the number of hours spent on serious literature in Russian schools with those spent in American and German schools, the difference is clear.

In the German *Realschule,* which includes grades 5 to 10, the number of hours devoted to literature is left largely to the discretion of the teachers. Some of them may feel that the students need more hours on grammar and spelling at the expense of literature; others may think differently. Per school year between 40 and 50 hours are dedicated to literature on the average. That adds up to between 240 and 300 hours in six years or, if one adds the fourth grade in order to compare with grades 4 to 10 in the Soviet school, to between 280 and 350 hours.

The German teacher of literature is not given a strict plan telling him which literary works he has to cover with his class. His assignment is more general, the German classics, the period of Naturalism, and so on. In contrast to the Russians who study, year in and year out, exactly the same novels, poems, and short stories throughout the entire country, the Germans of today have no obligatory literary fund in common. (This was different in my school days of 60 years ago.)

Parallel to this rise in the level of education is the growth of the population of the towns. During the last four decades the urban population has increased from 63 to 170 million people, and during the last 30 years, 60 million apartments have been built, with an average of 45 square meters of floor space.[1] One may view these official statistics with some skepticism. Yet, anyone looking down from a plane on Soviet cities can see their relatively small prerevolutionary core and the vast new housing areas sprawling in all directions. For people who like to read, it obviously makes a big difference whether they have (as my wife and I did in the thirties) one room in an overcrowded apartment shared with five other families or a flat of their own, even though a very small one by Western standards. As a general rule one might say for Russia: more living space equals more book space and more reading space.

---

1. *Narodnoe khoziaistvo SSSR 1980,* pp. 7, 455, 388.

Finally, available cash has increased, not so much in terms of wages, but in actual income, which includes all kinds of bonuses and earnings "on the side." People now have considerably more money with which to purchase books than they did some decades ago. In general, there are many more rubles in circulation than commodities to spend them on. This leads, of course, to speculation in rare durable goods. Those who have much money may line up to buy apartments or automobiles, or they can go to the jeweler. (I heard of a woman from the Caucasus who bought a golden necklace with diamonds for about eighteen thousand rubles.)

With less money to invest, one can bet at the races or buy books. The speculator's value of a book is relatively easy to establish, hence for some people, certainly a small minority, books have become, apart from their intrinsic value, one of the currencies of the land, as cigarettes were in postwar Germany. Some Soviet observers have compared a book owner in the USSR to a shareholder in a capitalist society.[2]

Better education, additional housing, more cash, these are, I think, the main material explanations for the reading boom in the USSR since the sixties.

To these, one more explanation, an immaterial one, must be added: the respect with which books were treated in Russia even at a time when few people could read continues today when practically all Russians are literate. And while the book until some decades ago had a practical significance only to the urban upper class and to the landed gentry, the habit of reading now has expanded throughout the countryside. I found this confirmed in the village libraries I visited.

The Paradox of the Bookstores

It is difficult to find meat in the shops and nearly impossible to get fiction in the bookstores. This frequent complaint may sound strange to a foreigner who compares the empty butcher shops with the crammed shelves of the bookstores, but it is true just the same.

To prove this, the next time you visit the USSR, go into any bookstore (except the *Beriozka*) and ask for any popular book written by one of the 24 authors discussed in this study. The odds are 50 to 1 that you will not find a single copy. (If you do, there is something wrong with my list!) Yet the bookstores are full.

---

2. *Literaturnaia gazeta* (henceforth *LitG.*), June 20, 1979.

The explanation for this odd contradiction is simple: there is no lack of books in general but a tremendous lack of the books people want to read, namely poetry (not dealt with in this study) and fiction. The books desired are, as we shall see, neither subversive nor smutty. So why is it that people cannot get them in the stores and only with difficulty in the libraries?

At first, Soviet comments on the reading boom were full of pride, calling the USSR "the most book-reading country in the world." New forests were cut down to produce more paper. But the hunger for books did not stop, and soon it became evident that the publishing industry was quite unable to satisfy the demand; it lacked both paper and an efficient distribution system.

The information concerning these two stumbling blocks is all taken from my fat file of clippings from Soviet papers dealing with the production and trade of books in the USSR. Specific sources are indicated. The size of this file and the content of the complaints show the tendency toward greater public participation in matters of general concern and the decreasing willingness to accept complacently whatever is decided on high. Perhaps the candor and vigor of the debate can be explained by the public's feelings that to fight for more and better books is nobler than to clamor for more jeans, necessary though these may be.

The decision on paper allocation for the printing of fiction is made at various levels of the planning apparatus. Four pivotal decisions have to be made before printing can start: first, how much paper is to be produced for books; second, how much of it will be allotted to fiction; third, how much of that will each of the various publishing firms of the country receive; and fourth, how much will each author be allocated.

The influence of public opinion on the first decision is probably rather weak; paper production rose sharply from 1940 to the early seventies but has stagnated lately and has even decreased since 1978.[3]

But the frequent protests in the press and the demands for a more generous allocation of paper for fiction cannot remain without some result. Fiction, including books for children, I was told, amounts to about one-third of the yearly book production at the present time. The most radical suggestion was made in 1976, no doubt with tongue in cheek: in order to eliminate the lack of fiction, cease publishing all other types of books![4] A most revolutionary thought, for its application would mean no more political books.

---

3. *Narodnoe khoziaistvo SSSR 1922–1982*, p. 203.
4. *LitG.*, Jan. 21, 1976

Another demand is to decrease the number of unwanted titles
printed and increase the number of books that are really in demand.
Forty-three percent of the books in specialized libraries, it is claimed,
have never been used.[5] In the public libraries operated by the Ministry
of Education, there are "hundreds of millions of books" that nobody ever
requests.[6] "The bookstores are crammed with books, but there is nothing [anyone wants] to buy."[7] "There is too much senseless duplication:
for example, why are 30 titles dealing with manners (*kultura povedenia*)
published in Moscow alone, and why are there 29 books on rhetoric?"[8]
And to sum up the complaints: much of what is published is unworthy of
the word *literatura* and is therefore properly called *utilitura,* a new word
meaning books good for nothing but wastepaper (from *util,* meaning
"reusable waste").[9] Even one of the senior staff members of the Lenin
Library in Moscow raised his voice against flooding the country with
"gray," or insignificant, books and demanded more books that were
truly in demand.[10] "Every year we order the books we need and every
year we get little of what we requested and much that we cannot use for
our readers," one librarian told me. "Somehow we try to manage," she
added with a brave smile.

This is not the place to examine the intricacies of book publishing
and censorship in the USSR, nor is there any need to do so because a
specialist from Oxford's Bodleian Library, Gregory Walker, has written
a detailed analysis entiled *Soviet Book Publishing Policy* (Cambridge,
1978). Some thoughts on this subject, however, are presented in Part IV
under the heading "The Authorities."

What To Do About It?

Some unhappy but wise booksellers, swamped with unwanted books that they cannot refuse, have found a way of selling them
after all: the customer gets the books he wants only if he also buys some
books he does not want.[11]

Perhaps in response to the numerous complaints, the powers that be

5. *LitG.,* Aug. 22, 1979.
6. *Sovetskaia kultura* (henceforth *SovKult.*), Sept. 21, 1979.
7. *SovKult.,* Nov. 14, 1980.
8. *SovKult.,* Nov. 14, 1980.
9. *LitG.,* Turn of year 1973–74, *A kostry vse goriat i goriat.*
10. *Komsomolskaia pravda,* Oct. 31, 1975.
11. *Pravda,* Nov. 11, 1980.

decided to print 100 million additional books in the field of fiction (including children's books) during the Tenth Five-Year Plan by reducing by 10 percent the production of other books.[12]

To improve the work of the libraries is of course an obvious way to put the available books to better use. It is my impression that the libraries are doing what they can (I shall have more to say on this subject) and that the problems they face are not of their own making but are beyond their control. The libraries are practically at the mercy of higher institutions for the books they receive, and they feel that often they do not get what their readers really want and need but rather what is allotted to them.

Some years ago it was decided to publish a Library Series of the most wanted books for sale exclusively to libraries.[13] On the whole, this works well; however, a number of the series intended for libraries ended up in the homes of VIPs.

The organizational reforms introduced during the seventies aimed at better service through the creation of several thousand well-equipped central libraries to which the smaller libraries are attached. But these reforms did not find much favor with local librarians. The installation of one more intermediary level, it seems, makes it harder rather than easier for them to obtain more and better books. For the inhabitant of a village or a small town it is, of course, far more convenient to get what he wants in his local library than to be referred to a central library a few hundred miles away. He is probably unfamiliar with the holdings of this distant library, and when he finally does find out about their collection and requests a book from them, the machinery is exceedingly slow. "It takes months (plural!) for the orders to get to the next central library." The technique of interlibrary exchange is also poorly developed. All this means "that for a long time (*nadolgo*) many advantages of library centralization will remain a theoretical possibility, a good idea lacking a basis in reality."[14]

Other suggestions on how to increase the supply of fiction to the population are more modest in scope, yet just as difficult, if not even more difficult, to implement.

Put an end to the careless transportation of rolls of paper! During an inspection (called a "raid," using the English word) it was found that many paper rolls were badly damaged in transport, some to a depth of ten centimeters, and that therefore much paper had to be discarded.

---

12. *LitG.*, Jan. 21, 1976.
13. *LitG.*, Aug. 22, 1979.
14. *SovKult.*, July 27, 1980.

Hence the "raiders' " demand: get better equipment for the transportation of paper rolls! After six years, the inspection was repeated: "We
discovered excellent machinery for transporting, loading, and unloading
the paper; exactly what was needed! We saw an impressive parade of
technology! However, we saw all that at the International Exhibition of
Paper Machinery . . . our own paper is still transported in trucks that
are also used for bricks, sand, and metals."[15]

Improve storage! Poor storage is said to be responsible for the loss
both of paper and of books. In one case tens of thousands of books, worth
53 thousand rubles, were ruined when sewage water flooded the cellar
in which they were stored.[16]

Increase the text page! Great reserves, it is claimed, can be opened
up by this simple method. By putting 10 percent more letters on each
page, one publishing house saved 55 hundred tons of paper, enough to
print 30 million brochures.[17]

The most promising method of printing more books while staying
within the planning limits seemed, for some years, to be recycling old
paper. The drive began in a number of cities during the second half of
1974.[18] Those who brought in old paper were promised two kopeks for
each kilogram and—this was the trump card—a coupon entitling them
to a book from the list of popular books for each twenty kilograms. (For
Russians, everything that is not readily available, be it butter or fiction,
is *defitsitno*.) The drive also had conservationist overtones: each one
thousand kilograms of old paper delivered to the state, it was claimed,
would equal four cubic meters of lumber and each million kilograms
would save 45 thousand hectares of forest.[19]

The idea sounded excellent, Soviet citizens by the hundreds of thousands brought millions of kilograms of old paper to the collection points
in knapsacks, carts, and automobiles, enough to produce, in the years
between 1975 and 1978, 24 million copies of additional books.[20] But
then one problem after another arose: the collection points were ill
prepared for the flood of paper. The millions of coupons handed out did
not bring the promised rewards because the distribution system did not
properly function in spite of the small number of titles that were to be
printed for the paper donors; to obtain "old paper" for recycling, crooks
stole paper that was used but not yet discarded, such as computer cards;

15. *LitG.*, Sept. 18, 1974.
16. *Trud*, Dec. 15, 1974.
17. *LitG.*, Sept. 18, 1974.
18. *LitG.*, Jan. 14, 1976.
19. *LitG.*, Dec. 25, 1974.
20. *Pravda*, Mar. 12, 1978.

some enterprising people printed fake coupons—40 thousand in Moscow alone—which they sold for two to four rubles a piece.[21] Also, some bookstores refused to honor coupons from the previous year even though their owners had not yet received any books. The papers were full of stories about disappointments and frustrations. One described with bitter sarcasm the tribulations of people in quest of Dumas's *Queen Margot*, one of the titles promised to donors of old paper.[22] But in 1983 I still saw collection points in Moscow.

Book Lovers' Fight and Plight

Eventually book lovers became exasperated with this mismanagement and the disregard of their wishes. For some time local circles of people interested in books had been meeting for discussions and lectures. Sooner or later, they started thinking about ways of obtaining books. The idea caught on. After a short while there were hundreds, then thousands of such groups. In October 1974 they merged into the All Union Voluntary Society of Book Lovers (*Vsesoyuznoye dobrovolnoye obshchestvo lyubitiley knigi*), calling themselves *knigolyuby* for short, a combination of the words *book* and *lover.* Theirs was one of the fastest growing nonpolitical organizations in Russia: after a few years it boasted ten million members. Their primary wish, however, remained unfulfilled. Buying books continued to be almost as difficult for them as for anybody else.

"The Society of Hunters," they complained, "or the Society of Hobby Fishermen offer their members all kinds of advantages—areas to hunt or fish, rifles, boats, fishing rods. But our Society provides no advantages; people are beginning to lose interest in it. Collecting dues becomes increasingly difficult." The resolution of August 1, 1977, demanding the production of more books, was agreed upon by the pertinent organizations but did not help much.[23]

Being unable to find enough fiction in the stores, readers did the next best thing: they started exchanging books, directly or with the help of ads in newspapers such as the supplement of *Vechernaya Moskva*. They also devised all kinds of tricks and unusual methods of obtaining books, mostly to no avail. When the Dog Breeders Society, for example, held a conference, it urged publishers to send them books, not on dogs, how-

---

21. *Trud*, Nov. 2, 1978.
22. *LitG.*, Dec. 25, 1974.
23. *SovKult.*, June 13, 1979.

ever. They requested classical and modern novels, and they actually received some copies.

If nothing else helped, some remembered the old saying, "All is fair in love and war," and turned it into, "All is fair in love and book hunting." As the reading boom rolled along, so did the wave of obtaining books by devious methods.

In one case a lover of books became a lover of Irina, the manager of his favorite bookshop. Cheerfully she supplied him with books taken from her store. To put their relationship on a firmer basis, they married and then, to improve the family income, started selling books from the store at black-market prices. When Irina was caught, she explained to the judges: "I did it because I loved him." But that did not help her much. Both she and her husband landed in prison.[24]

One Muscovite by the name of Krivdin, well known in the liquor department of Food Store no. 5, discovered a simple way of improving his finances. He sold books to that store's employees who then resold them to others. Krivdin's books came from the city's public libraries. After registering at each library, he could borrow up to five books, which he promptly sold. Written demands sent to his home address urging him to return the books were simply ignored. Because the checking system is rather haphazard, he received more than one borrowing card in some libraries—one in his father's name and others in the names of his nonexistent children. He successfully emptied the libraries' shelves of the books that were most in demand. Since there are hundreds of libraries in Moscow, Krivdin's supply was almost unlimited. Eventually, however, he was caught and sentenced to three years of hard labor.[25]

There were other cases: One Nikolay Kuzmenko, a graduate of the Department of History at Moscow University and an official in a ministry, was caught buying stolen books, including works by Shakespeare, Dickens, Mark Twain, Montaigne and even by Tacitus, Plutarch, Julius Caesar, as well as Flavius's *History of the Jewish War*. His entire apartment was filled with books, some were even stored under his couch. Kuzmenko had obtained most of his books from a young bookseller who carried them from the store hidden under his clothes. "Some people drink," Kuzmenko's mother said when he was arrested, "my son collects books."[26]

Another method adopted by some bookstore employees is to remove certain books from the boxes when a shop receives a new shipment and to replace them with the same number of easily available titles. In one

---

24. *Sovetskaia Rossiia*, Feb. 28, 1979.
25. *LitG.*, Sept. 13, 1978.
26. *Komsomolskaia pravda*, Dec. 4, 1979.

bookshop almost two thousand of the most desired books never reached the shelves. Sixty-three Moscow bookstores had signed receipts for the new edition of Dumas's *Collected Works*. In 27 of them all copies of this book had vanished without a trace. With one set of Dumas selling on the black market for about 80 rubles, these transactions netted a tidy sum.[27]

In bookstores they have learned to distinguish between two types of customers—buyers and readers. Buyers buy books not to read but to sell with a maximum profit. According to D. Khrenkov, editor-in-chief of Lenizdat, one of the country's leading publishing houses: "The buyers are squeezing the readers out of the bookstores." One such "buyer" attracted Khrenkov's attention: day after day he bought all the interesting books the store had just received and stashed them in his "bottomless bag." One day, Khrenkov said, the man spent about 50 rubles within half an hour, which means that he bought between 20 and 30 books.[28]

Three inspectors in Gorky who were checking local shops reported that they had fewer difficulties in grocery stores, where they had expected the greatest amount of trouble, than in the town's only bookstore. There, they explained, one could not buy a single good book, because "almost all books that came to the shop disappeared without ever reaching the counter, going to employees of the town's various trade organizations." When the team of checkers began to look more closely into this matter, the people who had benefited from such manipulations decided to fight back. One day, when a fresh book supply arrived, people began lining up before the shop in the early morning delighted by the sight of the books on the counter ready to be sold. Suddenly a woman, an employee of one of the local trade organizations, appeared and removed two stacks of books. When the three inspectors protested, she said: "It's none of your business!" Noticing people's anger, she phoned her superior to complain that she was being harassed by the controllers. He arrived on the scene and took away the controllers' documents. Henceforth the bookshop was not be be checked, they were told.[29]

Once a boom is on, the desire to obtain the goods in question soon becomes indiscriminate. "Get it!" is the main slogan. To explore to what lengths this bibliomania can go, the Leningrad House of Books made an experiment: one morning the rumor was started that in the afternoon a two-volume edition of Joe Rosinant would be on sale. Soon lines began to form by people eager to buy the book of the famous Frenchman, although they could not quite agree among themselves whether he was a novelist or caricaturist. Only gradually did it dawn on them that they

27. *SovKult.*, June 17, 1980.
28. *LitG.*, June 20, 1979.
29. *Pravda*, October 1975.

were being taken for a ride and that Rosinant was not an author but Don Quixote's horse![30]

Attempts to channel the black-market trade into secondhand bookstores run by the government have largely failed because these are forbidden to pay more than the original price, which is ridiculously low (an average of two rubles); they also very rarely have the books the public desires.

A gift from the powers that be to the lovers of books are collected works by subscription. When a bookstore learns that it will get several sets, let us say of the collected works of Alexandre Dumas, it hangs a sign at the entrance informing its customers that subscription will start on such and such a day at nine in the morning. Hours before, people begin to line up in front of the store. At nine o'clock they file in for registration and receive a number corresponding to their position in line. Subscription continues during the following days, but by then the chances of success are practically nil. When the first volume arrives at the store some time later, this is again announced by a sign at the door. If, for example, seven sets are allotted to that particular store, the first seven subscribers—out of perhaps two hundred or more—will get them. However, the newspapers complain that even quite a few of the subscription sets do not reach the customers but are set aside by the printing house or the bookshop for bartering for other rare commodities or for presenting to friends and VIPs.

Deficit is a frequently used word in contemporary Russian. It refers to everything that is not readily available, from meat to books. Wherever there is a deficit (this is also true in countries other than Russia) a black market emerges. Moscow's Kuznetsky Most, one of the main shopping streets in my childhood and still the address of many leading stores, is a favorite meeting place for book dealers, as are the residential entryways near leading secondhand bookstores (in Leningrad this is the *Bukinist* on Liteiny Prospect).[31] Some of the people with bulging briefcases are no doubt bona fide book lovers, looking for a Dumas or a Tolstoy in exchange for some volume that they do not need any more. But even they get into trouble when the police swoop down on the "speculators."

As a foreigner, I steer clear of such places. But from accounts in the Soviet press I know that the *Tales of Hoffmann* and Andersen's or Grimm's *Fairy Tales* can be found there as can the works of Cicero and Petrarch, *The Three Musketeers* for 25 rubles, Yevtushenko's poems (two volumes) for the same price, and Lord Byron's poetry (very popu-

---

30. *SovKult.*, Aug. 19, 1980.
31. *Komsomolskaia pravda*, Nov. 4, 1976.

lar and very rare) for 40 rubles. In a list of eighteen names involved in such book "speculation" I found physicians, chief engineers, artists, teachers, and theater directors.[32] A junior professor of philosophy was apprehended seven times.

This would prove true devotion to books, if we could assume that it was this force that drove these people to such places. However, such devotion cannot always be taken for granted. I have my own experience to contribute: two books, as I mentioned earlier, did not arrive at my Black Forest home although I had been standing nearby while they were packed together with several others in the same parcel. Apparently, somewhere along the line somebody wanted them for himself. One was a copy of the precious Proskurin that I had started reading, making notes in the margins, the other was written by Pikul. I had wanted it very much because of the controversy surrounding it. Not even *Beriozka* had it, so I mobilized all my Russian friends, offering two Jack London volumes in exchange. Finally, the day before my departure, I got a copy—and now it was gone.

Who is guilty for the lack of books that people really want? Shifting the blame is a favorite habit everywhere, not only in Russia. So it was only a matter of time before the heavily criticized bureaucracy adopted the clever ploy of blaming the plight of the book lovers on the book lovers themselves. They were accused of being antisocial egoists with private property instincts because they owned 30 billion books; they sat on them, hoarded them, and still demanded more and more. Such criticism began shortly after the reading explosion became widespread. One of the earliest attacks was published by *Literaturnaya gazeta* in 1974, "There, in the Bookshelf on the Second Row—Deliberations About People Who Collect Private Libraries and How They Do It."[33] The author, N. Zamokhin, mentioned a "malicious" (*oskorbitelny*) ditty that he once found to his dismay on the bookshelf of a "clever, solid, intelligent" person. In my translation it reads:

> Don't let your greedy eyes in my shelves roam,
> These books of mine cannot be taken home.
> Only an idiot would allow a friend to borrow,
> For this must lead to grief and sorrow.

Zamokhin's anger was not very effective; many years later I saw these verses on a shelf in a book lover's home I visited. But the offensive

---

32. *Komsomolskaia pravda*, Nov. 4, 1976.
33. *LitG.*, Dec. 4, 1974.

against book owners has continued ever since. These are some of the most frequent accusations: they buy books by the meter, because they need them "for the sake of prestige."[34] They say in the bookshop: "Give me some books with a blue cover for the price of some nine or ten rubles."[35] They need books because these are in fashion and in order to keep up with the Ivanovs (literally "to be like everybody and even better than the neighbors").[36] They find it more convenient (*komfortabelno*) to own books than to get them from the library.[37] They buy anything they can lay their hands on as long as it is *defitsitno* and proves their *intellektualnost*.[38] The books on their own shelves are "unemployed."[39] Therefore their home is a "cemetery of spiritual values."[40] For all these reasons the book owners behave "immorally" (*beznravstvenno*).[41] This has so far been the worst accusation.

On the other hand, book owners who allow others to use their treasures are widely praised. The Demichevs, a couple in Kursk, are held up for emulation: they own fifteen thousand books and lend them to about fifteen hundred friends and neighbors. How they manage to lead their professional lives and handle their library (which has more books and customers than some public libraries) we are not told. It seems a miracle.[42]

Lyudmila Fadeyevna, a physician, and her husband, an engineer, are another shining example. They own only those books that they need for their professions. Concerning other titles, Lyudmila has a very firm rule: "Buying a book means removing it forever from a wide circulation and robbing many others of the pleasure of reading it. A book's place is in the [public] library, not at home."[43]

The campaign against the "immorality" of book owners has deftly eliminated the danger of the huge book lovers' organization turning against the paper and print bureaucracy. Of course, its members still want more books, but they have been put on the defensive, frequently

34. *SovKult.*, Sept. 28, 1979.
35. *SovKult.*, Mar. 25, 1980.
36. *Komsomolskaia pravda*, Dec. 30, 1977.
37. *Pravda*, Mar. 12, 1978.
38. *SovKult.*, Oct. 26, 1970.
39. *SovKult.*, Nov. 16, 1979.
40. *Komsomolskaia pravda*, Dec. 30, 1977.
41. *Sovetskaia Rossiia*, July 22, 1979.
42. *Sovetskaia Rossiia*, July 22, 1979.
43. *SovKult.*, Sept. 28, 1979.

coupling their bid for books with the promise to let others use them too. Only a few fight back. One who did, preferred anonymity. In a letter to the editor he wrote: "Who gave you the right to point your accusing finger at my private library? It is my own, my personal library. I bought these books with money that I—take note—earned myself. Whoever extends his paw (*lapa*) toward my books, will be hit over the knuckles. Out of 100 people who exchange books with others, 99 are fools (*duraki*). I am not that naive."[44]

Another owner of a private library, a teacher by the name of M. Kotlov, was appalled to hear some of the arguments advanced against people like himself. How can one use terms such as *turnover* when speaking of books that, after all, are "a spiritual [i.e., not a material] treasure?"[45]

As an author myself, I have had some experience with the problems of printing and publishing in a number of countries; I know the weaknesses of our free enterprise system in this field, and so do the readers. Here I am concerned with the situation in the USSR where, according to a statement in *Literaturnaya gazeta*, only 10 percent of the readers' wishes for fiction are being satisfied in the bookshops.[46]

If, for whatever reason, the public's demand for a certain commodity outgrows its supply, the Western system has its own ways of reacting. One of them is inflation; the price goes up, and as a result the demand decreases. Alternatively, private initiative will find a means of taking care of at least some of the unsatisfied demand. Under the Soviet system these methods do not work because the government has a monopoly on production and distribution and because it is committed to a policy of stable and, in the case of books, extremely low prices. As long as there are enough books, this is fine. But there are not, and the very cheapness of a much desired and limited commodity gives rise to innumerable problems that the state cannot solve and private initiative is not permitted to address.

The enthusiasm of booksellers and librarians is admirable. But they must employ bureaucratic methods because everybody—with a few exceptions, such as writers—is a civil servant, and civil servants the world over are inclined to feel less responsibility in their jobs than private entrepreneurs and their employees. In a long and critical article, A. Rubinov accused the publishing houses of first printing useless books

44. *Sovetskaia Rossiia*, Oct. 21, 1979.
45. *Sovetskaia Rossiia*, July 8, 1979.
46. *LitG.*, Aug. 22, 1979.

and then of destroying them. He answers his own questions concerning how this is possible, thus (slightly abridged):

> Most of those who know the book trade and with whom I have talked agree that publishing houses, because they do not carry any financial responsibility, are free to ruin as much paper as they like. Nobody remembers a case where the government demanded amends for losses suffered by a publisher. The people working in the bookstores do not pay for the deficit; instead an anonymous [state] bank account that never complains bears this financial burden. This is an unparalleled paradox! One group of people sends good money to produce unsalable books, while the other one pays for this useless rubbish with money that doesn't belong to it. The government suffers losses, and the employees get their salary just the same.[47]

Even a man high in the book trade organization stated: "We are in favor of putting the relationship between publisher and bookseller on a business basis. Let the publisher decide how many books to print, and allow the book trade to pay only for the books actually sold."[48] This is excellent advice from a responsible citizen who does not fear that the Soviet system might collapse if his advice is followed. Is there any reason to ignore his sensible suggestion other than the bureaucracy's fear of reforms?

This question is posed by a non-Russian who can buy Soviet novels either in Western countries or in Moscow for Western currency. If he were a Russian citizen, he would feel sad—and angry.

---

47. *LitG.*, Aug. 21, 1974.
48. *LitG.*, Oct. 26, 1975.

3
The Road to the Top

Within about a fortnight after my trip in 1981 began, I had compiled a list of roughly 50 of the most frequently mentioned names of very popular novelists from the answers to my questions. Some two dozen of these came up with the greatest frequency, while there was less of a consensus concerning other writers whom I have called the runners-up.

To my surprise the answers I received were similar in cities and villages, in European Russia and Siberia, in bookstores and libraries. Among Siberians there was a certain bias in favor of Siberian authors and settings; they like to "cheer for the home team." But there is certainly no anti-Siberian bias in the capital: when I was in Moscow in 1981, I counted on its stages more than a dozen plays by or about Siberians.

The main reason why literary tastes are so similar lies in the cultural and intellectual centralization of the USSR, especially within its most important component, Russia. All over the country, from Smolensk to Vladivostok, people grow up with the same school curricula; in addition to their local paper, they read the central press from the capital and the leading literary reviews; they watch the same movies and the same serials on television. The more frequently the mass media deal with one and the same novel, the greater the number of people who become acquainted with it. Book reviews, on the contrary, were hardly ever mentioned as reasons for reading a book. They seem to be written by critics not for readers but for writers and for other critics.

Tables 2 and 3 list the 24 favorites and the runners-up alphabetically and show to which age groups the writers belong. Eighteen of the top 24 (counting the two pairs of brothers as one entity each) were born between 1924 and 1934, which means that their major writing

Table 2
The 24 Most Popular Soviet Authors

	Date of Birth		Place of Birth			Participated in World War II	Student in Gorky Institute
	1923 and before	1924 and after	Area	Village	Town		
Abramov, Fyodor A.	1920		near Archangel	yes		yes	—
Aitmatov, Chingiz		1928	Kirgizia	yes		no	1956–58
Astafyev, Viktor P.		1924	Siberia	yes		yes	1959–61
Belov, Vasily I.		1932	near Vologda	yes		no	1959–64
Bondarev, Yury V.		1924	Urals		yes	yes	1946–51
Bykau, Vasil U.		1924	near Vitebsk	yes		yes	—
Chakovsky, Aleksandr B.	1913		St. Petersburg	yes		yes	?–38
Dumbadze, Nodar		1928	Georgia	yes		no	—
Ivanov, Anatoly S.		1928	Kazakhstan		yes	no	—
Lipatov, Vil V.		1927	Siberia	yes		yes	—
Markov, Georgy M.	1911		Siberia		yes	yes	—
Nagibin, Yury M.	1920		Moscow		yes	yes	—
Pikul, Valentin S.		1928	Kagarlyk, Ukraine	yes		yes	—
Proskurin, Pyotr L.		1928	near Bryansk	yes		no	1962–64
Rasputin, Valentin G.		1937	Siberia		yes	no	—
Semyonov, Julian S.		1931	Moscow		yes	no	—

Shukshin, Vasily M.		1929	Altai	yes		yes	—
Simonov, Konstantin M.	1915		Petrograd		yes	yes	1935–38
Soloukhin, Vladimir A.		1924	near Vladimir	yes	yes	yes	1946–51
Strugatsky, Arkady N.		1925	Batum		yes	no	—
Strugatsky, Boris N.		1933	Leningrad		yes	no	—
Trifonov, Yury V.		1925	Moscow		yes	no	1944–49
Vainer, Arkady A.		1931	Moscow		yes	no	—
Vainer, Georgy A.		1938	Moscow		yes	no	—
Vasilyev, Boris L.		1924	Smolensk		yes	yes	—
Yefremov, Ivan A.	1907		near St. Petersburg	yes		no	—

SOURCE: Author's personal poll.

Table 3
The 24 Runners-Up

	Date of Birth	
	1923 and before	*1924 and after*
Adamov, Arkady	1920	
Alekseyev, Mikhail	1918	
Aleksin, Anatoly		1924
Ananyev, Anatoly		1925
Bogomolov, Vladimir		1924
Cherkasov, Aleksey	1915	
German, Yury	1910	
Granin, Daniil	1919	
Grekova, Irina	1907	
Honchar, Oles	1918	
Iskander, Fazil		1929
Kaptayeva, Antonina	1909	
Kaverin, Venyamin	1902	
Kazakov, Yury		1927
Kron, Aleksandr	1909	
Ketlinskaya, Vera	1906	
Nilin, Pavel	1908	
Rybakov, Anatoly	1911	
Sartakov, Sergey	1908	
Stadnyuk, Ivan	1920	
Tendryakov, Vladimir	1923	
Troyepolsky, Gavriil	1905	
Zakrutkin, Vitaly	1908	
Zalygin, Sergey	1913	

SOURCE: Author's personal poll.

occurred after Stalin died (in March 1953). About half of them attended Moscow's Gorky Institute of Literature. Seventeen are among the 290 members of the *pravleniye* (presidium) of the Writers' Union of the USSR, elected at its Seventh Congress in July 1981; missing are the names of Pikul and the two pairs of brothers, Strugatsky and Vainer, and, of course, those of the dead. Eight are in the Union's secretariat, its power center: Markov is chairman; Abramov, Aitmatov, Bondarev, Chakovsky, Dumbadze, Ivanov, and Proskurin are secretaries.

Glancing at the list of runners-up, one notices that their age distribution is the opposite of the first group. Only five were born after 1923. Their advanced age may well account for their lagging behind in popularity.

Chapter 13 discusses classical Russian authors, both old (up through Chekhov) and new. The list of new classics includes three living authors: Valentin Katayev (born in 1897), Leonid Leonov (born in 1899), and Mikhail Sholokhov (born in 1905), famous for *And Quiet Flows the Don*. All three were frequently mentioned by my sources, but only in connection with fiction they had written long ago.

The Writers' Union of the USSR has about ten thousand members, and each of them, by virtue of his membership, has a chance to be published, so how does a writer get to the top? In most cases he will move up a ladder of four steps.

As a rule one's literary career starts not with a book but with a periodical, preferably one of the reviews with literary inclinations to which an aspiring author turns first. Just as in old Russia, these are simply called the "thick reviews," or for obvious reasons, today they may also be called the "prestigious reviews." *Periodicals of the USSR*, published yearly in Moscow, lists 126 titles under "Literary Magazines," including 40 in Russian; about two dozen of these are of a national stature. Quite a few are published outside of Moscow, for instance *Sibirskiye ogni* (Siberian Fires) in Novosibirsk.

The usual circulation of reviews printed in Moscow and Leningrad runs between 100 and 350 thousand copies, but some, such as *Yunost* and *Smena*, go as high as 2 million. For a long time *Novy mir* (New World) was considered the highest quality review; its present circulation is about 350 thousand copies. Now this honor, so I found, is accorded to *Nash sovremennik* (Our Contemporary) with a circulation of 335 thousand. The illustrated weekly *Ogonyok* (The Little Fire), which has an even larger circulation, has helped some top writers to achieve their breakthrough.

The second rung on the ladder is the book. Many novels are first serialized in one of the reviews just mentioned; this was also the case in the old days, and Dostoyevsky often had a very hard time meeting the deadline. But only a book really makes a writer. If successful, a book will appear in several, often in many, editions, some of which may be published outside of Moscow. Russian authors take special pride in also being published abroad, especially in the West.

The popularity of an author is greatly enhanced if he reaches the third step—publication of a book in *Roman gazeta* (Novel Gazette). Printed on cheap paper and on large pages (about the size of standard American office stationery) and published twice a month in about two million copies, *Roman gazeta* presents popular prose works for the price of 60 kopeks. For some novels (or collections of short stories) one issue is enough, especially if they are somewhat condensed; others take two or even more issues. Aitmatov's works have appeared five times in *Roman gazeta*, thus multiplying the total circulation of his books from less than four million to about fifteen million copies.

Students of library science working at the Lenin Library were kind enough to check for me which of the 24 authors had had their books reprinted in *Roman gazeta*. The figures in parentheses indicate the number of issues devoted to each writer: Abramov (2), Aitmatov (5), Belov (1), Bondarev (6), Bykau (5), Chakovsky (6), Dumbadze (2), Ivanov (3), Lipatov (4), Markov (4), Nagibin (1), Proskurin (3), Rasputin (2), Semyonov (1), Shukshin (1), Simonov (5), Soloukhin (2), Trifonov (1), Yefremov (1).

Even more important for the popularity of an author is the fourth step: use of his book for cinema, television, or theater. Quite often when I asked someone why he read and liked a certain novel, the response was: "Because I saw it at the movies (or on television)." Three of Julian Semyonov's novels, serialized for television, are said to have been seen by 150 million, 57 million, and 37 million people, respectively. There is an additional way in which television promotes an author's fame: from time to time a lecture by a writer and the question and answer period following it are broadcast on nationwide television. Chakovsky seemed very pleased to tell me about one such occasion, which because of the obvious interest to the viewers, was repeated after a few weeks. But this only happens to authors who have made it anyway.

Not all the 24 have attained their great popularity using these four steps. Pikul and the two pairs of brothers, Strugatsky and Vainer, did not make *Roman gazeta*. However, the four steps are the general rule for a successful march to the top. That, of course, only explains *how* a writer gets there. The question remains: *why*?

In order to be called "most popular," novels and stories must reflect some fundamental tendencies in the population, perhaps even antedate them. To mention just a few: nostalgia (similar to the West) for the "good old days" when life was tough but simple (now it is still tough but far from simple and often highly confusing); the desire to learn more and to get a clearer and more objective picture of recent Soviet and world history, and of Stalin, than was possible from earlier black-and-white propaganda; an increasingly uneasy feeling that man's exploitation of the natural environment—which until recently was considered mankind's inexhaustible reserve—has gone astray; the strong desire, difficult for us to understand, to relive again the battles of the Second World

War; an interest in science and technology and hence in the new field of science fiction; the need for entertainment and relaxation that is growing steadily as working hours decrease and that explains the rapidly rising demand for whodunits. Around two lonely but mighty trees, Arthur Conan Doyle and Jules Verne, an entire forest of authors dealing with these equally recent genres is growing up in Russia.

In addition to new interests and concerns, nations also have literary traditions that survive revolutions. The expansiveness of Russia, both of the country and of its people's character, corresponds to the readers' sympathy for the epically broad and lengthy novel, the *epopeya*, as the Russians call it. The Western reader is often scared by fifteen hundred pages and the multitude of personages populating Russian prose, especially by their strange and unpronounceable names. For this reason I have mentioned as few as possible, relying instead on expressions such as "the kolkhoz chairman" or "the grandmother." Even if one and the same person is referred to by four names (given name, father's name, family name, and pet name—which often has little similarity with the given name, such as Sasha for Aleksandr) the Russians immediately know which character is meant. Fortunately for the less patient Western reader, Russian literature also offers a tradition of novellas and short stories in which Chekhov is perhaps the most influential figure; some of our 24 are actually best known for their short prose.

Another tradition still to be found in Russian literature is its value orientation. Here are a few values typically found in Russia's *classical* novels: bravery, honor, romantic love, loyalty (also toward tsar and government), patriotism, sense of family, chivalry, respect for the aged, humanism, piety, and the ability to sacrifice and to suffer. When the Revolution and Civil War turned the country upside down, strange, new values came to the fore such as class struggle, intense hatred of the class enemy as a precondition for his "liquidation," "proletarian internationalism," atheism, sexual freedom at the expense of the family. In the struggle against the "class enemy" anything was permitted, even if he was one's own father. But nowadays, in a process that began under Stalin, respect for many of the traditional values has reemerged in literature, as we shall see, under different historical conditions, of course, but with little change in substance. This change is being sensed and considered by most writers. In that respect, Soviet novels of today remind me more of the Russian novel of the nineteenth century than of the revolutionary literature of the twenties and thirties.

There is, however, one more question to be asked in connection with the rise to top popularity: Who decides how many copies will be printed of each individual author's work? In the West the answer is simple: as many as the market can bear. As long as there is a demand, publishers will publish. But how does it work in the USSR with her chronic paper shortage? Much to my chagrin I have no clear answer to this question because the decision-making process is involved and bureaucratic. As we have seen, a bookstore or a library places its orders with the publishing houses on the basis of their advance programs. Thus the publishers have some idea about what the market wants. With these figures in mind, but not exclusively on their basis, the publishing houses submit their demands for paper to the higher organs. But what happens then I do not know, and there is no need to speculate about it. This study is concerned with the popularity of authors and books, which in the USSR does not correlate with the number of editions and the size of the print run.

The road to the top requires—apart from talent—hard work and the perseverance to struggle upward, year after year, from step to step. It further demands a sensitive awareness of the prevailing tendencies in the nation, as well as, and this goes without saying, a good nose for what can and cannot be published at any given moment, and, of course, luck. Our 24 authors have all of these.

II
The 24 Authors

4
Being a Writer

The writer enjoys an extraordinary position in Russia, as this brief story may illustrate. Two Russian writers went fishing. Some boys from a nearby village asked who they were and seemed much impressed when the answer was writers. One of the writers caught many fish; the other none, and thus the boys concluded that he was a fake. How could he be a writer if he could not catch fish?

Konstantin Paustovsky, one of the modern classic writers mentioned in a later chapter of this book, recounted this story in his *Voronozh Summer* and made this comment: "For the boys, a writer is a truly legendary figure, unquestionably brilliant in all walks of life, a wizard with golden hands who knows everything, sees everything, understands everything, and does everything magnificently."

Although I am not a fisherman and am a foreigner to boot, I concur with Paustovsky. Formerly, many years ago, when asked about my profession, I said: "Professor." That was accepted by the Russians as a matter of course. But once, when I replied "writer," the reaction was totally different. "Pisatel!" people exclaimed with an expression of awe. Since then I stick to writer, reaping great respect, which, however, somewhat diminishes the moment I confess to being neither a poet nor a novelist but merely an author of books on international affairs. Still, I am a writer just the same.

The high regard for writers is a long-standing tradition among Russians. In the nineteenth century, their great writers served as the conscience of the nation. There have always been limits to what an author could say. People have learned to take this for granted and to read between the lines. There have also been ups and downs in the treatment of writers by those in power. During the thirties and forties a number of writers disappeared from view and some perished. In Khrushchev's time Solzhenitsyn was allowed to publish his first story (1964), still one of his best; later he was exiled (1974), others followed, with or against their will, and still others were imprisoned.

In order to publish legally and, that means, in order to remain a member of the Writers' Union, a Soviet author must refrain from writing "propaganda for war, racism, or antisovietism." These are not clearly defined terms and are open to different interpretations. The lines between "constructive criticism" and "antisovietism," for example, can be variously drawn by the authorities and also by the authors themselves, as the reader will notice.

Most intellectuals, including writers, wish to think not only about their personal problems but also about those of their country. Being sensitive people, they observe many wrongs in need of correction, many evils in need of attention. Those with a very strong desire to say so can easily get into trouble. Others who are mainly storytellers and who, above all, want to write for large audiences, to entertain them, but at the same time to help them in their lives by telling them about values that are permitted within the framework of the system, will have less trouble or none at all. Some writers—including some of the following 24—were once attacked and threatened and are now, although even more outspoken, winners of state prizes.

An author with millions of fans behind him and with a keen sense for the fine and often changing line that separates what is permitted from what is not, who finds the right style for transmitting his ideas and who shows that, whenever he criticizes, he does so not out of spite but out of patriotic concern, can almost be a law unto himself. But whatever he does, he will enjoy the Russians' respect, love, and awe for being a Writer.

Before describing the works of fiction especially popular among Russians, I shall introduce the 24 authors whom I found to be today's favorites. Although these men could not be more different, I have assembled some of them into groups, beginning with the two I have personally known longest; they and a third author write eagerly read novels relating to modern history. They are followed by three writers on World War II and four who are famous for their long family sagas; three writers lead in the field of short stories, three in mystery and science fiction. Three are not Russians in the proper sense of the word (a Belorussian, a Georgian, a Kirgiz). The others who do not readily fit into any of these six groups appear separately.

5
Three on Modern History

Of all 24 authors on my list, I have known **Aleksandr Chakovsky** longest. Born in 1913, he is the third oldest among them. One of his seniors, Yefremov, is dead, and I had no chance to meet Markov. My first encounter with Chakovsky was in 1945 through his first novel.

At that time I was living in Shanghai, on Avenue Joffre in the French Concession. On that same street was a Russian bookstore, the only one in all of Japanese-controlled East Asia that was allowed, throughout the war, to import and sell books, magazines, and newspapers from the USSR. There was, it seems, some understanding between Tokyo and Moscow, who were not at war until August 1945. I visited the store almost daily, and soon my bookshelves were bursting with Soviet books, including some recent novels that naturally turned around the war for the most part. All of them were strictly Stalinist and full of propaganda; the party was always right.

Only one novel was different: *Eto bylo v Leningrade* (That Was in Leningrade, 1945) written by one Aleksandr Chakovsky. It was different because it was intensely human and therefore almost unpolitical. The heroes' main interests are neither Stalin, who does not even figure here although his name crowds the pages of other contemporary books, nor the world revolution, nor the duty to increase steel production, nor even the hatred of the Germans. The two heroes love each other, and because of their love they seek to survive and naturally also to contribute to the victory. But the young war correspondent and his beloved Lida in beleaguered Leningrad are not marionettes dangling on ideological strings or parrots of *Pravda* editorials. This goes for the other characters, too. A wounded young lieutenant dies without uttering political slogans, and one of the heroes is encouraged to read the Old Testament: "There is much joy of life in it and a strong passion. Without these one cannot now live in Leningrad." While many starve or freeze to death in the cut-off city, a pianist in the Hotel Astoria survives because of his grand piano. "If you love something very much, you don't die."

Exactly ten years later, in autumn 1955, for the first time after the war, I accompanied Chancellor Konrad Adenauer on his only visit to Moscow. Among the events the Russians had planned to entertain their German guests was a reception by the Writers' Union of the USSR on Vorovsky Street. I went out of a feeling of nostalgia because in the midthirties my wife and I had lived in this building's servants' quarters (the best we could find in hopelessly overcrowded Moscow) and also because I wanted to meet some writers. The invitation had been signed by Boris Polevoy, a chairman of the Union and the author of a war book that had sold millions of copies, *The Story of a Real Man* (1946). I had not liked its all too didactic and moralizing character, but it was one of the most successful books of that time. While our small group sipped tea and cognac and ate cookies, Polevoy introduced his eight colleagues one by one. When he came to Chakovsky, I requested permission to introduce him myself. I explained to my countrymen that he had written what I considered the best Soviet novel about the Second World War and also gave a brief rundown of its plot. Polevoy might not have been too happy that I did not praise him instead; Chakovsky, however, seemed quite pleased.

He was less satisfied with my later reviews of two of his novels. In *Mirnye dni* (Peaceful Days, which I read in the 1950 East German edition), the earlier novel's heroes are united in freed Leningrad, but their happiness is marred by a black cloud. All Lida can think about is a new method of producing a special kind of steel in the laboratory where she works. She is disappointed that her man, after years of war, desires at least a little relaxation. He annoys her with his plea: "Not even the war could harm our love. Should it really flounder on account of the problem of developing extra-hard steel?" In the end, of course, he realizes (with the help of the local party secretary) that he is wrong to criticize her devotion to work. Lida accepts him again, and the two of them, together with an war-orphaned boy whom she has taken in, plant young trees in Leningrad's new Victory Park.

U nas uzhe utro (Here It Is Already Morning) was written to inspire the workers in the fish-canning industry on Sakhalin, the easternmost Soviet island, to work still harder. They are determined to do so, and one of them, in a symbolic gesture, "turns toward the sun. Its slanting rays touch his face softly. The morning begins."

We had a few little skirmishes concerning these two novels and my review of them when we met on various occasions, first in the editorial office of *Inostrannaya literatura* (Foreign Literature), which is the Russians' window on literary life abroad and which Chakovsky led from 1955 to 1962, then at the offices of *Literaturnaya gazeta* where he served as editor-in-chief. His work in this smart and lively weekly to which I have subscribed since the thirties keeps him very busy, and I admire his writing, in spite of his commitments, two very long novels, *Blokada* (Blockade)* about the blockade of Leningrad, a sequel to *That Was in Leningrad* mentioned earlier, and *Pobeda* (Victory)* about the Potsdam Conference of 1945.

Chakovsky was born in St. Petersburg in 1913 the son of a physician. He has been a professional writer ever since he completed his studies at the Gorky Institute of Literature in 1938. A man of medium height with a slight build, of slow speech and movement, he knows English but prefers to speak Russian with me. "We have known each other for a long time," he began at our last meeting in 1982, "and even before we first met we had both been writing for many years, so there is no need to beat around the bush." The trouble with Western interviewers, he added, was their own or their publisher's desire to make something sensational out of every conversation. Some time ago he had granted an hour-long interview to an American journalist (he mentioned his name). But when he read the man's story in the paper, he found only marginal questions discussed, not the essence of their conversation.

I sympathized with him, having had similar experiences in the course of my life, and thanked him for his willingness to receive me just the same. As for myself, I was primarily interested in his novels, I explained, but naturally I also wanted to talk to their author, who was, as of course he could guess, quite high on my list of the most popular fiction writers in Russia. We talked about *Victory*, which I had recently read, while his secretary brought tea, cookies, and chocolates. Through the windows of his office on one of the top floors of the journal's comfortable building I saw the snow-covered roofs of the smaller neighboring houses.

We agreed that Russian readers were definitely interested in novels dealing with contemporary history, especially if they create the impression of describing these events more or less as they actually happened. I mentioned Semyonov as an example of an author using this genre. But we did not agree on another point I raised: "You have obviously read a

---

*Indicates the books that are summarized in Chapter 13, "The Authors and Their Books."

lot of material about the conference," I said, "official documents as well as the memoirs of the participants such as Churchill, Truman, Bohlen, Byrnes. For your Russian readers all this is largely new and exciting. Why did you not tell them in a bibliographical note what material there is and perhaps even whether you have presented the statements of the leading men at the conference verbatim or as you imagine they might have spoken?" He answered that this was not done in novels. Well, it was up to him, I said; but this was not an ordinary novel, it was a novel concerning an event of utmost historical significance, and, because of the millions of copies read (the novel was also reprinted in *Roman gazeta*), it would shape the image Russians have of the conference for many years, perhaps even for decades. We parted amiably.

While Chakovsky is the writer I have known the longest, **Julian Semyonov** is the man I know best. My indirect acquaintance with him began one evening in Moscow, in the winter of 1973. While walking home from the Lenin Library, I noticed that there were few people in the streets, even the usually overcrowded buses seemed half-empty. My hosts, the German ambassador and his wife, made the same observation but could offer no explanation. So I asked their cook, who seemed surprised at my question. "Didn't you know they are showing an episode of the *Seventeen Moments of a Spring* on TV?"

I hurried to the television set and sat absorbed in the program for a good part of the evening. I saw at least parts of the remaining episodes and the twelfth and last one I watched in its entirety. The novel had been published in *Komsomolskaya pravda*, I recalled, but I had not read it, and only now did I learn that at that time people had fought over the copies. Eventually and with great difficulty I obtained the book from which the film was made. It had the same title and a man named Julian Semyonovich Semyonov as its author.

The story is a thriller, a political thriller to be more precise: a Russian who grew up in Switzerland and therefore speaks German perfectly is working for the Soviet secret service in Germany under the name of Stirlitz. He has infiltrated Hitler's elite guard, the SS, and is rising high in its ranks. *Seventeen Moments** is the story of his adventures in Germany during the last months of the war. There Allen Dulles, at that time the top man in Europe for the OSS, also appears in some scenes. The makeup of the actor who played him in the film was so excellent that I believed the director had used a clip from an old documentary when he appeared for the first time.

The Russians are avid television fans, and they have liked serials ever since they saw the dubbed Russian version of the *Forsyte Saga*. But the *Seventeen Moments of a Spring*, I was told, held the record at that time: between 50 and 80 million people watched the 70 minutes of each sequel. Julian Semyonov, well known even before, was a trademark when the series was only half over, and "SS leader Stirlitz" was everyone's idol, especially the ladies'. The fact that he was played by Vyacheslav Tikhonov, one of the country's most popular actors, added to the serial's appeal. Once in eastern Siberia, someone said to me in a restaurant: "You know, you almost look like Stirlitz." Rarely have I felt so flattered.

A few years after I had seen the *Seventeen Moments* in Moscow, the phone rang in my Black Forest home. The public relations man from the Soviet Embassy in Bonn informed me that a new correspondent for *Literaturnaya gazeta* had just arrived from Moscow and wanted to meet me. Would I receive him? "Certainly," I said. We have a special relationship, that paper and I. By far the most lively journal published in the USSR, it is also the one that attacks me most frequently (for being on good terms with China, for one thing). When I asked for the man's name, "Semyonov," was the reply.

"Which Semyonov?" (There are so many in the USSR; one of them at that time was even the Kremlin's ambassador to Bonn.)

"Julian Semyonovich Semyonov," the man from the Embassy said.

"The one who wrote the *Seventeen Moments*?"

"None other."

I was delighted. "By all means send him up. He can stay at my house."

When he arrived a few days later, together with one of his countrymen, I welcomed a heavyset man, not too well shaved, not too elegantly dressed, in his late forties—something between a bear and an army captain in a Lermontov tale. Our discussion lasted well beyond midnight and continued the next morning—the first of many that have followed in the years since. He has stayed at my Black Forest home several times, once with one of his teenage daughters, as I have stayed, since his return to the USSR, in his dacha on the outskirts of Moscow.

Semyonov is a tireless researcher who tries to observe the people and the documents as well as the places he writes about with his own eyes. When I drove him to Nuremberg, he was not satisfied until he had seen all the important sites of the Hitler era including the hall where the war crimes tribunal was held, which was especially unlocked for us, and the building where the executions had been carried out. But there are also sites he wants to see simply as a Russian, without intending to use them in his books; together we went to Baden-Baden where Turgenev and Dostoyevsky lived and to Badenweiler where Chekhov died.

Eventually I learned that a shadow lay over Semyonov's life. In the sinister year of 1937, when he was six years old, one of his uncles was arrested, and in 1947 at the age of seventeen he saw his father being taken away, a professional officer who had fought with distinction in the war against the Germans. The many petitions the young man wrote on his behalf to various organizations only brought trouble down upon his own shoulders. His father was not freed until 1953. In the meantime Julian Semyonov studied at the Moscow Institute for Oriental Languages, concentrating especially on Persian. But the life of a scholar did not appeal to him; he wanted to see the world and to write. In Russia and Siberia, in China and Afghanistan he worked for newspapers and magazines; he even spent several weeks at the North Pole.

Then came his first books. The detective story *Petrovka 38** was made into a play that was produced in almost a hundred theaters. In 1964 he published his first Stirlitz novel and immediately captured the readers' imagination. Others soon followed, showing the master agent busily working for the Russian fatherland. So far a dozen films and seven television serials have been made from his novels. Some of the serials were broadcast more than once; *Seventeen Moments* was shown three times. Hardly a Russian has not seen that serial at least once.

Semyonov's fans wanted more and still more Stirlitz stories. The hero's latest appearance, in *A Bomb for the Chairman,** is again set in Germany, mostly in West Berlin, in the autumn of 1967. But, now 67, Stirlitz is no longer the center of attention. By now a dignified professor of modern, especially German, history at Moscow University, he appears here and there, but it is he who solves the novel's puzzle in the end.

Although Stirlitz, with rare exceptions, has to deal with Germans, there is surprisingly little anti-German sentiment in Semyonov's books. Instead, an undercurrent of sympathy pervades his work. I once asked him about it; after all, Hitler's Germany had been a deadly enemy of Russia's and had inflicted terrible harm on his people. He offered a number of reasons for his sympathetic tone that many Russians might share. The Germans are Russia's most important neighbors; the two nations have a long tradition not only of cooperation but also of war; a powerful German influence upon Russian intellectual life has existed for centuries. Then he added a very personal experience: "At the end of the war, my father, an administrative official with the Soviet occupation forces in East Germany, was stationed in a small town near Berlin. Then in my teens, I played a lot with German kids. I liked them and learned from them some things that amazed me. Often we went fishing in a small river. My German playmates took a yardstick along, much to my amazement. The custom was that small fish had to be returned to the water; only those longer than eight centimeters could be taken home. I marveled and thought to myself: our Ivans still have a long way to go before they learn this kind of orderliness." How many times I heard him quote the old German saying, in German, of course: *Ordnung muss sein!* (There must be order.)

Like Stirlitz—and most Russians—Semyonov is an ardent Russian patriot; he likes patriots in general and is puzzled to see only a lukewarm variety of patriotism in Germany today. Russians are Russians for him, even if they are emigrés, "Russians like I am," he calls them. One of his heroes plans to display in a historical museum the pictures of the tsars, including that of the last one, as well as those of his leading ministers, Witte and Stolypin. When he encounters opposition, he says: "It is impermissible to fear the history of one's own government." Stirlitz no doubt expresses the author's feelings when he remarks about a Russian emigré: "Without a fatherland a writer perishes." Patriotism is the driving force in Stirlitz's life, too. He risks his life for a *socialist* fatherland, to be sure, but for the *fatherland* just the same; one could imagine him in a similar role in the Germany of the First World War when the tsars ruled Russia.

As for me, I feel somewhat uneasy with Stirlitz for two reasons. First, he is proud of being a *Chekist*; he sees himself in the line of agents of an organization *(Cheka)* that ceased to exist in 1922, although its task was taken over by similar organizations using different acronyms (among them GPU and, lately, KGB). These organizations and their common ancestor, Felix Dzerzhinsky, still evoke terror in many Russians, certainly the older ones. By calling himself a *Chekist*, Stirlitz puts the halo of his own heroism on a tradition that for us in the West seems best characterized by executions and prison camps. Second, Stirlitz is a spy, and I have always felt antipathy toward that profession. I realize that spies are a fact of life and that one's own spy is a hero. The Soviets even use a different word for their own spies, *razvedchik*, meaning "scout" in the military sense. Their spies are noble scouts (for peace, of course), while other nation's spies are abominable. My objections to spies may be questioned by many readers in the West, for in today's novels in the style of Le Carré or 007, they are heroes, too, as much as Leatherstocking and Hawkeye once were for me.

In addition to Chakovsky and Semyonov, a third author on my list rode to success on his historical novels, with the difference, however, that he chose to explore Russia prior to the Revolution. I knew very little about him, until, on one of the first days of my stay in Moscow in 1981, I witnessed a dispute between two Russian writers concerning his work.

One called him a shady character, greedy for cheap sensations; an un-scrupulous pirate of other people's ideas who would lift whole pages from their works without giving them credit; a charlatan who, far from serving the cause of literature, only catered to the public's poor taste; a rabid nationalist; and an anti-Semite to boot. The other disagreed. That man, he said, performs an important service for the Russian reader by informing him of vital events that have been neglected until recently and that the people need to be cognizant of in order to understand the world of our time. "Borrowing" from other people's writings is legitimate for a writer of fiction.

The quarrel concerned a novel by a man with the curious name of **Pikul**. (The final letter is a so-called soft *l*, pronounced approximately like the *L* in Lucia.) Strangely enough—and most unusual for Rus-sians—neither of the two quarreling writers knew Pikul's given name. It started with a *V*, they thought, and they had no idea what his father's name was, although knowledge of the patronymic is a must for Rus-sians. They were not even sure of their colleague's national origin; he must be from one of the Baltic republics, they guessed. My curiosity aroused, I checked various encyclopedias but found no entry. Finally, in the Lenin Library, I saw his catalogue cards: my two friends had been right about the *V*, Valentin was his name. But his father's name was not mentioned, and only by chance did I learn that it was Savva, making his full name Valentin Savvich Pikul.

To be sure, some of Pikul's prose had been printed in Soviet monthlies and in book form, and some had been reviewed (not enthusi-astically), but I had read nothing about his work that prepared me for the keen interest and the lively discussions I encountered later on my trip.

Why was I so unprepared for Pikul's popularity? Because it is one thing to study Soviet literature from one's desk in California or Ger-many and another to look in Russia for the echo of these literary produc-tions in people's minds.

Pikul did not respond to the letter in which I asked him for some information about himself. But eventually I learned a few things from other sources: he traces his origin to the Ukrainian village of Kagarlyk, some 80 kilometers south of Kiev. His father joined the navy, served on a destroyer, and died at Stalingrad when the navy sent many of its men to the defense of the city. His mother came from ancient Pskov, the west-ernmost city of Russia proper, close to the Estonian border. Born in 1928, he spent his early youth in Leningrad but had barely finished the fifth grade when the war started in 1941. In the following spring he was evacuated with many other children from the beleaguered city and came to a *unga* school (from the German word *Junge* in *Schiffsjunge*, "ship's boy") on the distant Arctic island of Solovki. He served on a destroyer until the end of the war. (A quarter of a century later he published a book about these boyhood experiences: *Malchiki s bantikami* (Boys with Ribbons, meaning the ribbons on their sailor hats). Like many young veterans he felt the urge to become a writer when the war ended; at that time he was seventeen. He produced, so he says, three novels that he burned. The fourth one was published, *Okeansky patrul* (Ocean Patrol) and later rewritten into *Requiem for Convoy PQ-17*.* He now lives in Riga, I am told.

Among his later novels I found that three were most frequently discussed: they all deal with Russian diplomacy in the eighteenth and nineteenth centuries and with the end of the tsars' empire. His desire, he once said, was to describe the main events of Russian history during the last four centuries. To do this, according to his calculations, he would have to live to the age of 125; I wish him luck.

6
Three on World War II

Of the three leading writers who have won their fame from novels on World War II, I have met two, Bondarev and Vasilyev. Neither of them means very much to Western readers, but for Russians their names are household words.

Yury Bondarev, whom I first saw at the Writers' Union of the Russian Soviet Federated Socialist Republic on Komsomolsky Prospect, does not look the way one would expect a writer of war books to appear. He had a very civilian and almost melancholy appearance and a good-natured warmth in his eyes as they met mine in his small office. I felt I could still sense in his eyes some of the weariness caused by the thousands of kilometers he had marched as a young artillery officer in heavy battles all the way from Stalingrad to Prague.

Born in 1924 in Orsk at the southern end of the Urals, he came to Moscow as a child and was seventeen when Hitler invaded his country. He spent the following years in the artillery, first as a soldier, later as an officer. After the war he entered Moscow's Gorky Institute of Literature. He wrote his first stories and some poems in the style of Esenin and Blok. And then he himself became a writer.

Bondarev belongs to a group of Soviet writers who were still in their late teens when the war began and who spent years in the thick of battle, experiencing countless close encounters with death. At a very early age, they took on strenuous responsibilities, thought much in between and maybe even during battles, and returned with the intention of writing in order to keep alive what they had learned and, with peace restored, to turn over a new leaf in their own and their country's existence. Quite a few of them joined Moscow's Gorky Institute of Literature. (Please consult Table 2 for more information.) From the midfifties onward, the war generation produced a large part of the novels that quickly became and to this day remain the favorites of the Russian reader. One of these men was Bondarev.

His first novel had the fitting and almost programmatic title *Yunost komandirov* (The Youth of the Commanders, 1956). (We would say, "The Youth of the Officers," but after the Revolution of 1917 the officers in the Red Army were called *komandiry* to distinguish them from the tsar's officers. Only during the Second World War was the old term restored.) The book was greeted by friendly reviews, mainly, Bondarev thinks, because the critics felt obliged to say some nice words about a promising young writer. ("So young and already the author of a real novel!") But it did not make a big splash. "For us, 1956 was the year of one book that overshadowed all others, Dudintsev's *Ne khlebom yedinym*" (Not by Bread Alone, published in *Novy mir* in autumn of that year).

I liked these words. Bondarev was the only one of the authors I visited who referred to the author of that courageous novel, which, even more than Ehrenburg's *Thaw*, broke the ice, teaching young writers how to see and describe their country quite differently from the way it had been done hitherto. Since then, Dudintsev has rarely been published or mentioned.

Bondarev's first big success came with *Bataliony prosyat ognya* (The Battalions Are Asking for Fire, 1957), his second with *The Last Shots** (1959). The last of his big war novels was *Hot Snow** (1970). In between he wrote *Silence** (in two parts, 1962 and 1964) and *Rodstven-niki* (Relatives, 1969). Both had civilian themes but included some military scenes, as did his two later novels, *The Shore** (1975) and *Vybor* (The Choice, 1981).

Bondarev did not hurry me, and the secretary who had been helpful in arranging the meeting brought refreshments. Like any writer he wanted to hear my own impressions of his books before commenting on them himself. The success of the *Batallions*, he felt, was due to the new and realistic tone in which it described the war. In October 1943, two battalions with a foothold on the western bank of the Dnepr were sacrificed in order to confuse the Germans. *Battalions* recounts how this affected the men in these battalions as well as those in command of the operation. (Bykau, one of the 24 most popular writers and himself an author of war books, once said: "We all come from Bondarev's bat-

---

*Indicates the books that are summarized in Chapter 13, "The Authors and Their Books."

talions.") But there was also negative criticism because Bondarev described the war as a horrible ordeal and a tragedy rather than as a succession of uplifting events. He even showed men in uniform who could not live up to their responsibilities. After *Shots* was published, he was told that he should not have allowed his young hero to die. The first review of *Snow*, he continued, was quite hostile for similar reasons, but then the mood shifted. Anyway, he had by now, especially due to *Silence* and the film made from it, such a firm hold on his audience that reviews did not matter much.

When we came to *Shore* during our discussion, I rose and said: "As a German I want to thank you for this novel." He stood up too. We shook hands and sat down again. I then asked him about the Russian reaction. Not once in the many letters he had received concerning *Shore*, he said, had he been criticized for making a German woman the heroine. On the contrary, some people thanked him for providing a portrait that allowed them to revise their previous image of the Germans. (When I saw the dramatized version of *Shore* on the stage of the Maly Theater a few days later, I noticed a young officer and his female companion sitting right behind me, an artillery man as Bondarev and the hero in *Shore* had been. During the intermission, after the scene in which the officer almost killed his sergeant for misbehaving toward German civilians, I turned around and asked the young man how he felt about the scene. Without hesitation he answered: "I fully endorse the officer's action.")

I asked Bondarev about the nature of his fan mail. With a twinkle in his eye he named five different groups. First, enthusiastic agreement, admiration, thanks. Second, "Your book, comrade writer, is good but the end (or some other part) is awful, how could you . . . " Third, our youth is tempted by wickedness anyway, therefore it is wrong of you to write about extramarital love, rape, military desertion, and such signs of decay. Fourth, please let me talk to you for just twenty minutes, I have a darn good theme for your next novel. Fifth (only from women), "Your hero (the name of one of Bondarev's many heroes is mentioned) has profoundly impressed me. Now I measure all men by him, and I can't find a single one that is his match. What can I do? Please help."

Naturally, Bondarev had also been criticized for creating (in *Choice*) a not altogether unsympathetic picture of a former prisoner of war in Germany who chose to remain in the West. Bondarev explained that on his travels abroad he had occasionally met Russian emigrés; he considered their behavior wrong, but he had found strong characters among them: only such could stand the strain of emigré life.

He was not surprised when I said that *Relatives* had never been mentioned to me by his fans. Which of his novels did he like best? He did not want to answer; they were all his children. But he named the largest number of editions: *Snow* had 30 in the USSR and 29 abroad (including Eastern European countries); *Silence*, 10 and 29.

When I asked him about "his teachers," he mentioned Lev Tolstoy as expected, calling him the greatest storyteller of our time and the man who taught him how to think. Next he spoke of Thomas Mann, and he also added Chekhov and Turgenev, the Frenchman Zola, the Englishman Oscar Wilde, and the American Thomas Wolfe. More directly he called himself a student of Konstantin Paustovsky (see my discussion of the new Russian classics), who in his seminars at the Gorky Institute, had insisted that a novelist should first study and understand the mood *(nastroyeniye)* of the people and only then attempt to describe it.

Finally I asked him what he wanted to express in his work.

"I want to investigate attraction and repulsion, the good and the bad. What is life and what is death; what is love and what is hatred. Beauty, ugliness, self-sacrifice, jealousy, conscience, cruelty, valor, repentance— these are all landmarks along the road to truth. The eternal problems remain the same in art at all times; the world changes but man has changed very little. Maybe that is why the ancient Greek comprehension of man is still interesting for us."

Of the many speeches given at the Seventh Congress of Writers in 1981, I liked Bondarev's best *(Literaturnaya gazeta,* July 7, 1981). He spoke about symptoms of the moral decline he had noticed in the West in words that many of us might use. Then, in front of millions of viewers and readers, he added that, bitter as it was to confess it, certain worrying symptoms could be found in the USSR too. "The idea of the good life sometimes ends with the dream of urban conveniences; whatever you may feel about the joys the city can offer the soul, for very many people a soft easy chair is preferable to the soft grass on a sunny slope. . . . It is very likely that our best moral anchors . . . and the firm and the eternal [forces] that nourish our souls, were created not in the era of atomic energy but, surprisingly, in the past." He took architecture as a sad example: "Why do we tirelessly build rectangular cities with gigantically wide and windy streets, copying the soulless 'romanticism' of skyscrapers, the spirit of a foreign monastery?" Turning next to man's destruction of nature, he characterized him as a "murderer of nature" and warned in vigorous words against continuing to follow this road, "because there will not be a second earth nor a second sky for us."

Boris Vasilyev comes from a family of hereditary officers, friends told me before I met him. And that was the way he looked, slim and disciplined, in spite of the war wounds that had impaired his vision and hearing for quite some time.

By telephone we debated where to meet for lunch. As one possibility,

I mentioned my room in the Hotel National with its view of the Kremlin and Red Square. He had no objections. My announcement of whom I intended to entertain in my room caused a small sensation among the staff in the hotel restaurant: "Vasilyev? Boris Vasilyev? The writer?" When he arrived, the floor lady herself escorted him to my room, and the waitress who brought us first the menu and later our food had made herself especially pretty, it seemed to me.

The description of his family background had been correct. As far back as his relatives could remember, his male ancestors had been tsarist officers of medium rank, small nobility in the Smolensk area. His grand-father, also an officer, Vasilyev said, was killed in a duel in 1902. When I looked a bit puzzled, he added without a trace of irony: "A lady's honor was in question." His father had fought in the First World War as a tsarist officer. After the liberal February Revolution of 1917 he was elected representative of his regiment, and a year later without much ado, he became a *komandir* in the Red Army. The family tradition of service for Russia continued under the Red flag. His son, my guest Boris, entered the military service as a matter of course, but he experienced only the defeats and retreats of the war's first year. When the turn-around came, he was in a hospital in northern Russia.

During and after his recuperation, he felt like writing about the war but could not summon the courage, "Writers are chosen ones," he ex-plained his thoughts at that time, "extraordinary and important people who understand the soul of their nation and can speak for it, seers, often martyrs." He mentioned names from a long list of Russian poets and writers who had been imprisoned or had given their lives for people in difficult political circumstances.

"How could I, an insignificant, junior officer, sit at the same table with Tolstoy, be it even at the far end? My last courage vanished when I saw the flood of books about the war published year after year by men who had been in the thick of it to the end, who knew each single battle. Nor did I feel sufficiently educated; I had not been to the university; I was just a simple army engineer. The only thing I finally dared to do was write a play. *Officers* I called it. They made a film from it which was often shown and asked me to write more scenarios. I did. But with films you remember only the names of directors and actors, not those of the scriptwriters. For the public I remained an unknown."

Then, once more, Vasilyev overcame his apprehensions. Almost a quarter of a century after the end of the war, when it seemed that all that could be said about it had been said long ago, he wrote his first story, *Dawns Are Quiet Here.** *Yunost* published it in 1969, printing 1.8 million copies. With its descriptions of the fighting and suffering of a sergeant and his women-soldiers, it became an overnight success. One edition after the other was printed; a film was made that is still shown; seventeen different dramatized versions were staged at countless theaters including some abroad (even one in Japan); and it was made into an opera. His more mature story *His Name Was Not Listed** was almost as successful and was dramatized on many stages.

"In these books I have said what I wanted to say about the war. It is necessary to say it because some of our youth have begun to forget from where we came, to forget about the people-saints who gave their lives in the name of the future. War is primarily a human drama for me. Strategy I leave to others. My heroes became involved in the war as in any other catastrophe. Once in it, all their physical and spiritual forces were challenged and mobilized. Yet, the war remained for them a strange environment from which they return, if they survive, into their normal world. Other authors let their heroes lead their full life in the war and describe the campaigns and battles in great detail. I don't. Some people have reproached me for changing subjects and styles; some even told me that I did not have a style of my own. But I don't think this is a mistake. A work's style depends on its content. I could be a different author with each novel. Anyway, my *Do Not Shoot the White Swans** was far removed from the war. It was also made into a play and an opera. Later I even wrote a historical novel about the war with Turkey [1877–78] and a short autobiography."

At about the same moment we noticed that the Kremlin's shadows on that winter evening were growing longer. Before he left, he put two of his books on my table, a Russian author's most precious gift.

Not long after the beginning of the war between Germany and the Soviet Union in 1941, a poem began making the rounds among the many thousands of Russian emigrants in Shanghai, the Chinese port city where I was then living. It was very simple and so unpolitical that it immediately caught on not only with the relatively few pro-Soviet emigrés but also with the many anti-Soviet (and at that time pro-German) Russians. The first line, which was repeated throughout the poem, merely said: *Zhdi menya* (Wait for me). For the millions of Russian women to whom the poem was addressed, these unpretentious lines expressed the overwhelming sentiment of the time: we shall wait for each other until the war is over, no matter how long it may last. The poet's name was **Konstantin Simonov.**

Several years later, still in Shanghai, I read Simonov's first book. With many other Germans, I was interned in Kiangwan Camp near Shanghai. A friendly U.S. officer gave me the armed services edition of

Simonov's *Dni i nochi* (Days and Nights); the English translation had just been published and sent to U.S. military libraries and PX book-shops. Written in 1943–44 and hurriedly printed by the monthly *Znamya*, the novel became an immediate success in Russia and the allied countries. It described the heroic exploits of one Captain Saburov during 70 days of fighting in and around Stalingrad: how he unmasks and strangles a Russian traitor with his own hands; how he falls in love with a nurse. The story ends with the Soviet counteroffensive, which led, in January 1943, to the encirclement of an entire German army and to the decisive Soviet victory.

Simonov, born in 1915, was the son of a soldier in the tsarist army. After attending a factory school, he enrolled in the Gorky Institute of Literature in Moscow from 1935 to 1938. His first poem was published in 1934, his first drama in 1939. During the war, he served as a corre-spondent for the army daily *Krasnaya zvezda* and later visited the United States. He was cautious in his political life. After the party decree of 1946 he loyally wrote polemical dramas such as *Russky vopros* (The Russian Question, 1946), which played in New York and was rather critical of America. He received six Stalin prizes.

But his fame rests on his war novels: *The Living and the Dead,** with its two sequels, and the three-volume work *The So-called Private Life: From the Notes of Lopatin,** the third volume of which was pub-lished in 1978.

I found it difficult to talk about Simonov with Russians who still have personal memories of the war and postwar years. Since his first wartime poems, his *Wait for Me* or *You Remember, Alyosha, the Roads of Smolensk?*, which everybody knew by heart, and after his *Days and Nights*, Simonov has been a writer of unusual esteem.

"During the war I was a child, evacuated from the danger zone to the rear," a highly educated Russian lady told me. "At that time Si-monov was the first to open my eyes for poetry. A thing like that you never forget for the rest of your life."

About controversial episodes in Simonov's biography, there was no way of talking with her or any other Russians. He is the only writer of his generation whose life's work has been published in ten well-edited volumes. He died in 1979.

7
Four with Epopeyas

Of the four men who have written an *epopeya,* as the Russians like to call long family sagas in the style of Galsworthy, I came to know three, Abramov, Proskurin, and Ivanov.

Meeting **Fyodor Abramov,** who lived with his wife in Leningrad, was not easy. There are no telephone books in the USSR. Eventually, through the Writers' Union in Moscow, I obtained the phone number of its branch in Leningrad, and there I learned that Abramov was recuperating from a serious operation in a recreation home in Komarovo, 40 kilometers west of Leningrad. That is where I found him and where I had a much more leisurely talk with the Abramovs than would have been possible in the busy city. We had something to eat and drink, including a bottle of Pepsi-Cola the hostess managed to get from somewhere, on the assumption that this was what a chap from the Western world wanted. (I have never liked the stuff, but I did not tell her that.)

I had barely finished explaining my project when Abramov reacted with more enthusiasm than I had heard so far from any of my 24.

"A great idea! Why didn't any one of our people think of it?"

He said this even before I had shown him my list (in which he found himself, hardly to his surprise, right under *A*).

Abramov was born into a peasant family in 1920 in the province of Archangel, in the forests of northern Russia, where he also grew up. But he did not look like a villager; he was of slender build, with the face of an intellectual and quick eyes. Lyudmila Vladimirovna, his wife of thirty years, looked even less like a peasant—she could have stepped right out of a Tolstoy novel.

After a short while, the atmosphere in the small room was so friendly that I decided to summarize for my host what I had written about him in the draft of my book. "I am not asking you to be my censor," I said with a laugh. He raised his hands in horror. "But I would like to be corrected if I have a fact or two wrong." What I told him was more or less the following:

One year after Stalin's death, an article in *Novy mir* (1954:4) caused a good deal of furor in Russia and abroad. Its title was "People of the Kolkhoz Village in Postwar Prose" and Fyodor Abramov was its hitherto practically unknown author. "Hitherto *totally* unknown author," interrupted Abramov. I continued. The anger he provoked was due to his debunking the shellacked and prettified existing village literature that was so far removed from the actual situation in the kolkhozes. The author weathered the storm and nine years later fired his second shot: in January 1963 the Leningrad review *Neva* published a story whose title is taken from a Russian expression that has been translated as "around and about."

This story caused a stir similar to that of the *Novy mir* article of 1954 and for much the same reason: his criticism of agricultural policy. After that, Abramov practically disappeared from view for several years. Rereading the story today, one finds it difficult to understand the excitement of two decades ago. In the meantime we have become used to much tougher criticism, some from Abramov himself. But at that time *One Day in the "New Life"** pushed the author onto the road to fame, and to some notoriety.

At the age of eighteen, Abramov had taken up the study of literature at the University of Leningrad. In 1941 he volunteered for the army; he was wounded twice during the heavy battles around Leningrad. After the war, he concluded his studies with a dissertation about Sholokhov, the author of *And Quiet Flows the Don*. From 1956 to 1960 he served as professor of Soviet Literature at his alma mater. Since then he has been a full-time writer.

Like Proskurin and Ivanov, he is primarily known for one big *epopeya*, entitled *Bratya i Syostry* (Brothers and Sisters). The novel is impressive for the honest and courageous way in which the author describes the problems of a Soviet village over a period of about three decades. It is, however, not just a novelized treatise on Soviet agriculture; it is excellent literature.

A dramatized version of the fourth volume, called *The House,**

---

*Indicates the books that are summarized in Chapter 13, "The Authors and Their Books."

premiered on the stage of Moscow's Gogol Theater. Friends advised me not to go. They said: "Wait for the reviews; maybe the new play isn't worth seeing, and the Gogol Theater is at present not one of the best."

I went anyway and found it worth my while. At that time I had not yet read *The House*, although I was familiar with the first three parts of the Pryaslins' story. When I left my winter coat at the cloakroom, I asked the attendant what I should expect—a war story, a comedy, or a tragedy.

"It is an intense drama," she answered. "You have to think yourself into it." She was quite right. The following day I borrowed the novel from a friend.

After I had reached this point, I summarized for Abramov what I had written about *The House* (see Chapter 13) and was pleased to hear from him that he approved of my decision to confine myself to telling my readers about the last part of his tetralogy. Each one of the four parts, he said, at first had evoked negative criticism, but gradually the climate changed in his favor.

When I asked about his duties in the secretariat of the Writers' Union, he explained that most of the work was done by full-time secretaries; the burden on writers serving as secretaries was light. Later, talking about the war, he mentioned the two severe injuries he suffered during the early part of the battle to defend Leningrad against the German army. These disabled him for the rest of the war (the first to his left arm, the second to both legs). But, he quickly added, he owed much to the culture of my country. "Schiller was an inspiration for me from my early youth."

When it got dark, the Abramovs walked me back through the fresh snow to the train. Within an hour the *elektrichka* took me back to Leningrad's "Finland Station."

It came as a profound shock when I read Abramov's obituary in *Pravda*, which called his death a "heavy loss for Soviet literature" (May 17, 1983).

I met **Pyotr Proskurin** at the House of Writers on Herzen Street. In prerevolutionary times, this building was a Masonic Lodge, and it still retains a somewhat pretentious dignity with rooms on different levels. For ordinary Muscovites it is considered a great honor to go there; besides, the food is good and relatively inexpensive. We had barely sat down at a quiet table near a window when a pleasantly smiling blonde appeared with the menus; for her, too, working in the Writers' Union was a good job—better than serving in any old restaurant. After all, some of the most respected people in the USSR dine here. (The House of Scholars is a similarly exalted place.)

Proskurin was hungry; I was not. But because he did not want to eat unless I did, I ordered a small dish of mushrooms (real mushrooms from the forest, not from a sunless cellar), and he a regular meal. Between us we split a bottle of red wine from the Caucasus.

Proskurin has a strong build and open, somewhat heavy features. Our conversation quickly picked up when I asked him about his life. He was born in 1928 in a village in the typically Russian area of Bryansk. As a boy he lived through two years of German occupation, an unforgettable and harrowing experience that has affected much of his writing. After the war he served for several years in the army and then went to the farthest Far East, to the North Pacific peninsula of Kamchatka. Three and a half years as a lumberjack and truck driver in this out-of-the-way place left the second strong mark on his life and supplied him with material for many of his stories, the best known being *Taiga*, an adventure in the north Siberian wilderness.

His first stories were published in 1958 while he was living in the Far Eastern city of Khabarovsk. Next he entered the Gorky Institute of Literature in Moscow and, after completing the course of study there in 1964, moved first to Orel and then back to Moscow. For the last two decades he has concentrated on writing. His breakthrough, so he told me, came in 1960 with his first novel about the war, *Glubokiye rany* (Deep Wounds). The reviews, even in the important *Literaturnaya gazeta*, were friendly. Other novels followed in quick succession. Unsurpassed in popularity is his two-part *epopeya*, *Fate** and *Thy Name.**

When I asked him about the meaning of the second title, he replied that he had taken it from the Bible, "Hallowed be thy name." Noticing my surprised face, he added: "Why not? The Bible is one of the oldest expressions of human wisdom."

I agreed, I said, but wondered about the connection between this Bible quotation and the novel's plot. His book, he said, deals with man; hence the title might be understood as "Thy Name Is Man." I left it at that and remarked that in addition the novel hinted at a number of pre-Christian religious customs. The heathen element, he answered, was still alive in Russia, mainly in the village, of course, and therefore it played a role in his novel.

I raised another issue. "You have described Stalin with the detachment of the novelist. May I know your personal opinion of him?"

The image of Stalin, he said, was still controversial. The writer's task is to describe people without passion, be they high or low; he himself had not been in Moscow in March 1953 after Stalin's death became known and had only heard about the wild excitement in the streets of the city. He was a soldier then, stationed in a garrison near the capital. Personally, he was against using slogans or poster rhetoric (*lozungi i plakatnost*) to describe people; therefore he had attempted a differentiated, multifaceted picture of Stalin; the readers must form their own opinion. Many had thanked him in their letters for courageously tackling such a difficult problem.

In his latest novella, *Chyornyye ptitsy* (Black Birds), which takes place exclusively in Moscow's art circles, is a curious scene that I also inquired about. An unusually gifted young composer is killed early in the war. After some years his widow becomes the mistress of his friend, a married man. He too is a composer but far less talented than the one who died. One day he tries to steal the draft of an incomplete composition that his friend has called "Prayer to the Sun." In her desperation the woman, very ill at that time, implores her dead husband to help her protect his work. He appears, comforts her, and lightly touches the sheet of music causing the notes written on it to disappear. The horrified friend dashes from the apartment into a snowstorm.

How was that to be understood, I asked. Was this sorcery? Am I supposed to believe in hocus-pocus? After hesitating for a moment, Proskurin responded that the reader should find his own explanation. I was not satisfied. To be sure, I said, with a high fever the woman might have imagined seeing her dead husband, but how could notes written on a sheet of paper vanish? Again Proskurin hesitated. Then he suggested that perhaps the friend was close to madness with feelings of guilt and remorse and simply imagined that the notes had vanished.

After we finished eating and conversing, Proskurin accompanied me along the snowy street until I caught a bus to my hotel.

Another writer of a vast *epopeya* of contemporary Russian history is **Anatoly Ivanov**. His main novel contains about as many pages as Proskurin's and covers more than fifty years. It also consists of two parts that appeared at different times but under one name, *Eternal Call.**

It took several phone calls to the office of the monthly *Molodaya gvardiya* (Young Guard) where Ivanov is the editor-in-chief. But finally I got him on the line. A mutual friend had already mentioned my interest in him, so he agreed to come to my hotel room without much ado. However, he did not want anything to eat, he announced, and when I saw what a heavyset man he is, I could understand why. Ivanov has what one might call a typically Russian face and easy manners; there was no trace of that nervousness Soviet citizens sometimes display in the presence of a foreigner from a *kapstrana* (Sovietese for capitalist country; *strana* means "country"). Indeed, he had no reason to be nervous. As the author of one of the most highly valued novels, dramatized for screen and television and known to at least half the Russian population, his reputation is as weighty as that of an entire university department.

After he ensconced himself on the sofa, we shared some small talk. I told him that my grandfather, who lived in Moscow for many decades, used to give some of his parties at this very hotel in the old days. Then we turned to my subject—to him. First I told him what I knew of his life. Born in 1928 in eastern Kazakhstan, not far from the border with the Altai region, Ivanov was too young to fight in the Second World War. After it was over, he studied journalism at the University of Alma-Ata until 1950, then served in the army, and ended up working for a local Siberian newspaper. At 24, he joined the party. In the late sixties he moved to Moscow, where he has been in charge of the influential monthly *Molodaya gvardia* since 1972.

"Would you tell me the story of your success," I asked, "from your start as an unknown staff member of a Siberian newspaper to your present position as one of the most widely read Russian writers?"

He settled back comfortably and then began his tale. At 27, he summoned his courage and sent a short story, "Alkiny pesni" (Alka's Songs), to *Sibirskiye ogni* (Siberian Fires), the literary magazine in Novosibirsk.

I had read the story and remembered it because of its touching simplicity. The heroine of the title, an orphaned young woman, falls in love with a fellow villager. But he is married and has children, so she puts her feelings into songs that she makes up and sings daily in the village. Gradually he too is drawn to her, until in the end he wants to leave his family to be with her. But, as happens quite often in Russian literature, she is the stronger of the two. At the last moment, before they both fall into the abyss, she renounces him. When he refuses to let go of her, she says: "You have a family, go to them. Go. You cannot do otherwise. Nor can I." She leaves, singing her farewell song, while he remains, listening as it fades away.

The editor in Novosibirsk found the story appealing; he published it (1956) and showed it to his colleagues at the local radio station. They liked it so much that they sent some of their people to Ivanov to suggest that a 90-minute radio play with music be made from the story. It was a great success. The Youth Theater of Novosibirsk dramatized the story, and the play ran for a number of years; the municipal theater even turned it into an opera. In the end, the story reached television. Not a bad start for a young provincial journalist.

His first collection of stories came out in the same year, named of course after his famous debut. Two years later, his first novel appeared, and many others soon followed. The central television network became interested and turned one of his novels into a seven-part series; it also adapted *Eternal Call*, making two series of nineteen parts all together and winning state prizes. When in 1981 his *Collected Works* appeared in five volumes, Ivanov had definitely established himself as one of the country's leading authors, collected works being considered a crowning achievement.

Not surprisingly, Ivanov looked quite happy as he told me the story of his success. Then, at my request, he explained his various official functions to me: he has held high positions in the Writers' Union since 1965. Since 1981 he has also been one of its secretaries and one of the few who enjoyed the privileges of this position without being expected to do any work, leaving him free to write.

Asked about his literary ancestors, he mentioned, like so many of his colleagues, Lev Tolstoy in first place, then the relatively conservative Leskov and Kuprin, and finally a fellow-Siberian, Mamin-Sibiryak. Before leaving he offered to send me his latest novel *Vrazhda* (Enmity). I was quite touched when he actually brought the novel to me himself on the following day; an event that, incidentally, greatly enhanced the floor lady's respect for me.

Vrazhda is an *epopeya*, too, once again set in a Siberian village and full of action. The class struggle aspect is a bit thick for my taste, but in the end a granddaughter of the wicked exploiter marries a grandson of the decent peasant—for once, a happy ending.

Another writer of *epopeyas*, the fourth among the 24, is **Georgy Markov**. I had seen his name many times; for almost 30 years he has been one of the leading functionaries in the Writers' Union of the USSR and has served as its first secretary since the death of Konstantin Fedin in 1977. The addresses and speeches he has delivered at important writers' meetings could, I guess, easily fill a large volume.

Power over colleagues does not always bring popularity. Members of intellectual professions in more than one country, I have found, tend to look down on the secretaries or chairmen of their organizations and regard them as bureaucrats and necessary evils rather than as colleagues of equal stature.

Sometime in the sixties, I bought a copy of Markov's first novel, *Strogovy* (The Strogovs),* in a secondhand bookstore in Munich. It was unusually well printed and illustrated, quite suitable for official presentations at factory anniversaries and similar occasions. But for a long time I did not get around to reading it; its bulk, almost four pounds, discouraged me.

But once I began interviewing the general reader, Markov's name came up time and again. Soon it was clear that he belonged among the top 24. In 1982, I hoped to meet him to discuss his books and his role in Russia's literary life. But because of his heavy schedule of official duties, he did not find the time to see me.

Georgy Markov is one of the surprisingly many Siberians on my list. He was born into a peasant family in 1911 in the province of Tomsk, near the center of Soviet Asia. In his early youth, so I am told, he was a shepherd. Later he attended extension courses at Tomsk University and in the midthirties moved to Novosibirsk. In 1935 he began writing his first novel. But the war interrupted his work; like thousands of his colleagues, he spent the war years as a correspondent at the front. He finished *The Strogovs* in 1948, and after he won the Stalin Prize for this novel, he devoted himself to writing. In 1976, he received the Lenin Prize for the novel he had written in the early seventies, *Sibir* (Siberia),* his book most frequently mentioned to me.

8
The Short-Story Trio

One weekend while I was visiting Semyonov at his dacha some 35 kilometers south of Moscow in a place called Krasnaya Pakhra, he phoned his neighbor **Yury Nagibin**, also on my list, and suggested that he see me. One of Semyonov's daughters showed me the way. We walked along the street where Semyonov lives between walls of snow with snow-covered gardens and dachas on both sides, turning once to the left and once to the right. Another few steps and my young guide set out to return home. A dog barked. I was there.

Nagibin and his wife, Alla, were alone. She is a friendly, quiet woman. Nagibin, a man in his early sixties, has a furrowed face and calm, thoughtful eyes. He took me to a large room upstairs. The snow muffled all outside noises, and the houses stood quite far apart. It was very quiet. Mrs. Nagibin brought us tea and the kind of jam (*varenye*) the Russians like to eat with it, as well as two pieces of a rich pie. Then she left us alone.

I told Nagibin that my introduction to his work came toward the end of 1956, that memorable year when the Russians learned about Khrushchev's damnation of Stalin and felt encouraging signs of thaw and spring. At that time, an almanac under the title, *Literaturnaya Moskva*, appeared in Moscow and brought frowns to the faces of the country's literary guardians. Their ire was especially directed against two pieces by a man whose name I had not heard before, Nagibin.

Nagibin smiled the way people do about events long ago but did not comment. Instead he told me a bit about himself. Born in Moscow in the hungry year of 1920 into an educated family, he was introduced to the world of books by his mother early in life. He was so captivated by one of the first novels he read, *The Three Musketeers*, that with three of his friends he formed a little band of the Four Musketeers to repeat the adventures of his heroes or even to improve on them. In the war he was first a political officer, then, after being wounded, a correspondent for the newspaper *Trud*. During this time his first stories appeared, war stories, of course; some of them were also published in book form. He married Bella Akhmadulina, Yevtushenko's former wife. Now he was married to Alla.

His literary breakthrough, he said, came with "Trubka" (The Pipe), a story published in *Novy mir* in 1951 when he was 31 years old.

"Why did this piece capture the public's attention?" I wondered.

"Because its totally unpolitical character was most unusual at that time," was his reply. It is indeed an unpretentious tale told by a grown-up gypsy about his childhood with a gypsy clan, once again with a grandmother, a babushka, as the heroine. Soon it was turned into a radio play, then into a film, *Trudnoye schastye* (Difficult Happiness). This success gave him a strong boost, and two years later his first volume of stories was out.

When I told Nagibin that I was especially fond of his "Ekho,"* he seemed pleased; he is convinced that it was precisely this story that won him many friends in Russia, although the film made from it, he said, was not good.

His next success, Nagibin told me, came quite unexpectedly with a story that recounts an older man's love for a younger woman. (I had read it without being much impressed.) In the end—in fact, in the story's last line—the man decides to return to his wife ("Srochno trebuyutsya sedyye volosy" [Gray Hair Urgently Needed]). What really surprised him, Nagibin said, was the public's reaction. Even two decades later I could see it in his face. The vast majority of his fan mail came from women, many of whom were outraged by the story's ending. "How did you dare to allow the man to betray his love! He is a coward, afraid to venture forward into a new life, a measly skunk!" From this one might infer that these Russian women would opt for love in a conflict between love and marital duty.

But the most exciting experience, Nagibin reported, had been with his "Predsedatel" (The Chairman), a scenario he had written at the request of a film studio. But even before the film was finished, a violent quarrel erupted among the higher-ups. When the film was banned because it featured the serious problems in Soviet agriculture, the battleground shifted to the Central Committee. The events around

---

*Indicates the books that are summarized in Chapter 13, "The Authors and Their Books."

Khrushchev's fall additionally complicated matters. It was rumored at that time that Brezhnev, Suslov, and Mikoyan were in favor of permitting the film to be shown and that Kosygin and Shelepin were against it. Eventually, the film's supporters won, and it became a sensational success. (I have not seen it myself; it was not shown abroad, not even in Eastern Europe.)

This film and many others made from his stories accounted in large measure for his popularity, Nagibin said. He reckons that some three dozen films are based on his tales. But he does not think much of lecture tours—too tiring and time-consuming. He is happiest living and writing right there in his dacha.

Chekhov's popularity notwithstanding, in Russia the novel was traditionally esteemed more highly than the short story; it also corresponded more closely to the monumental style of the Stalin epoch. Novellas and short stories were considered just incomplete novels. Nagibin told me that his father-in-law from a previous marriage, a well-known industrial manager, had once called him lazy because he wrote short sketches instead of novels. Nagibin's (and Shukshin's) work has contributed to a change in climate. In 1981, most unusually, a four-volume collection consisting exclusively of his short stories was published.

Much of his fan mail concerns his widely read stories about children. The tenor of these letters is frequently: "By reading them I was reminded of my own childhood. Unfortunately youth today is much worse than it was then." He did not know much about the present young generation, Nagibin confessed; he had heard that young people were different but not necessarily worse now and that they yearned for a simple life; he knew of a case where a gifted young man preferred the work of a carpenter to the career of an official. On the whole, however, mankind has not improved over the last hundred years, he thought. In science and technology we have advanced far beyond our ancestors but not in ethics: too much corruption and thievery and too great an urge for power.

Nagibin did not show much interest in politics, national or international. His only question about Germany concerned Böll, whom he admired. At the end of our talk, he walked with me back to Semyonov's house through the snow.

The other leading short-story writer among my 24 is **Vasily Shukshin**. I never met him, for he died in 1974. The Russian public became fully aware of him in that year, too, due to the sensational success of the film, *Kalina krasnaya*,* released a few months before his death. He had directed it, using his own script and starring in the main role. After his untimely death and the film's release, he became a writer of national stature. In the year after his death, his film scenarios and two collections of his stories were published, one in one volume and the other in two volumes, for a combined print run of 500 thousand copies.

Shukshin was an endlessly talented person. He wrote stories, novels, plays, and film scripts, made films, and acted in them. Whenever I mentioned his name, I saw warmth and love in people's eyes. In addition to his last film, his fans always emphasized his short stories, whose full value was now better appreciated.

Born in 1929, in a village in the Altai region, not far from the Chinese border, Vasily Shukshin had a hard youth. Both his father and his stepfather died when he was young. As a teenager he worked during the war in a Siberian kolkhoz, then as an unskilled laborer on various construction sites. After serving in the navy (1949–1953) and working for a year as a schoolteacher in his native village, he decided to make a big change in his life: he moved to Moscow. He was then 25 years old. From 1954 to 1961 he was a student and assistant at the cinema institute. The first film he made on his own won the Golden Lion at the Venice Film Festival in 1964. Other films followed, but he was not allowed to make the one film he really wanted to make—a film about the robber and folk hero Stenka Razin. So he put his ideas into a novel about him. All the while he continued to write short stories, more than a hundred in all.

If someone asked me who is the most Russian among the 24, I would answer without hesitation: Vasily Shukshin. In his short stories I put him on a par with Anton Chekhov, one of my favorite authors in modern world literature.

One of the characters in the story "Veruyu" (I Believe) says with reference to the poet Esenin: "People lament that Esenin only lived a short life. Just as long as a song. If the song had been longer, it would not touch the soul so deeply. There is no such thing as a long song."

Vasily Belov (pronounced Belóv) is among the youngest of the 24. He was born in 1932 in a typically Russian village near Vologda. After he left school, he first worked on the kolkhoz, then as a carpenter. After three years in the army (1952–1955), he studied five years at Moscow's Gorky Institute of Literature (1959–1964) and then moved to Vologda, the capital of his native region. His first stories did not cause much of a stir, though they appeared in book form. Then suddenly in 1968, he became famous with his *Carpenter's Tales*.* Whenever his name was mentioned, so was this book, and quite justly so, for it is a joy to read.

Other stories followed; some were collected into a small volume called *The Dawns Are Kissing.**

One of the most frequently discussed pieces of the blossoming village literature was his *Commonplace Affair.** Another, *Kanuny* (The Evenings Before) tells in great detail about a village in northern Russia prior to the collectivization, and in a collection of what he called "Ocherki o narodnoi estetiki" (Essays on popular aesthetics), published under the collective title *Lad* (Harmony) in various issues of *Nash sovremennik* in 1979–80, he lovingly described the old forms of life in the village and the harmony with nature in which the peasants had once lived. I shall not present this work because it is a cultural history, rather than literature in the proper sense of the word. But for some people I talked to (not many had read it yet), it seemed to represent the peak of Belov's writing so far, almost an encyclopedia of the old (and rapidly disappearing) Russian village, based entirely on his own experiences or on the reports of eyewitnesses, such as the chapter on folk dances with songs (*khorovody*). *Harmony* made such a deep impression that it was quickly awarded the State Prize.

Although Belov is only one of many members of the presidium of the Writers' Union of the USSR, he complained in *Literaturnaya gazeta* (November 11, 1981) about the annoying burden this honor places on him: two or three meetings per week, he wrote, though perhaps necessary in themselves, take too much time; they interrupt creative work and make fresh ideas wilt before they ever even blossom. Many of the other 289 members may feel the same way; several said to me with a tone of irritation: *Zasedaniya* (meetings), always *zasedaniya!*

9
Three on Mystery and Science Fiction

I only had time to see one of the two Brothers **Vainer**, and it so happened that it was the older one, Arkady, whom I met. Maybe it would have been just as interesting and amusing to visit Georgy. Anyway, I remember with pleasure the time spent with Arkady Vainer.

He lives in an apartment house not far from Moscow's Garden Ring (*Sadovaya*). After I rang the bell, the door was opened by a curious figure: a stocky man, dressed in a multicolored Uzbek robe (a bit similar to our bathrobes) with an embroidered Uzbek skullcap on his head, whose eyes were full of humor and curiosity. That fellow might have been an Uzbek himself, and I wondered whether I had come to the wrong address. But the man greeted me by name and asked me to step inside. I entered a large room that extended from one outer wall to the other and probably originally contained three rooms. The interior partitions seemed to have been removed, and now one section was the dining room, another the living room, and a third the library. The easy chairs were comfortable; my host sat in his like an Uzbek chieftain, exuding good nature. After his wife returned from work (in cancer research), she joined us for a little while before disappearing into the kitchen.

The conversation was easy. Vainer told me about his and his brother's road to the genre that had made them famous—whodunits. Both were born in Moscow; he in 1931, Georgy in 1938. Both studied law. Arkady then joined the militia (our police), working as a detective in the famous building at Petrovka 38, while Georgy became a journalist. One evening while chatting with some friends, Arkady outlined a complicated criminal case he was working on. The others were fascinated and suggested that the brothers make a novel out of it. They hesitated, saying they did not have any talent for writing books. But one of those present, Julian Semyonov (one of this book's 24), asked them to furnish just the bare outlines of the case; he knew some experienced chaps who would do the rest. The brothers started writing the outline, but before they knew it, they had written a full-length book manuscript. *Nash sovremennik* published it in 1965 under the title, *Chasy dlya mistera Kelli* (A Watch for Mr. Kelly). A detective by the name of Tikhonov ably solved the case. The story was a medium success. The breakthrough came two years later, when *Ogonyok*, the mass weekly with a circulation of two million copies, printed their second story, *Oshchupiyu v polden* (Groping at Noon). Detective Tikhonov again did his stuff, this time pursuing a Russian who had acted as executioner for the German occupation power during the war. Their third crime story, *Ya, sledovatel* (I, the Inspector) also published first in *Ogonyok*, was made into a film and a television show.

From then on, the Vainers had luck on their side and are today, I found, the most popular of the Russian detective story writers. They differ from others, as the reader will notice in Part III, by giving to their crime stories, especially to *Visit to Minotaur** and *Medicine for Nesmeyana,** a historical and European dimension, thus putting them on a plane above the ordinary cops and robbers stories.

For us, Arkady Vainer said, the crime story is but a method for reaching the people. If we succeed, and we have been read and seen by many millions, we can transmit some of our ideas to them, because the reader will internalize them easily under the cloak of the whodunit.

However, the literary aspect comes first. By no means do they consider themselves "engineers of the human soul," as Soviet authors were once supposed to be, or as tools for changing human nature for political purposes.

I inquired whether Brothers Vainer was simply a pen name or whether they really worked together. Arkady explained their routine. Together they outline the entire new novel as well as each individual chapter. Then they divide these among themselves. From here on they write independently, meeting regularly in order to read each other's chapters, to work on them and sometimes to throw them into the wastebasket. They are so pleased with this method that they have decided to try a remarkable experiment: to write a novel together with the other two writing brothers, the Strugatsky. The author would then be Brothers Vainer and Brothers Strugatsky. I am curious how that will work. By putting two and two together the result may be more than four,

---

*Indicates the books that are summarized in Chapter 13, "The Authors and Their Books."

because the Strugatskys have a very large following too, though in a different field.

Before I started this study I had read nothing by the Brothers **Strugatsky**, for the simple reason, though painful to admit, that I am not a science fiction fan. Only when their names appeared again and again on my lists did I try to familiarize myself with their work. This is not an easy task, because their oeuvre is very large and practically not available in the USSR, not even at the *Beriozka,* although all their stories—save one, *The Ugly Swans*—have appeared there. They are sold out both above and under the table. But the fact remains that of all the literary fields mentioned in this book, this is the one I am personally least interested in. Of course, this is beside the point. What matters is that many Russians love science fiction and the Strugatskys lead the field.

As with the Vainers, it was the older Strugatsky I met. His name is also Arkady. To visit him, I rode the Moscow subway to the last station in the southwest of the city and, after a five-minute walk through thawing snow, took the elevator to the seventeenth floor of an apartment house. Arkady Strugatsky met me at the door and escorted me to a room with a magnificent view of the city's last blocks of houses and a distant forest. There were bookshelves along the walls, a sofa bed, a writing desk, and a table, where we sat down. Arkady Strugatsky wore a dark turtleneck. He had wavy hair, a round face with a mustache, and friendly, somewhat cunning eyes behind his glasses.

Briefly he told me about his and his brother's life. Their combined age is a little larger than that of the Vainers; Arkady was born in 1925 in Batum (on the Black Sea), Boris in 1933 in Leningrad. They came from an educated home; their mother was a teacher, their father an art historian employed for some time at Leningrad's famous Hermitage Museum. The father had joined the Bolshevik Party in 1916 and was, during the Civil War, commissar of a Red cavalry brigade; he died in Leningrad in 1941 during the murderous first winter of the blockade. While serving in the army, Arkady studied at the military language school, specializing in Japanese. He then worked as a translator of Japanese at various institutes in Moscow, including one devoted to scientific-technical information. Brother Boris studied astronomy and joined the staff of the Pulkovo Observatory near Leningrad, the Russian Greenwich. By the end of the fifties, the brothers had teamed up as writers of science fiction, while continuing to work in their old specialties—Boris at Pulkovo, where his wife is employed too; my host as a translator of Japanese texts (currently he is working on medieval writings). To his regret, he mentioned in passing, he had never been in Japan.

"How do you do it," I asked, "writing novels together while living so far apart?"

"That's simple," he answered. "As a rule we meet every month for one week either here or in Komarovo near Leningrad, where you visited our friends, the Abramovs. Each time we write one or two chapters and go on when we meet again."

"How does this work in practice?" I wanted to know.

"Boris lies on the sofa bed over there, while I, being the better typist, sit at this table with the typewriter. We talk, I type, then we talk again, and in the end neither knows which word he contributed and which the other. That works fine. After almost a quarter of a century we are used to it."

Each of the two seems to have enough imagination for five, and their intellectual acrobatics are remarkable, as the summary of four of their novels in Part III will show.

When I asked why *The Ugly Swans* had been published only abroad, my host for once showed some irritation. "Whatever a Soviet author writes," he said, "you in the West always try to smell veiled criticism of the Soviet state, and if a manuscript does not appear in print here, you speak of censorship. But Boris and I are not writing our novels in order to complain about the lack of meat in our shops; we are concerned with much bigger problems—ecology, genetics technology, the survival of mankind. Now about *The Ugly Swans*. The manuscript had already been accepted by a Moscow publisher. But then somebody got hold of a copy and sent it abroad where it was printed in a Russian emigré journal hostile to the USSR. After that there was no chance for its publication in the USSR. That's all."

He confirmed the plan to collaborate on a novel with the Vainers, but that was, he said, still some way off.

As I walked back to the subway, I passed a collecting point for waste paper; people were lined up on the street with their bundles. Being empty-handed, I was allowed to enter. Inside, people were crowding around a big scale, which they carefully watched. After a package was weighed, the contributor received a coupon. On the wall hung a poster listing the books one could get for each 20 kilograms of waste paper; it still promised Dumas's *Queen Margot*.

Years before the Strugatskys published their *Far Rainbow** (1964), another Russian author had begun to win a growing audience with fantasy stories, **Ivan Yefremov**. His early life and education had as little connection with his later literary life as that of the Brothers Strugatsky. Born in 1907 in a village near what was then St. Petersburg, he showed an early predilection for science, especially in connection with fantasy. In his later life he often spoke of the strong influence Jules Verne had on him. He had read the Russian translation of *Vingt mille lieues sous le mer* and *Voyage au centre de la terre* as a child. He studied paleontology, later adding geology to his field and receiving a Stalin Prize for his scholarly work. As a geologist he participated in the first reconnoitering of eastern Siberia directed toward building a new railway line from Lake Baikal to the Lower Amur on the Pacific to be called BAM (Baikal-Amur Line).

I wrote about the BAM from Moscow as early as 1934. At that time the new railway was directed against Japan. Later the plan was put on ice because of the Second World War and the rise of the then friendly and seemingly obedient Red China. Bitter hostility toward Peking raised the issue of its construction once again. Its purpose remains the same: to have a railway to the Pacific that is farther from Manchuria, now under Peking's, then under Tokyo's, rule. In 1982 when Yefremov would have celebrated his 75th birthday, the suggestion was made that one of BAM's future stations be named after him. There is also, in Moscow, a Committee for the Study of Yefremov's Legacy.

Other expeditions combining his geological and paleontological interests took him to the Caucasus, central Asia, Yakutia. But the Gobi Desert expedition brought him the most recognition. There he and his colleagues found dinosaur remains, the famous Graveyard of the Dragons. All the while he wrote scientific articles, later adding stories and books in which he combined the knowledge he gained in his scholarly work with his lively interest in history. His greatest literary success came in 1957 with his futuristic space novel *The Andromeda Nebula*,* published just as the Soviets (and hundreds of millions abroad) were fascinated by the first Sputnik, a very powerful promoter for the novel. Yefremov loved to write about the future and about the past, as his last novel, *Thais of Athens*,* reveals.

When heart failure forced him to abandon his scholarly work, he concentrated on writing novels. Death came in 1972, when he was only 65. But even a decade later, his name was mentioned very often to me. A new edition of his *Thais* published shortly before my arrival in Moscow in 1981 sold out immediately. In *Beriozka* they had just two copies left, I bought them both, one for myself, the other for a Russian friend who seemed almost overwhelmed by this rare gift.

10
Three Non-Russians

The following three authors have only one thing in common: they are not ethnic Russians. In temperament and subject matter they are far apart. None of them lives in Moscow.

By language and character **Vasil Bykau** is closer to the Russians than the other two. Next to the Russians (or Great Russians) and the Ukrainians, the Belorussians (literally White Russians) are the third and smallest Slavic group within the borders of the USSR. (In Russian translations of his books Bykau spells his name Vasily Vladimirovich Bykov.)

Born in 1924, Bykau spent his youth as a peasant boy in a village near Vitebsk in Belorussia, not far from the old Polish border. When he was seventeen and just starting art school, the war began. He joined the army as a volunteer, saw heavy fighting, was believed dead (in the Ukraine his name is included on a memorial over a mass grave of Soviet soldiers) but managed to survive, and remained in uniform for ten years after the war. Only then did he begin his literary career. Since the late fifties, his works have appeared in quick succession—fourteen novels so far, in addition to more than ten novellas. He lives in Minsk.

His subject has always been the war described in realistic, nondogmatic, patriotic terms. His patriotism differs little from that of Russian writers: Hitler did not distinguish between Belorussians and Russians, although at least some of his men tried to see the Ukrainians as something apart. Of course, Bykau disliked the German invaders who devastated his Belorussian homeland, but he reserves his special antipathy for those of his countrymen who did the Germans' dirty work for them, as is especially clear in *Sotnikov*.* Bykau also portrays a man erroneously suspected of collaboration in *Obelisk** and one who has not lost his dignity while a prisoner of war in *Ballad of the Alps*.*

Belorussia, occupied by the Germans in the first days of the war, was one of the last areas to be liberated. Consequently Bykau's novels, more than those of Russian writers, deal with the problems of people in occupied territories and in prison camps.

In 1983 I intended to take the train from Moscow to Germany and stop over in Minsk, the capital of Belorussia, to pay a visit to Bykau. Then the crucial West German elections were set for March 6, and I had to take the plane to fulfill my civic duty. But fortunately I managed to get Bykau's private phone number and was able to hold a 45-minute long-distance conversation with him. While we talked, his wife was kind enough to check the dates of his books' first printings, which I had been unable to discover. "No objection," he said, when I told him that in my book I intended to spell his name in his native Belorussian rather than in Russian.

Then we talked about his books. Among other things I mentioned my appreciation for the restrained tone in which he described the German enemy in his war books. This, he said, had been his intention.

Asked about his further plans, he explained that he intended to continue writing about the war; the war was also the subject of a new story soon to appear in the review *Druzhba narodov* (Peoples' Friendship). When asked about his literary mentors, Bykau mentioned, as many others had done, Lev Tolstoy in first place, then Dostoyevsky and Chekhov; as for foreigners, he cited Remarque, Hemingway, and Böll. Next time, he said, I must visit him in Minsk, he would like to take me around.

Though far removed from the center of Russia and only conquered in the nineteenth century, Georgia has always had a romantic appeal for the Russians. Towering mountains attracted the inhabitants of the plains; southern sunshine and an abundance of fruits lured the people from the cold and often bleak north. The long battles of conquest against the valiant tribes have a firm place in Russian literature, thanks to Pushkin, Lermontov, and Tolstoy. In a way, Georgians represent for the Russians what the Italians typify for the Europeans north of the Alps:

---

*Indicates the books that are summarized in Chapter 13, "The Authors and Their Books."

easygoing, pleasant, witty, gallant, but also fierce and fiery and great storytellers.

The best known of Georgia's present-day writers is **Nodar Dumbadze**. Being primarily interested in Russian literature in the proper sense of the word, I had not paid much attention to him and was surprised to discover his name appearing so often on my lists. He wrote this brief summary of his own life in 1981: "Hard youth, early loss of parents [it seems they were arrested during the purges], bitter recognition of this irreparable loss and, at the same time, the realization that there are many good, decent people around. The war, a test for the entire nation, was perhaps hardest on the young people who suffered from hunger, privations, lack of attention, . . . later golden university years, love, friendship, disillusionment, treason."

This brief autobiography is important because Dumbadze is honest enough to say that all the central figures in his works are reflections of himself. Incidentally, even in the distant mountains of the Caucasus, Dumbadze was reared on Tom Sawyer, Huckleberry Finn, and the heroes of Alexandre Dumas. Among his later literary teachers, he mentioned Lev Tolstoy, Thomas Mann, Faulkner, Sholokhov, and, of course, the idol of all Georgian writers, their Homer, Rustaveli. As a Georgian, Dumbadze is, like his mountains, a favorite of the Russians.

More than a thousand miles separate Bykau's Minsk from Dumbadze's Tbilisi, and another fifteen hundred miles divide Tbilisi from the little Soviet republic of Kirgizia. Here, in a tiny nation on the border of China, hardly known except to anthropologists and geographers, one of the Soviet Union's greatest authors was born and lives. Imagine a Navajo Indian writer appearing for years on the best-seller lists in the United States—the phenomenon is just that peculiar. **Chingiz Aitmatov** is also one of the most translated Soviet novelists; his latest novel, published in one of Moscow's literary reviews in November 1980, turned up less than a year later on the West German market as a hardcover book in German.

Aitmatov was born in a small Kirgizian village in 1928. When he was nine years old, he lost his father, a party man since the Revolution, in the purges, so he grew up in his grandmother's care. At the age of thirteen, school ended for him because of the war. He was mobilized for various duties on the home front, since all adult men were away at war. Those hard and bitter years of his boyhood deeply affected Aitmatov. One of his recurring themes is the wartime suffering of the civilian population, especially women and children. He immortalized their anguish in *Early Cranes*,* *Mother's Field*,* and *Dzhamilya*.* In one of his shortest stories, "Soldatenok" (Soldier's Boy), a mother watching a war movie with her fatherless son draws his attention to one particular soldier who dies while fighting against the German tanks, pretending it is his father. From that moment on the boy has the father whom he so sorely missed.

Following the war Aitmatov went back to school; in 1953 he graduated from the Kirgiz Agricultural Institute as a specialist in livestock. After writing on the side for a few years, he entered the Gorky Institute of Literature in Moscow in 1956. His first collection of stories was published in 1958, and soon afterward *Dzhamilya* carried his name throughout the USSR and far beyond; the first German edition appeared in 1962. From then on he was a full-time writer. His stories have been published and republished singly and in collections many times over.

Aitmatov's first full-length novel appeared in a literary review late in 1980 under the title *A Day Lasts Longer Than Eternity*.* When I arrived in Moscow a few weeks later, the novel was the talk of the town. A Russian friend lent me his copy, acting as though he were entrusting me with a bar of gold. Fearing that some Aitmatov fan might disappear with it, I barely dared to leave it in my hotel room.

Aitmatov wrote his first pieces in Kirgiz; they were later translated into Russian and from there into other Western languages. *A Day* he wrote directly in Russian.

The rise of Aitmatov, and a number of other writers from the Soviet Asian republics, is due to the quick development of these nationalities in recent decades. In the old days, they barely had a national identity; they were Moslems rather than Kirgiz or Tadzhiks. Now their newly acquired national feeling seeks literary expression. For a man with as wide a horizon as Aitmatov, a purely Kirgiz patriotism, strong as it is, cannot suffice. Hence he embraces what I would call a global patriotism and a feeling of responsibility toward humanity as a whole. It finds expression, apart from his latest novel, in an interview published last year in *Literaturnaya gazeta* (January 13, 1982) under the title "Not Coexisting Means Not Existing." The interviewer did his utmost to pressure Aitmatov into admitting that class struggle is the only road to peace, but to no avail. Using the biblical legend of the great Flood as an example, Aitmatov asserted that mankind was once again threatened by destruction. "Under these conditions," he declared, "we must find a common language for people irrespective of the world to which they belong." His interviewer insisted that class struggle has by no means lost its topicality, and it should not be buried with bells ringing; he even mentioned El Salvador and the wicked Americans in his argument. True, true, Aitmatov acknowledges, but he holds his ground: people on the other side also know that a war would be "an act of suicide." This is, he is convinced, "understood everywhere."

11
. . . And Five More

The last 5 of the 24 do not fit into any of the previous six groups. Hence each of them—alphabetically—is treated by himself.

Viktor Astafyev is a Siberian born in 1924 in a village near the Yenisey River in the region of Krasnoyarsk. His mother died when he was eight; his father was sentenced—for reasons not mentioned—to prison work on the White Sea Canal, where countless people died of privations. Viktor lived with his babushka, his mother's mother, and she is the warming light of his childhood, immortalized in many of his stories, the best known of which is "The Horse with the Pink Mane."* Nobody is dead, he once said, as long as he lives in the memory of someone still living. Later he shifted for himself as one of the millions of *bezprisornye* (homeless children) of the early thirties until he was put into a *detdom,* a children's home, in the town of Igarka. At that time Igarka was largely inhabited by dispossessed kulaks, the somewhat wealthier peasants, who had been exiled to Siberia. In 1942 at the age of eighteen, he went away to war. He was wounded twice, and while recovering the second time he was attached to a home regiment and happened to be on guard when the news of victory came. Overjoyed, he shot five bullets into the air just to celebrate and, as a result, was locked up by an outraged sergeant who had not spent a day at the front. So, while all of Russia was celebrating with vodka and kisses, he was confined to the guardhouse—not for long, of course.

Astafyev married, got a job in the Urals as a locksmith, and started writing stories mainly derived from his own experiences. In 1953 at the age of 29, the first volume of his stories appeared. From 1959 to 1964 he attended the Gorky Institute of Literature in Moscow. *Novy mir*, then the most respected literary review, published one of his stories in 1967.

Although Astafyev has also written about the war in his very popular *Pastukh i pastushka* (Shepherd and Shepherdess), most of his stories and novels deal with young people, especially *The Last Bow** and *The Theft.** *Starodub* is also about an orphan who sneaks into a village hidden in the depths of Siberia that is inhabited by Old Believers, a very strict, secretive, and independent-minded sect. A number of his stories about adults written in the first half of the seventies were published under the title of one of them, *The Tsar Fish.**

Vil Lipatov's young heroes are somewhat older than Astafyev's, but Lipatov is more didactic and moralistic. Astafyev just narrates, in a somewhat detached and autobiographic way, and is little interested in teaching lessons. Lipatov, on the other hand, has a strong pedagogical bent.

Vil Lipatov lived only 52 years (1927–1979). Of the relatively numerous Siberians among "my" 24, he was born farther east than any of them, in Chita. His parents belonged to the middle intelligentsia—his father was a journalist, his mother a teacher. From the name they gave him we can deduce that at the time of his birth they wanted to show their allegiance to Lenin: Vil stands for V-ladimir I-lyich L-enin.

After completing his studies at the Institute of Education in Tomsk, he too became a journalist, working for *Sovetskaya Rossiya* and moving to Moscow in 1967. In the early seventies he was a member of the secretariat of the Writers' Union of the Russian Republic and of the presidium of the Writers' Union of the USSR. His death in 1979 is still considered a major loss for Russian literature. As with Shukshin who died in 1974, the frequency with which his name was mentioned may reflect people's sorrow at his untimely death. The Russians are loyal readers.

Valentin Rasputin, born in 1937, is the youngest among our 24, yet he clearly belongs to the top group of writers in the eyes of most of those I questioned. Millions have read at least two or three of his four most important novels, and many have reread them.

Among Russians, an author's popularity and people's compassion for him are more closely related than perhaps anywhere else, and the misfortune that befell the young author in March of 1980 added, so it

---

*Indicates the books that are summarized in Chapter 13, "The Authors and Their Books."

seemed to me, to the noticeable warmth reflected in the words and facial expressions of his readers. The incident was bizarre: he was attacked in front of his house in Novosibirsk, of all places, by four men who demanded his blue jeans, of all things! When he refused, they hit him over the head with a metal pipe. He had to be hospitalized and sent to Moscow for two operations. People spoke in hushed voices about rumors that he had suffered brain damage and amnesia as a result of the blow. Some even indicated the possibility of political motives behind the assault. As far as I was able to ascertain, it was just a case of mugging. But even in 1982 Rasputin complained that he needed much rest and was not yet entirely his old self. Among the stories he has written recently is one that takes place in a hospital: in connection with his operation, the narrator tells of a somewhat mysterious occurrence or dream concerning a girl named Natasha (in *Nash sovremennik*, 1982). The author has many, many millions of well-wishers, and I am among them.

Rasputin is generally included among the "village writers." But I have used other categories in this study, and he does not fit comfortably into any of them. Thus I feel justified in treating him as a *samorodok*, a man of and by himself.

Born in eastern Siberia, he spent his childhood in a village along the Angara, and that river and its people have never left him. After studying in the department of history and philosophy at the University of Irkutsk until 1959, he worked as a journalist and published his first stories. But what caught the attention of critics and readers alike was his first novel (relatively short as all his novels are) *Money for Maria* (1966).* That this was not just beginner's luck became evident as his subsequent novels appeared one by one. Including *Maria* there are four that have a firm place in millions of Russian homes and in still more Russian hearts: *Period of Grace* (1971),* *Live and Remember* (1974),* and *Farewell to Matyora* (1976).* Four highly praised novels within a decade. Dramatized versions of three of them were playing on Moscow stages in 1981. I have also seen one of his short plays, *Vstrecha* (The Meeting [of two people]), on the Small Stage of the Yermolova Theater on Gorky Street and a movie made from one of his novels in Moscow's Metropole cinema. *Vasily and Vasilisa*, the title of novel and movie, bears the names of the two heroes. Although it sounds like a musical, it is one of Rasputin's sad true-life stories about a peasant and his wife who make each other miserable and only realize their closeness at the moment of his death. At the end of the movie, as I moved with the crowd into the street, I saw women with red eyes holding hands with the men accompanying them.

I find it amazing that Rasputin, who was born twenty years after the Revolution and is truly a son of Soviet Russia, should be so extraordinarily fond of old Russia, more correctly, of old Siberia. The intensity of his attachment to the old values sounds almost desperate at times, as if he wanted to hold tight to something that is irretrievably slipping away.

I met **Vladimir Soloukhin** at a Moscow dinner party. Although only about a dozen people were present, it was still too many for me to have a good talk with him. He was also, I felt, not too happy with me. When the conversation turned to "my" subject, present-day Soviet literature, he showed annoyance. Yet, he had no reason to shy away from that subject because he is very much a part of the Russian literary scene; he would not be on my list if he were not. He may have resented finding himself on a list together with some authors of whom he does not think very highly. But it also seemed to me that he did not like my seeking out the most popular authors rather than the most valuable ones. Evidently he had expected to find in the German guest a man with whom he could discuss some of his favorite subjects, such as the role of history and culture in the life of modern nations, and was disappointed to meet a man whose interest in popular opinions rather than intrinsic values must have made him appear hopelessly Americanized.

Before I had a chance to explain the purpose of my study, he got up and moved to another table. I was sorry because I am certain we could have had an interesting discussion on the very topics that are close to his heart. I would have asked him to analyze the reasons for his enormous popularity in view of his being far removed from the literary mainstream in his ideas and style. I would also have expressed my respect and appreciation for his personal contribution to the preservation of Russian cultural treasures that are dear to my heart, too.

I have called Pikul the only nationalist among the 24. I would call Soloukhin the most consciously Slavic or, as the historians say, the most Slavophile, and therefore the one most critical of the West among the 24. Not knowing him well, I cannot even guess at the reasons behind his attitude except that he was born in the center of ancient Russian culture and tradition not far from the architecturally beautiful town of Vladimir to the northeast of Moscow and once its rival for supremacy among the Russian principalities. (If you, dear reader, travel to Moscow, take the bus trip to Vladimir through beautiful countryside and skip the visit to a Moscow factory.)

Soloukhin was born in 1924 into a peasant family in the small village of Olepino that he still calls the place dearest to him. One of his interviews in *Literaturnaya gazeta* (July 29, 1981) even carried the caption: "Of course, in Olepino!" (This was his reply to the question where he could write best.) When he was four years old, his sister, then sixteen, was confined to her bed for several months because she had damaged her back in an accident. During that time she constantly recited aloud the verses of Pushkin and Lermontov, and his mother knew many poems by other Russian writers by heart. Thus Soloukhin explains his early love for poetry.

The war began when he was seventeen; he spent three years in the army. Then—until 1951—he studied at the Gorky Institute of Literature. His first book of verses appeared in 1953. At that time he worked as a journalist for *Ogonyok* reporting on voyages inside the USSR and abroad. The first book that revealed the unmistakable quality of Soloukhin's prose and message appeared in 1957, *Vladimirskiye proselki* (Byroads of Vladimir),* followed by *Kaplya rosy* (Dewdrop, 1960),* *Mat-machekha* (Mother-Stepmother [or the plant Coltsfoot], 1964), *Pisma iz russkogo museya* (Letters from the Russian Museum, 1966),* *Chyornyye doski* (Black Boards, 1969),* *Slavyanskaya tetrad* (Slavic Copybook, 1972),* and *Vremya sobirat kamni* (A Time to Gather Stones Together, 1980).*

Throughout, as will be clear from the summaries of some of his books, he fought courageously to preserve the old traditions, including the traditional Russian language. It angers him that Soviet dictionaries have declared thousands of "clear, beautiful, and expressive" words to be "colloquial (*razgovorny*) or local," thus disparaging them as unfit for literature. In defiance of this judgment he uses such words with special delight and emphasis.

People who follow Russian intellectual life will remember that Soloukhin denounced Pasternak in 1958 after the latter had received the Nobel Prize for Literature for his *Doctor Zhivago*. And in the United States his attack on the exhibition of American architecture arranged by the U.S. government in Leningrad has not been forgotten; he even asked why this "sleek and vulgar" show was permitted. It would be wrong, I think, to see something "Stalinist" in Soloukhin's attitude. Soloukhin's position is one of opposition to what he considers the evils of modern civilization, and to this extent he is anti-Western, not as a Communist, but as a Slavophile. The struggle between the *zapadniki* (from *zapad,* meaning "West") and the Slavophiles who see the Slavs, especially the Russians, as superior to the "decadent West" has never ceased. Dostoyevsky reflects the latter point of view. Pasternak's liberalism, his being awarded the Nobel Prize, the exhibition of American architecture, and, for that matter, my strange interest in the popular acclaim of Russian authors are in his eyes symptoms of an attitude that he considers dangerous for his holy Russia.

Personally I am no friend of either-or absolutes and do not believe that you must be anti-Western to love Russia. My feelings, however, are beside the point. What is worth noting is Soloukhin's large following among Russians.

Before he died in 1981, **Yury Trifonov** wrote nine novels of high quality, beginning with *The Exchange** in 1969. (One of them has not yet been published.) Most were translated into Western languages and, of course, into the languages of many nationalities in the USSR. Trifonov's was an extraordinary outburst of genius and hard, dedicated work.

I met Trifonov briefly in late February 1981 at the Taganka Theater where the dramatized version of *The Exchange* was playing. I expected to meet with him at length during my next visit, but he died, only 55 years old, a few weeks after that evening at the Taganka. Instead, one year later, I met with his widow, Olga Romanovna. Together we went, in his memory, to the dramatization of his *House on the Embankment** at the same theater. Later I had two long talks with her about the great writer. She was his closest companion during his last and most productive period.

The first book by Trifonov that I read, *Studenty* (The Students, 1950), I had obtained in Moscow in 1956. Ever since I published my *Youth in Soviet Russia* (in German in 1932; in English in 1933), I had been interested in Russia's younger generation, and Trifonov was 25 when his novel about Soviet students appeared. I am embarrassed to confess that I did not sense his extraordinary, then still hidden talent. But his widow told me that in later years he did not like *The Students* very much himself.

During the following years I lost sight of him. But with *The Exchange*, Trifonov arrived at the front of the Russian literary stage and has remained there to this day. In Part III I shall summarize most of his novels since 1969. The major omission is *Neterpeniye* (Impatience, 1973); it tells of the Russian terrorists who killed Tsar Alexander II in 1881 and is, I find, less typical of the master than the books to be discussed.

I confess to a certain prejudice in favor of Trifonov: he is more closely linked to the city of my birth than any of the other 23 writers. Although two decades apart in age, we grew up in the same Moscow neighborhood. The house in which my (German) grandfather lived with his wife and twelve children, one of them my mother, and his chocolate factory were both on the same embankment of the Moskva River. Halfway in between stands the house immortalized by Trifonov in his *House on the Embankment*. In my days the street was called Sophia's Embankment after a church dedicated to her. Now it bears the name of a communist saint, the Frenchman Thorez. But even today the old people still use its former designation. As a child, I frequently walked through the public garden on the island formed by the river and a canal, and the house where my parents lived was not more than four minutes walk from there. In the thirties, as a young journalist, I visited Karl Radek in Trifonov's house on the embankment. (Then one of the best German specialists in the top echelon of the party, Radek later fell victim to the purges.) Incidentally, Stalin's daughter Svetlana also lived in this house during her last years in the USSR.

This novel appeared in *Druzhba narodov*, a journal to which I did not subscribe, so when I arrived in Moscow, I had not read it yet. Since everyone mentioned it to me, I wanted to read it but could not find it anywhere. My friend's copies were all *na rukakh,* somewhere in circulation among their friends, and in the public library I found that some fan had removed from that issue the pages on which Trifonov's novel appeared. In the editorial office where I was sure I could get it, they just laughed at me: apart from their own archive copy there was not a single one left. Only in the German Embassy was I finally able to borrow this journal.

Trifonov was born in Moscow in 1925. In 1937, at the age of twelve, he had a traumatic experience that he shared with several of the 24 authors. He described it in a small book *Otblesk kostra* (Reflection of the Fire, literally "of the Stake," 1965), which is the story of his father. Valentin Trifonov was a leading Bolshevik. He had joined the party in 1904 at the age of sixteen and was one of its top men during the Revolution of 1917 and the ensuing Civil War and one of the founders of the Cheka, the secret police. Through diligent research in archives and old boxes of documents and letters, Yury Trifonov collected what he could find about his father's role in those chaotic years. What he found (including two of Stalin's letters to his maternal grandmother, also a revolutionary) he put into that remarkably vivid account written in his inimitable style and full of documentary material. After the Civil War, his father, like so many Bolsheviks, held numerous high positions: in the oil and energy field, the Supreme Court, the military mission to China, the economic mission to Finland.

In the opening paragraphs of *Reflection of the Fire*, the novelist states the reason behind his interest in his father's life with a reticence that is astonishing considering that he is describing his life's greatest catastrophe: "One night men in uniform appeared at our dacha [near Moscow] and arrested my father. My sister and I slept; father did not want to waken us. Thus we could not even say good-bye. It was the night of June 21, 1937."

Much in Trifonov's work becomes more understandable when this event is taken into consideration. That night a world collapsed for the boy; its darkness never quite disappeared throughout the 44 remaining years of his life. Trifonov is, I think, the most somber of the 24; he and Aitmatov are the two who tried most intensely to cope with the Stalinist past, delving deeply into the minds of people who lived through this period.

When he was accused of forcing people to abandon their illusions and to engage in *samokopaniye* (self-digging, that is, self-searching or self-analysis), he answered that this had been practiced since the days of Socrates. "It is a serious occupation for soul and mind, an education of the emotions that is the task of literature." When asked why he liked writing about the unsuccessful ones (*neudachniki*), he explained that these were precisely the people who, because of their lack of success, were searching for something and hence moving toward self-discovery (*samoraskrytiye*). He hated clichés above all; "life is the anticliché," he said. He also refused to do what some of his readers demanded, namely to make things clearer in his novels, to dot the i's and cross the t's in English parlance, and he calmly told them: "I never could explain what I wrote." (These quotations are from his last interview a few weeks before his death, *Literaturnaya gazeta*, March 25, 1981.)

As was my habit with the authors I interviewed, I asked Olga Romanovna about some of her late husband's favorite authors. "Among foreign authors, in his youth he loved Balzac and enjoyed Hemingway. Thomas Mann remained with him for a long time because he found him akin to Dostoyevsky. And Dostoyevsky was closest to Yury Valentinovich. About the author of *The Demons* he said: 'He foresaw the contradictions of the twentieth century.' With Chekhov, he had a very intimate relationship—too intimate to talk about. Bunin's books stood on his shelf, and he once traveled to Grasse (France) to find the house where Bunin had lived. In the evenings he used to read Zoshchenko to me, also Nabokov who, he thought, had in many ways expanded the frontiers of Russian prose."

When I asked how he felt about the frequent accusations that his novels were too melancholy and lacked optimism, she told me that in such cases he often explained the role of literature through a quotation from Aleksandr Herzen, "We writers are not the healers (*vrachi*), we are the pain."

12
Other Authors

From the outset I asked the Russians I talked to, random individuals as well as people working in libraries and bookstores, about their preferences among not only contemporary Soviet authors but also two other groups: Russian classics and foreign writers. Although those questioned dwelt mostly on contemporary Soviet authors, my primary interest too, a pattern soon emerged with regard to the other two groups.

I divided the Russian classics into those of the prerevolutionary period, the "old classics," and those whose fame rests on the books they wrote during the roughly 25 years after 1917, the "new classics." The findings in these two categories reveal less about the Russians today then do their preferences among contemporary Soviet authors; hence two brief sections may suffice, one for the Russian classics, old and new, and one for the foreigners. Those wishing to learn more about the role of foreign literature in the USSR might read Maurice Friedberg's *A Decade of Euphoria: Western Literature in Post-Stalin Russia, 1954-64* (Bloomington and London, 1977).

Many of the early Bolsheviks read a great deal—in tsarist prisons, in Siberia, in Western exile. Compared to workers and peasants, they were intellectuals who respected the literature of Russia and of the West. After 1917 many prerevolutionary books disappeared, and many were used as fuel during the hungry winters of the Civil War. But while no policy of book burning was inaugurated, there have been many purges of books considered harmful, mainly of those dealing with politics (in the broad sense of the word), religion, and philosophy; fiction was hit less hard. (The role played in this context by Lenin's widow, Nadezhda Krupskaya, has been described by the late Bertram D. Wolfe in his article in *Survey* [Summer 1969].) The last great book purge occurred in the late forties.

Since the mid-fifties, conditions have improved, largely thanks to the intelligence and diligence of thousands of Russian librarians. More often than not they defend their attitude by referring to Lenin's statement of October 8, 1920, in *On Proletarian Culture* attacking "all attempts to invent a special [proletarian] culture" and instead demanding that "everything of value during the more than two thousand years of the development of human thought and culture be integrated into proletarian culture."

Yet, the development of a more tolerant attitude toward world literature was a hesitant process. Take the full acceptance of Dostoyevsky for example. For quite some time he was considered morbid and his influence dangerous. But the growing clamor for his works led to the publication of some individual novels and finally, the big event, of his *Collected Works*, including the *Demons*, that devastating critique of radical left movements. I well remember one morning in Moscow in the midfifties when I went to the special bookshop near the old Art Theater where on that day subscription was opened. My appearance caused much merriment among the booksellers: the subscription had been completed an hour before I arrived for people who had been waiting in line overnight. And here I was strolling in at eleven o'clock, thinking I could still get one!

Since that time, even though there are never enough *copies* to go around, the number of available *titles* from the literature of the past, both Russian and Western, has grown considerably.

The Classics

After the first two or three weeks in 1981, I realized that there was not much point in asking people to indicate their preferences among the Russian classics: they made three plusses after most of the nineteenth-century authors on my list, only few received less. Russians would read all of the old classics if they could only get hold of them. They were more selective about the newer ones. I divided the 24 top names into "old" and "new" classics, somewhat arbitrarily since no clearly established demarcation line exists (see Table 4).

Among the old classics, Pushkin, Tolstoy, Lermontov, and Chekhov are the most loved, in about that order. The novels of Dostoyevsky, one of the giants of Russian literature in Western eyes, lack some of the entertainment and beauty that the Russians crave and that the works of the top four supply in full measure. Dostoyevsky may be somewhat less well known because he was taboo for so many years and was attacked as

Table 4
Authors of Popular Russian Classics

Old	New	
Chekhov, Anton	Bulgakov, Mikhail	Paustovsky, Konstantin
Gogol, Nikolay	Bunin, Ivan	
Goncharov, Ivan	Ehrenburg, Ilya	Tolstoy, Aleksey
Dostoyevsky, Fyodor	Fadeyev, Aleksandr	Shishkov, Vyacheslav
Lermontov, Mikhail	Fedin, Konstantin	Sholokhov, Mikhail
Leskov, Nikolay	Gorky, Maksim	
Pushkin, Aleksandr	Il'f, Ilya and Yevgeny Petrov	
Tolstoy, Lev		
Turgenev, Ivan	Katayev, Valentin	
Saltykov-Shchedrin, Mikhail	Leonov, Leonid	
	Ostrovsky, Nikolay	

a "reactionary" and a religious philosopher; also, reading him is heavy going. Rasputin, however, mentioned him as his favorite author. Leskov has experienced something of a renaissance in recent years, but this has not been strong enough to lift him into the very first rank. For the somewhat restrained enthusiasm for Gogol, I have no convincing explanation except that his irony is essentially merciless and depressing.

Gorky, Alexey Tolstoy, Paustovsky, and Leonov are firmly established, in about that order, among the new classics. Bulgakov and Bunin, both partly taboo for a long time, have the attraction of being almost like new discoveries; the books of Fadeyev, Fedin, and Ostrovsky live off their officially sponsored fame during the Stalin period.

The popularity of native classics is far greater in Russia than in Western countries, even more so than in England or France, the most tradition-conscious of the great Western nations. Why is this so? One might surmise that, due to their strenuous living conditions, Russians love their classics for their beauty, harmony, and elegance. But this is not enough because quite a few of them do not satisfy such desires. My assumption: people who grew up with Pushkin and Tolstoy approach literature in later life differently than those whose childhood fare included endless hours of comic books and television shows.

Finally there is one more way in which the classics have an effect on the Russians of today: many contemporary Soviet novelists write within the tradition of classical literature. Almost all of them acknowledge this indebtedness, partly because it is true, but also because they know that their readers like to hear them offer such recognition. The mystique connected with the name of Pushkin or Tolstoy is bestowed on a writer who declares himself to be their spiritual descendant. Pushkin, whether mentioned by name or not, is perhaps the most influential inspiration. His prose, especially his *Captain's Daughter*, is a model for Soviet authors who try to emulate his realism. Turgenev teaches the art of describing, through the narrative, the soul of the Russians, of landowners as well as of simple peasants; the melody of his *Sportsman's Sketches* can be heard in many a village author's prose. The epics, the *epopeya*s, take their cues from Tolstoy; it is a rare novel about the Second World War that does not aspire to emulate *War and Peace*. Many of today's best short stories remind the reader of Chekhov's masterful prose and spirit.

The classics also live through their understanding of the hero. As in English, the word *geroy,* the Russian equivalent, has two meanings: a person known for heroic deeds and the leading character in a novel, who need not have heroic attributes and may in fact be a rather nasty individual. There have been periods in Soviet literature when the hero had to be a person of heroic deeds and proportions who never wavered and always did the right thing (right according to the official interpretation of communism at that time). This was not the hero of the nineteenth-century Russian novel for whom Lermontov set the pattern in his *Hero of Our Time* (1840). The use of the word *hero* in the title has been debated almost since its publication, for Pechorin is not a hero in the first sense of the word, nor are Turgenev's, Tolstoy's, or Chekhov's protagonists. They are all heroes in quotation marks, people with good and bad sides, in other words—human beings. More properly Lermontov could have called his book "A Man of Our Time," but by calling Pechorin a hero he established one of Russia's most durable literary traditions. If the reader thinks back to the leading characters of the stories described in this book, he will find that most of them are heroes in the Pechorin tradition; in fact, in my view the transformation of the leading character in Russian literature from a Korchagin (*How the Steel Was Tempered*) to a Nikitin (*The Shore*) is the single most important difference between Stalinist and post-Stalinist literature.

But one very typical nineteenth-century hero can rarely be found in today's novels: *lishny chelovek*, the superfluous one. He came from a well-to-do home, often from the nobility, and lived off the money his serfs earned for him. Feeling unsure of himself and his place in life, superfluous and hence guilty, he was often bent on exculpating himself by supporting causes, leftist causes more often than not. The superfluous ones have moved from feudal nineteenth-century Russia to our late-bourgeois West, where they are still trying desperately to find the meaning of life.

But other characteristics of the Russian classics have survived: the inclination to examine not only the factual but also the moral aspect of an issue, a certain reticence about discussing sexual matters, the propensity for portraying women in a positive light. Pushkin, more than anyone else, contributed to this tradition by creating Tatyana in *Eugene Onegin*.

Turgenev and Tolstoy, except in the latter's concluding phase, have also advanced a favorable view of women. Often the woman has clearer and more strongly felt emotions than the man. While he is torn between his professional-public and his private life, the woman is *tselnaya,* from *tsely,* meaning "whole, complete, total, undivided, integral, solid." Again Pushkin's Eugene and Tatyana come to mind as prototypes.

Another inheritance from the classics is patriotism. Despite all the critical remarks about political and social conditions found in the 111 works, pride in Russia, in her people, landscape, history, and art, is always there, if sometimes only in the background. This kind of patriotism is usually linked to obedience toward the existing authorities. The soldiers in Pushkin's *Captain's Daughter* died without making great speeches and in a matter-of-fact, disciplined way. So did the young lieutenant in Bondarev's *Last Shots.*

Thus a Russian is doubly exposed to his classics: first directly by reading them, then indirectly by finding many of their traits reflected in the writings of contemporary authors.

The Foreigners

The following passages allow only a glimpse at a fascinating intercultural issue. All they offer is a number of names mentioned to me by people and librarians, regardless of the intellectual and social status of the readers. But while practically all Russians read Chakovsky or Semyonov, the fans of Dumas and Faulkner most likely belong to quite different groups. These differences are not treated here.

One knowledgeable Russian librarian told me: "The level of popularity a Western writer enjoys among us Russians corresponds to the level of our interest in his home country." To which she added: "Interest in a country does not necessarily coincide with sympathy for it." To which I might in turn add: interest in an author depends to some extent on the availability of his works, which is not a matter for the reader to decide.

Among contemporary foreigners, the Americans clearly take first place for the very reason the librarian mentioned, and Arthur Hailey with his *Airport* was number one among the Americans at the time of my questioning in 1981 and 1982. When I asked why, the answers were more or less alike: "For a long time," people said, "we used to think that novels about the economy were rather boring exhortations and generally poorly written to boot. Then along came Hailey and proved that it was quite possible to write a book about an economic topic in a fascinating and, at the same time, informative way. In our country, we have millions of airplane passengers, but not one of them ever knew what happens behind the scenes at an airport. Now Hailey has told us. In addition we have learned a lot about that strange country, America. Entertainment, suspense, information—these three ingredients make Hailey's novels some of our favorites."

Similar judgments might be made about many other contemporary U.S. authors. Those mentioned to me most frequently, some of whom are known in Russia for just one novel, were (in alphabetical order): James Baldwin, Truman Capote, James Clavel, Theodore Dreiser, William Faulkner, John Gardener, Ernest Hemingway, James Jones, Sinclair Lewis, Norman Mailer, Joyce Carol Oates, John O'Hara, Philip Roth, J. D. Salinger, William Saroyan, Irwin Shaw, John Steinbeck, John Updike, Kurt Vonnegut, Robert Penn Warren, Thornton Wilder, Richard Wright.

Perhaps a list composed by some American readers of names especially close to their hearts would not differ too much from the one presented here. The majority of leading writers in the United States— and, for that matter, in the West in general—are often critical of our bourgeois society and hence inclined to show its seamy side; this makes them acceptable to Soviet censors. They are even allowed some descriptions of sex as long as this can be construed as presenting Western decadence. However, no matter what they write, they are finished if somewhere along the line they have abandoned the Faith as Howard Fast did by writing his *Naked God* in 1957. He was promptly excommunicated.

Second and third places in the reader's interest are shared by writers from Germany (West) and Great Britain. The Russians want to know what the Germans are really like, this people who, barely 40 years ago, advanced in a few months to the gates of Moscow and Leningrad and to the summits of the Caucasus. They are especially curious about the people in that part of Germany about which they know relatively little, the Federal Republic. Since the war, there have been several waves of reading German literature. The Thomas Mann wave mainly arose in connection with his *Buddenbrooks*, for the Russians love long family sagas, as we have seen. Erich Maria Remarque fascinated them as a storyteller, and his *All Quiet on the Western Front* exercised a strong influence on Soviet war literature. In the long-lasting Heinrich Böll wave the Russians were pleased to discover the "good German." This was followed in turn quite unexpectedly by a Hermann Hesse wave, caused mainly by his *Steppenwolf*, which, a decade later than in America, caused a stir in its Russian translation. Among the other well-received German-language authors are Max Frisch, Günther Grass, Peter Handke, and Siegfried Lenz.

Among the British I found no authors clearly in the front row. The names most often mentioned to me, in alphabetical order as always, were: James Aldridge, Archibald Cronin, Graham Greene, William Golding, Norman Lewis, Iris Murdoch, and Evelyn Waugh.

Whenever I inquired about contemporary French authors, the name mentioned first was that of Georges Simenon, the master of a hundred brilliant detective stories. The other favorites are: Louis Aragon, J. P. M. Hervé-Bazin, Albert Camus, Antoine de Saint-Exupéry, Maurice Druon, Robert Merle, Françoise Sagan, and Jean Vercors.

Italy follows at some distance as country number five. The leader there is still Alberto Moravia. Although he cannot be called a fighter for the Cause, he is welcomed for his description of Italian social problems. To judge from the people I questioned, Italy "has no great literature" at this time. Perhaps the Russians, conservative and averse to any kind of chaos as they are, feel somewhat irritated by the constant pell-mell of the political and cultural scene in Italy.

Other European countries do not have a large Russian clientele for their fiction, neither the Scandinavian nor the Iberian writers, nor the authors of Asia, Africa, or Latin America, although some reviewers do their best to popularize them. The one exception is Gabriel Garcia Marquez, who was much read long before he received the Nobel Prize in 1982.

Repeatedly I was told that the Japanese have advanced in the readers' interest; some even spoke of a Japanese wave. However, for the time being their fiction is still considered somewhat exotic. Among the best known writers are Kobo Abe and Yasunari Kawabata.

As far as the classics of world fiction are concerned, their authors' nationalities probably mean little. Four of them are very high in the readers' esteem: the Frenchmen Alexandre Dumas and Jules Verne, the Englishman Arthur Conan Doyle, and the American Jack London. The hunger for copies of Dumas novels is insatiable; if they are at all available on the black market, then hardly below 40 rubles. (The official price is around 4 or 5 rubles.) The adventures of chivalrous men and beautiful women in a totally different world, that of romantically feudal France, exert a tremendous attraction. I met people who had read practically every Dumas volume and who could banter around names of Dumas heroes I had never even heard of. Jules Verne lures with his science fiction that is impressive, well told, yet not burdened with technical details. Jack London was one of the first foreign authors to reach the Russian mass reader after the Revolution. The cannery laborer, sailor, tramp, socialist soapbox orator, gold seeker, and prolific writer was considered a "good American" and soon became a favorite of the Russians, not because of the semiproletarian circumstances of his life, but because of the vitality and exotic excitement of his books. I need not elaborate on the reasons behind the popularity of Doyle's Sherlock Holmes; he is as alive as is that other immortal brainchild of a writer, Odysseus.

Other much read classical writers from the West are Hans Christian Andersen, Honoré de Balzac, James Fenimore Cooper, Daniel Defoe, Charles Dickens (and his contemporary Wilkie Collins), Leon Feuchtwanger, Gustave Flaubert, Victor Hugo, Heinrich Mann, Guy de Maupassant, Edgar Allen Poe, Robert Louis Stevenson, H. G. Wells, Emile Zola, Stefan Zweig.

When in 1974, as mentioned earlier, the Soviet paper industry wanted to entice people into collecting wastepaper, how did it lure them? By offering one copy of Dumas's *Queen Margot* or Doyle's *Hound of the Baskervilles* or Simenon's *The Maigret Stories* or Wilkie Collins's *Woman in White* or Hans Christian Andersen's *Fairy Tales* for each 20 kilograms of paper.

Those members of the Russian intelligentsia who read the lesser known foreign authors are probably subscribers of the monthly *Inostrannaya literatura* (Foreign Literature), which prints foreign works in full or abridged and has a circulation of about 400 thousand. Its staff consists of specialists on the literatures of the most important countries. In conversations about foreign authors one can easily spot subscribers; this journal offers a way of learning about Western literature, and people interested in the subject read it with the care one would accord a rarity. Some of them are better informed about world literature than many intellectuals in the West.

III
Their Books

13
The Authors
and Their Books

The 24 authors considered in this book have written, among them, hundreds of novels and stories. From the start, I asked the people I interviewed to list their favorite writers and the novels or stories they liked best. Only these, 111 in all, will be described in some detail on the following pages, giving the reader a chance to form his own opinion.

Not everybody will agree with my synopses. Retelling stories is, in a way, similar to reporting on public events or accidents where various witnesses sometimes have quite different impressions. I have emphasized what seemed essential to me.

The question of why these writers and these books are so popular will always occupy the reader's mind as it has mine. In addition to preliminary reflections at the end of some of the synopses, a more comprehensive answer to this question will be attempted in the Conclusions.

Here then, in alphabetical order by author, are summaries of the most popular books by the most popular authors.

Fyodor Aleksandrovich Abramov

The novel with the title that has been loosely translated as "around and about" (English title, *One Day in the "New Life"*†) tells about a day in the life of the chairman of kolkhoz New Life. He visits the homes of the kolkhoz members in order to persuade them to bring the fodder into the silo from the soaked meadows despite the heavy rains.

---

†For Russian titles, see Appendix A. For English titles, see Appendix B.

What he finds there and what he thinks about are depressing. Many of the former inhabitants have abandoned the village for good. Left are the very young and a very few able-bodied kolkhozniks who, however, are already on the lookout for better jobs. Even an invalid freed from kolkhoz work is, without a pension, better off than a kolkhoznik because he produces onions and cucumbers for the market on his tiny private plot. All villagers prefer to putter around in their house and garden rather than to work for the sickly kolkhoz. The only ones the chairman is really pleased with are some jolly milkmaids, but he suspects that soon they too will marry and leave. His prompting meets with little enthusiasm until, in a drunken mood, he says something that the peasants take as a promise for higher payment by the end of the year. That brings them out in full force.

The Pryaslins appeared over a period of almost two decades and consists of four parts: *Brothers and Sisters* (sometimes also used as the title for the entire novel), *Two Winters and Three Summers*, *Roads and Crossroads*, and *The House*.

The story takes place in a village on the bank of the Pinega River in the far north, to the east of the White Sea harbor of Archangel. The first three volumes cover the war and the early postwar years amidst unbearable hardship and poverty. Most of the men have gone to the front, and few have returned; the country is poorly administered; the desperate desire to find a better life somewhere else drives people away, draining the kolkhoz, the collectivized village, of manpower. There is nothing pretty about the village and its inhabitants except the majestic beauty of the wild forests all around.

The story's hero, Mikhail Pryaslin, is a teenager growing into manhood, who loses his father in the war. He is hardworking and dependable. He too could have left the village and easily found a better position, but he stays because of his overriding feeling of responsibility for his mother and his younger brothers and sisters. He represents the ideal of a strong-willed, practical, and decent lad, motivated by what he considers his duty, not by any ideology.

The House shows the Pryaslin family about two decades later. Abramov spent five years working on this last part of his saga, and it is his most mature and also best known book. It can be read without previous knowledge of the first three volumes, although it still concerns the same village. To be sure, some characters in the first volumes are dead, and some new ones appear, but the center of the stage is still held by the Pryaslins.

Mikhail, now 44, is no longer the young hopeful whose courage and strength had once decisively contributed to the survival of the village. He is still the hardest worker (now for the state-run sovkhoz the kolkhoz has become), but his leadership qualities, so badly needed during the war years, are now resented as a burden by the others. His energetic pace of work brings him respect but not love. However, he has also begun to think of his own interests and has built a new house for himself next to the old family house that is falling into disrepair. He calls it "the most important thing." It is the first of several fateful houses that appear in the last volume and give it its title. Another peasant says proudly that he intends to build a house for each one of his sons, a "village in the village," so that his family may live on "forever" and adds, "Now you understand what I am living for?"

Sad to say, the loving oldest brother who cared for the younger ones has become a coldhearted egotist. He respects only one of his sisters. She has married a Moscow VIP who, so he learns when he visits her, "drinks only champagne"; in addition to a city apartment, she owns an elegant dacha and a car and even has a servant.

But he has completely cast off his sister Liza, whom he loved so much when they were young. She was married to a charming good-for-nothing who left the village; her son died in a fatal accident. After living alone for a long time, she had a brief affair with an army officer who was quartered in her house while his unit was stationed in the neighborhood. When he left she was pregnant. Tormented by feelings of guilt and unwilling to hurt her lover, a family man, she never asked for child support and cared by herself for the twins she bore. Because of this, Mikhail broke off all relations with her although she lives only a few yards away in the house her father-in-law gave her after his son abandoned her.

Neither does Mikhail find any real contact to his two unmarried younger brothers who return to the village after a prolonged absence. It irritates him that they refuse to boycott Liza and that the younger one is an epileptic. Mikhail has also become estranged from his wife though they continue to live together, and he finds it difficult to understand his teenage daughter who has entered the age of flirtations.

The real catastrophe befalls the Pryaslins when Liza's good-for-nothing husband returns after twenty years. Having tramped all over the Soviet Union and having lived with many women, he has fulfilled, so he announces laughingly, his duty to his fatherland; he has sired an entire company and maybe even a battalion. Out of sheer wickedness, he chases Liza from her house because, so he explains, having borne two bastards out of wedlock she no longer deserves to live there. When her younger brothers start repairing the ruined old family home, Liza is killed by a falling beam. This tragedy finally brings Mikhail to his senses; feeling responsible for her death, he takes the two orphans into his house.

Not less moving or lifelike are the stories of many other villagers whom Abramov has carefully observed and brilliantly described. *The House* almost bursts with peasant life, love affairs, hard labor, vodka, and a gallery of unforgettable characters. There is the old man, once the village priest, who after returning from many years in labor camps, becomes a slightly crazed guardian of traditional values. He utters the words that underlie the book's title: "Man builds his true house in his soul. And that house can neither burn nor be flooded. It is stronger than bricks or diamonds." In a scene that could almost come from Dostoyevsky, he kneels before those with him, asks to be forgiven, leaves the house, gets severely hurt by falling into a pit, and dies after persuading the doctor not to treat him because he wants to die "like a human being." Then there is Dunayev, now over 80 years of age, whom they call *epokha* because he has been in the thick of everything that the epoch had to offer, from enthusiastic support for the Revolution and the First Five-Year Plan to many senseless years in prison camps. His wife, "the great sufferer" to the villagers, is unhappy about his madness yet follows him loyally and lovingly everywhere; she was mad enough herself to search for him on foot in all the prison camps of Siberia until she actually found and even freed him.

There is the epileptic brother who, reminding the reader of Dostoyevsky's *Idiot*, radiates love and brotherhood in a world full of hostility and conflict. He is happiest with children, loves those who suffer, and falls into convulsions at the sight of wickedness. The adjective *saintly* is employed for him several times.

What is most amazing is the nostalgia the villagers feel for the terrible years of the war. In the author's words:

> God forbid that once again we should experience starvation as we did during the war and the following years. God forbid the return of those awful times. *And yet, and yet.* Never was there as much happiness and joy in the Pryaslin family as in those distant unforgotten days. . . . The old women, the soldiers' widows, the unlucky ones, you would think, would grow weak and tremble at the mere reverting of their gaze. They had eaten grass with their children, have received death notices [from the front], paid taxes and war bonds, worked from sunup to sundown, ragged and barefoot—*And yet*—whenever they meet, what do they talk and chat about? What do they remember most? How they once lived and toiled. . . . And why do we not move forward? Perhaps we

have forgotten how to work in the old way and have not yet reached the point where we can master machines. [Emphasis mine.]

Many things have changed for the worse: peasants don't keep cows any more, preferring to buy milk in the store; the new houses in the village are ugly and boring compared with the old-fashioned ones; the Pinega River, "which had once been like a mother to us," is silting up— its fish are gone. An old peasant woman asks: "Could it be that good people are only born in hard times and that they are ruined by a good life?"

Nostalgia for the bad times during and after the war, for the years of suffering and hunger in one of the most popular and most read novels? Remarkable.

Chingiz Aitmatov

By *Early Cranes* Aitmatov refers to the young village boys who had to do the work of their fathers and older brothers during the war, somewhere in the mountains along the Kirgiz-Kazakh border. It tells of people whose thoughts are mainly with their loved ones at the front, who fear the worst and often enough learn the worst. The fascists are terrible, and the war must be won, of course. But the fight against them is in a way like the fight against frost and hunger in the village. Everybody does what has to be done, without any slogans, simply to survive.

The hero is fifteen years old. His father is away at war, so he lives with his mother and younger siblings. After finishing the seventh grade, he and the other strong boys are sent to plow up virgin land in a distant and lonely valley. This involves great hardships, fighting horse thieves, wolves, and each other. Interwoven is a tender love story involving the young hero and a girl from his school whose father and brother are also at war. As long as they were in school together, he barely noticed her, but in that faraway mountain valley his thoughts consistently turn toward her. Nothing happens between the two except that the boy writes an awkward love letter and has his younger brother deliver it to the girl and then she, in turn, gives him a little scarf with his initials stitched on it and a shy smile.

In *Mother's Field*, a lonely woman, a Kirgiz as almost all of Aitmatov's heroes and heroines are, pours out her sufferings to a field where she has worked all her life; she has lost her husband and all three sons in the war. One of the scenes in this novel is unforgettable. The war is just over, victory won, and the rumor gets around that the returning soldiers are coming. The entire village turns out for the welcome, driven by hopes and fears, for the news of casualties had traveled unreliably to the distant Kirgiz mountains. Only a single man jumps from the car that briefly stops at the fork in the road near the village.

> No one in the crowd said a word; everyone gazed in silence and wonder at the road along which a solitary soldier with a greatcoat and a kit bag slung over his shoulder was advancing. He was getting closer but still no one moved. There was bewilderment in every face. The soldier was getting closer and closer. Then he stopped uncertainly, for he, too, was shocked at the sight of the silent crowd at the edge of the village. . . . A barefoot girl standing in the front of the crowd suddenly shouted: "It's my brother! Ashiraly! Ashiraly!" And tearing the kerchief from her head she raced headlong towards him.
>
> "It's Ashiraly! It's him!" others shouted and then everyone, young and old alike, rushed towards the soldier.
>
> A great force picked us up and carried us on its wings. As we ran towards the soldier with open arms we carried our lives to him, all that we had lived through and suffered, the torture of endless waiting, our sleepless nights, our heads turned gray, our young girls grown old, our widows and orphans, our tears and moaning, and our courage—all this we carried to the victorious soldier. And suddenly realizing that we had come to welcome him, he broke into a run. [From Aitmatov's *Short Stories* (Moscow, n.d.)]

In *Dzhamilya* the heroine is a young bride who was married to a man now at the front; she feels loyalty toward him but nothing more and falls in love with a wounded soldier endowed with a beautiful voice who has been sent home and is as lonely and as shy as she is. She runs away with him, an unheard-of event in patriarchal Kirgizia, and rather reprehensible in Soviet literature.

One of the archetypes in Aitmatov's stories is a boy in his early teens, Aitmatov's own age during the war. The teller of Dzhamilya's story, her young brother-in-law, was then a boy of fifteen; he does not betray her love for the stranger as he should have done for the sake of his brother's honor.

A most touching portrait of a boy is that of the young hero in *The White Steamer*. He never gets near the ship on Kirgizia's beautiful Lake

Issik-Kul. He can only see it from his high mountain abode, but he imagines his lost father works there, and in his thoughts he speaks with him. This belief and the stories about ancient Kirgiz history that an old man tells him keep him going in his tough life as a homeless child until, again following his imagination, he becomes a fish on the way to his father and drowns.

Next to *Dzhamilya* the best known of Aitmatov's novels is *Good-bye, Gulsary*. For the former he received the Lenin Prize, for the latter the State Prize. This is a powerful novel about the love between the Kirgiz Tanabay and his horse Gulsary, or rather the kolkhoz's horse. As a young man, around 1930, Tanabay was a fiery Communist, believing that a new world was emerging, that the wicked past had to be spat out and destroyed to make room for the glorious future. Then he had even voted with those who declared his half brother, who was a little better off than the others, to be a kulak, which meant seven years in Siberia. With honor Tanabay had been through the war, he was twice wounded but in good shape when he returned to his wife and young son. In his village he was highly respected as an excellent herdsman, and Gulsary, the best horse in the kolkhoz, one that he himself broke in, was the swiftest in the herd, a winner of races.

But Tanabay was a hot-tempered man and a disappointed one, too. Returning from the war he had high expectations: "Not only Tanabay but everyone else in those days lived on the feeling of victory as if it were bread—after victory they'd have everything." This was not so. "They lived in the same way—there were no funds at the kolkhoz; everything was handed over [to the government] at a loss—milk, grain, and meat." In those postwar years everyone was poor, and so was the government.

Disappointment and frustration make Tanabay a difficult man. He is furious at the seignorial bureaucrats who are now in charge of the kolkhoz and at the local party organizations. Instead of looking after things themselves, they issue orders with "illegible signatures" that affect the lives of people and herds. Gulsary is taken from Tanabay to serve the new kolkhoz chairman, one of those disagreeable and incompetent bureaucrats. In the end, Tanabay even loses his job with the horses and is sent to tend sheep under abominable conditions for the flock. When he rebels, he is expelled from the party by people mainly interested in intrigues and in furthering their own careers. "What a fool I was. I have used up my life for the sake of the kolkhoz, for the sake of the sheep and the lambs. . . .Now I'm a dangerous element." (From *Farewell, Gul'sary*, trans. John French [London, 1970.])

The man and his horse both suffer. Gulsary is taken away from his beloved master and from the mares he is beginning to woo. When he refuses to serve the new chairman and time and again breaks loose to return to Tanabay and his herd, he is gelded and gradually reduced to pulling carts and serving as the children's plaything. He dies of exhaustion by the wayside.

In the end, a silver lining appears on Tanabay's cloud. Representatives of a new and better generation are moving up in the party. One of them, the young secretary of the county's party committee, suggests that Tanabay apply for party membership once more. But Tanabay is tired and bitter. On the last page the book vaguely hints at the possibility that Tanabay might apply after all. But even if he does, it would hardly affect his wasted life.

This book is not hostile to the party or to the Soviet state, but it is somber and critical. The two voices with which the author speaks, those of Tanabay and Gulsary, are the voices of energetic, buoyant, freedom-loving beings whose love of life is reigned in and destroyed by stupidity and malevolence. They both fight against bridles and vileness—and they both lose. Yet they are the story's real heroes together with the wide, wild grasslands of Kirgizia.

The Russian theater likes to produce novels on the stage, not always to the novel's advantage. But some novelists have written plays of their own, and Aitmatov, the master of prose, is among them. This study is not concerned with plays, but it is with Aitmatov, whose play *The Ascent of Fujiyama* is one of his major works. I saw it shortly after it came on stage, in Moscow's Sovremennik Theater.

Fujiyama is a mountain in Kirgizia, named after the holy peak in Japan, because of the similarity in shape. At the top of this peak in central Asia what might be called a class reunion is held: four men, classmates in school, comrades-in-arms in the same regiment during the war, meet here decades after the end of the war. One of them, Mambet, now a schoolteacher, speaks with the voice of Aitmatov, we soon notice. Three of their wives later join them as does their old schoolteacher, a woman who retired years ago. All eight are Kirgizes, but in Moscow they were all played by Russians; perhaps the director wanted to show that their problems concerned everyone.

What was planned as a joyous affair turns into a tragedy. To pass the time, the group decides that on this occasion everybody must tell the truth. One of the wives, an actress by profession, begins with two confessions. The first is a minor one: as a child, she once stole out of need. The second makes her shed tears and throws a shadow over the group: years ago, to keep her figure and to preserve her carefree life, she had an abortion. Since then she has never become pregnant again. Although this is sad for her, it is hardly of general interest for the audience. The confessions continue, and we soon sense that these are not just a number of unrelated events in the lives of these people. There seems to be a mystery that troubles and pains the four men. As the play unfolds, we learn their secret: in 1942, when they joined the army as volunteers, there were five of them. The fate of this fifth man, Sabur by name, weighs heavily on the conscience of the other four.

Sabur, the most gifted among them and the local people's pride and joy, was a poet who made a name for himself early on. One day after hard battles, when the regiment had pursued the retreating Germans to the Soviet frontier, Sabur was overwhelmed with longing for his Kirgiz mountains. Had they not all done their duty in expelling the enemy from Soviet territory? Had not the time come to bring an end to the slaughter on the battlefields? Gripped by such emotions, Sabur read a poem he had just composed to his four friends. Mambet, who still remembers it, recites it now, on the top of the mountain.

> When the bugle stops blowing,
> The shadows arise of those who were killed,
> And in endless rows
> They come marching to me.
> What am I to tell them?
> Which words to console
> Those who were killed in this gigantic war?
> Death made equals of them.
> They are just people and dead.
> Each is a son of man,
> Now neither marshal nor private.
> What am I to tell them,
> Those who have gathered together,
> Among whom there are now
> Neither ours, nor theirs?
> Who, on high, has invented
> The fate of these generations?
> And where does the suffering end
> In the ocean of humans?
> What am I to tell them,
> Those who have gathered together?
> And does it matter to them
> In their distant beyond?
>
>   [Translation mine.]

What was the meaning of this poem? Pacifism? Cowardice? Religion? In the midst of war, how could Sabur say that "there are now/Neither ours, nor theirs?"

On the following morning, the military police arrested Sabur and confiscated everything he had ever written. He refused to renounce his poem. His request to be sent to the front with a penal unit was denied. Not one of his four comrades spoke up for him—that might hurt him more than help, they consoled themselves. Sabur was sentenced to Siberia. Many years later he returned "from there" a useless alcoholic, obstinately declining to meet his comrades of yore.

Which of the four had informed the military police? It had to be one of them. Only they had heard the poem—in Kirgiz, which nobody else around could have understood.

The truth on which the friends had agreed for that day is not revealed. Aitmatov leaves the question open, his drama is not a whodunit where the criminal is handcuffed and taken away with the motto "crime does not pay" ringing in his ears.

Besides, could one really speak of guilt? Had it not rather been a duty to denounce the author for his pacifist verses? Or was it the betrayal of a friend, of a poet "who had understood, there at the front, the depth and tragedy of human life and who [in his poem] had tried to state a great and eternal truth?"

The old teacher, shaken by what she has learned about the pupils she once loved so much, tells them upon leaving that she had formerly believed life in a socialist state would be "like clean water in a mirrorlike lake." Now she knew better. She too had not defended Sabur. "From now on I cannot live in peace. You should not either. Farewell."

There is nothing in this play remotely connected with class struggle, with the glorious fight of the collective versus the individual, with dialectical materialism. Aitmatov's message is clear: all humans are involved in guilt, and the difference between friend and foe loses its meaning in view of the sufferings on both sides. In death all are alike. Admirable thoughts.

On the same high literary and ethical level is Aitmatov's latest novel, *A Day Lasts Longer Than Eternity*. It moves on two totally different planes: a whistle-stop in the desert of Kazakhstan and outer space. The author's heart is with the Kazakhs, cousins of the Kirgizes. With loving care he describes their small world, essentially three families. Two of the men are railway workers, Kazangap and Yedigey, and one is a teacher, Abutalin. In addition there are some figures from ancient Kazakh lore and a noble camel, which plays a role similar to that of Gulsary in an earlier tale.

At the beginning of the novel, old Kazangap dies and his friend Yedigey, then in his fifties, decides to bury him according to old Kazakh tradition in a sacred burial ground. While riding on his camel the twenty-odd miles to the cemetery, followed by a tractor bearing Kazangap's body, Yedigey ponders his life and that of his friend. In a number of scenes from the past, Yedigey relives the years of work and poverty, of heat and dust in summer, of storms and snow in winter.

During the period prior to the funeral day, that day that lasts longer than eternity, remarkable events have taken place in space. The United States and the USSR have together embarked on a grandiose enterprise for space research, carried out in complete and scrupulously observed equality, even to the extent of using an internationally acceptable language. The program is called Demiurge (from classical Greek), meaning "workman" or "creator" and the space lab, *Parity*; the ship from which the operations are conducted, *Convention*, is a mighty aircraft carrier, run by men of both nations and stationed exactly halfway between San Francisco and Vladivostok.

For some time now, *Convention* has not received any signals from *Parity*. Two space shuttles are sent up to check, one from Nevada and one from Kazakhstan; Yedigey's observing the launch of the latter links the two levels of the novel. The astronauts in the shuttle find the space lab empty, but a letter awaits them: the crew of the *Parity* has accepted an invitation from a distant galaxy and has left on a spaceship that came from there. The governments in Washington and Moscow clearly have a problem.

Now the scene shifts back to Kazakhstan. Sad memories fill Yedigey's mind on his way to the burial ground. Kazangap had suffered much in the days of collectivization because his father, wrongly accused of being a bloodsucking kulak, had been exiled to Siberia. Being a kulak's son was not easy. Abutalin, the teacher, suffered a no less tragic fate. In the war, he was captured by the Germans, escaped to Yugoslavia, fought bravely with Tito's forces against the Germans, and finally returned home. When Stalin's relations with Belgrade soured in 1948, he was arrested. He did not live to benefit from Khrushchev's amnesty, for he died shortly before Stalin's death.

As in his drama, *The Ascent of Fujiyama*, Aitmatov returns to the problem of Stalin. Again and again he grapples with it. And the past is not over yet. Men's spiritual needs remain disregarded. In the huge deserts of Kazakhstan with their wide-open spaces, it is precisely the ancient cemetery that is being incorporated into the Cosmodrome, as the Russians call their space center. When Yedigey and his friends arrive, they are chased away by a tough, young lieutenant who has the same name as the secret police officer responsible for the young teacher's arrest and misery.

Yedigey buries his friend on another hillock, turning his head toward Mecca and reciting the ancient prayers. Later he tries to win back the burial ground for its traditional purposes by legal means. Will he succeed? The author leaves the question open without offering much hope. Modernization is likely to win the battle against tradition; even many of the young Kazakhs do not care for the old ways any more. This is also true of Kazangap's own son, who has only scorn for Yedigey's insistence on a traditional burial for his father.

Nor has Aitmatov cheery news in connection with outer space. The former *Parity* crewmen send signals from their host galaxy: we have found a wonderful and enviable civilization here, a utopia turned reality. The governments in Washington and Moscow come to one and the same conclusion. They order that all contact with these men be stopped and the earth be ringed with American and Soviet killer satellites capable of destroying all attempts to contact earth from outer space. In other words, they are afraid of any changes.

But the man from Kirgizia has more in mind than the problems of the Soviet Union and the relations between earth and universe. By bringing to life haunting myths of ancient central Asian tribes, he adds one more dimension to his book. Narrating the disaster that befell their distant ancestors when their enemies turned them into *mankurts*, creatures without a memory and thus mindless slaves, this great Asian writer raises a warning voice against the general drift in the modern world, of which the USSR is but a part, toward an increasingly rootless and hence soulless civilization. Aitmatov speaks not just to the Kremlin, he addresses us all.

Aitmatov does not divide people into good and bad; they all have their trials and tribulations, their ups and downs, but he clearly favors those with a potential for good, those who try to be decent and to do the right thing, not necessarily according to the values of the Kirgiz or Soviet traditions, but according to human values that have validity beyond a given society. These people carry their values in themselves, some from the very beginning, some after accepting them from others whom they love and admire.

There is no political propaganda in Aitmatov's stories, though many of his characters accept the ideals of communism, mainly those ideals enunciated in the early years. Some feel disappointed by their later application and hope for a better future; others pay no attention to it whatsoever.

Ascent and *A Day* carry impressive humanitarian messages, and

Aitmatov's stature in the USSR is so great that his truly cosmopolitan works meet with no serious criticism. The central party organ, *Pravda*, published a friendly review under the title, "The World of Man—Man in the World" (January 14, 1981), only mildly rebuking the author for putting the peace-loving USSR and the warmongering United States on a level of parity. Aitmatov stood his ground. In a statement in the form of a preface, which he may have written in anticipation of criticisms such as these, he deplored the arms race and all actions directed against the human individual by those who harbor imperialist aims. He refrained from putting the blame for the explosive situation on the West and explained that his outer space chapters were meant as a warning to all mankind.

Viktor Petrovich Astafyev

Like some of his writer-colleagues, Astafyev affirms the autobiographical background of most of his stories. In some he has changed neither the names of the places nor those of the people involved. On the following pages, three of his best loved books, those mentioned to me repeatedly, will be presented.

The Last Bow is not a novel (*povest*), as the title page indicates, but rather a collection of 24 stories written during the years from 1957 to 1977. These stories deal with the personal relationships among simple, decent folk in Siberia. The "I" is usually Astafyev himself, but the heroine, more often than not, is his grandmother, his babushka. In "The Horse with the Pink Mane," a story that practically every Russian knows, the narrator chronicles his boyhood with his grandparents in a Siberian village. His one great wish at that time was to have a ginger cookie decorated with a horse of sugar with a pink mane, since these cookies were all the rage among the village children. When babushka sends him to pick berries for her to sell, the neighborhood boys challenge him to share what he picked with them. He fills the basket with grass and adds just enough berries on top to conceal his wrongdoing. At first babushka praises him for his effort, but she discovers the ruse when she tries to sell the berries in town. Babushka is very angry and broken-hearted over her grandson's wickedness; in her mind's eye she already pictures him as a criminal in chains. He feels dreadful remorse and pleads for her forgiveness. Grandpa does not interfere. After a while he goes out and brings back a ginger cookie with the white horse and the pink mane. "Take it," he prompts the dumbfounded boy, "don't look like an idiot. But if babushka finds you cheating again . . ."

In the "Siberian Polonaise," babushka tells the boy the story of the blind Polish violinist who lives in the village and plays beautiful melodies. He is the son of Poles who were exiled to Siberia because of their opposition to the tsar's rule over Poland. They died in exile, and the orphaned boy grew up in the village. When the violinist dies, the people decide that his instrument must be sold. But at the last moment the boy puts it in the Pole's coffin to be buried with him.

The title story in *The Last Bow* concludes the book. The narrator comes to his Siberian village to visit the guardian angel of his orphaned childhood, babushka, now 86 years old. Everything is still as he remembers it from last time, and she greets him as if he had just been away briefly. Shortly afterwards she dies. The news reaches him in the Urals, where he is working then. His boss will not give him time off to attend her funeral. That would only be granted, he said, if his father or mother had died. Years later, the storyteller mused: "How could the man know that my grandmother was for me both father and mother, everything that was dear to me in this world. I should have sent him to where he belonged [meaning to hell], should have left my job, sold my last slacks and shoes, and hurried to her funeral. But I did not do that. At that time I did not realize the immensity of the loss I had suffered. If it were to happen now, I would crawl on all fours from the Urals to Siberia to close babushka's eyes, to give her my last bow."

With some exceptions, the entire book is written in praise and memory of his grandmother, perhaps even in praise and memory of all Russian babushkas.

Hundreds of thousands of Russians must have spent years of their youth in a Siberian orphanage (*detsky dom*, *detdom* for short, meaning "children's house"). These orphanages housed not only orphans but also children of parents who had been exiled for any old reason and were often separated from their spouses and from their children, especially during the twenties and thirties. Astafyev, as we know, had been among these orphaned children. His *Theft* describes life in a *detdom* on the edge of a Siberian town mainly engaged in lumbering and navigation. The author calls it Krayesvetsk (town at the edge of the world), but it is the Arctic port town of Igarka at the mouth of the Yenisey that he has in mind. The orphanage inmates are boys and girls up to fifteen years of age. The action takes place between 1939 and the start of the war in 1941.

The novel has two heroes. One is the boy Tolya (from Anatoly), an autobiographical portrait of Astafyev himself to a large extent. His mother died long ago; his father was sent to a forced labor camp. He spent his childhood with his granddad and, after his death, was brought to the *detdom*. We watch him develop from one of the ordinary *det-domovtsy* into a youngster with character and the strength to face tough challenges.

Repnin, the head of the *detdom*, is the novel's other hero. An ideal father to the boys and girls entrusted to his care, this man devotes his entire life to an educational task encumbered by the dark and tragic backgrounds of many of his pupils, some of whom have been held by the police for all kinds of crimes, but especially for theft. The other towns-people, though mostly exiles themselves, take all *detdomovtsy* for crimi-nals, an attitude that breeds a gang atmosphere among the orphanage's inmates.

There are indeed some criminal elements in the house, among them a cripple, one of the older boys who derives his power indirectly from his close relationship to the house's bully. Many a horrible story is hidden in the children's lives. Young Zoya, for example, lived with her mother, who had been working as the only woman in a fishermen's camp, doing whatever was needed. After her mother's death, two of the fishermen kept the girl for their sexual pleasure. When the police learned about their doings, they were arrested and the girl landed in the *detdom*. After a while she adjusts to her new life and becomes a first-rate student. When one of her nonorphanage schoolmates makes ugly remarks about her past, the *detdomovtsy* almost beat him to death. A very shy and preadolescent love starts developing between Zoya and Tolya, who tries hard and, it seems, successfully not to have any "dirty" ideas about her.

Astafyev probably remembered a hundred episodes and stories from his own life in a *detdom*. He selected some that were suitable for show-ing character development in moments of crisis. The central story is the one that gave the novel its title, a theft and its consequences. Thursday was the day of the *banya* (bathhouse) for the *detdomovtsy*, a great occa-sion for wild fun. At the end of one of these Thursdays, some of the boys stole several days' worth of entrance fees, 800 rubles, from the bathhouse cashier, a woman. (These old rubles are now worth 80 new rubles because of the currency reform of 1961.) Of course they are suspected, but a thorough search of the orphanage ends without success. Some of the older boys who share a room have a terrific drinking orgy and otherwise enjoy their ill-gotten wealth, while the cashier, suspected of having swiped the money and trying to blame the boys, is put behind bars. Her two young children arrive at the orphanage. Now the theft is no longer a joke—it has jailed the mother and orphaned her children. Nobody knows better than the *detdomovtsy* what being an orphan means.

While the real culprits try to shrug the matter off, Tolya decides to correct the injustice himself. First he takes what is left of the stolen money (only 380 of the 800 rubles) from its hiding place, which leads to a life-and-death battle between him and his friends on the one side and the cripple's gang on the other. Tolya prevails. Next he starts working for money in his free time. But he soon realizes that to earn the missing 420 rubles in this way would take an awfully long time. Reluctantly he agrees when one of the boys suggests that the missing money should be obtained by theft.

The story of the second theft is extremely well told. Three of the boys zero in on a well-to-do *damochka* who appears to have obtained her money by devious means and is now buying a fur for 500 rubles in an *univermag*, the Russian equivalent of a department store. They know exactly how to do it from their previous experience: the money the women put on the cashier's desk suddenly disappears, "as if a cow had licked it up." Not only are the ruble notes gone, so are the thieves: they might as well have been swallowed by the floor. Tolya feels bad about the new theft but not too sorry for the *damochka*, obviously a *spekulyantka*, and delivers the 800 rubles to the police. The innocent woman who had been suspected and imprisoned is released, and her two children can return home.

When I spoke to Astafyev fans, they usually mentioned one particular angle of this novel as being especially interesting. Repnin, the housefather, had been an officer in the tsarist army in his younger days and fought against the Reds in the Civil War. Except for a few people high in the party and in the local administration, nobody knows his secret until someone gets at Repnin's personal file. The children, above all Tolya, are deeply upset. Their whole world seems to be going to pieces. Tsarist officers, they had been led to believe, were wicked killers and torturers of innocent women and children. How could their beloved and highly respected housefather have been one of these terrible people?

Obviously, the author chose to break a taboo and to show a decent, even admirable ex-tsarist officer. He lets Repnin defend himself by remembering how he once told the young and leather-jacketed investigating commissar: "I am a Russian officer! Proud to have served my fatherland in the way the honor and conscience of a Russian officer demanded! After all, Lermontov [the great poet] was one of them, so were Kutuzov and Suvorov [outstanding tsarist generals in whose honor high decorations were named in the Second World War.] And who are you? What right have you to run my country?" And when the interrogator demanded to know why he had not gone abroad after the Revolution like the others, he shouted: "My country is here. I have no reason to go abroad and no one to go to. And if you don't like my being here, shove off and go to the devil!"

The moralistic and propagandistic angle is rather subdued in this novel. Tolya's maturing into a responsible person is explained by the potential for growth within him that was promoted by the pedagogical talents of a man still proud of having been a tsarist officer and determined to serve his fatherland under whatever flag.

It is simple to ascertain why Russians like to read *The Theft*. Not only the Russians love stories about groups that fate or chance has brought together in a hotel, aboard a ship, on a "wayward bus," in a fraternity, or in an orphanage; such topics are among the favorites of authors and filmmakers around the world. *Boys' Town* was an especially popular movie, not only in America; the German counterpart about a girl's boarding school, *Mädchen in Uniform* (Girls in Uniform), was equally in demand. So too was a recent Australian film about a girls' school from which some pupils mysteriously disappeared during an excursion to the nearby Hanging Rock. As in *The Theft*, these three plots revolved around the relationship between the inmates and society and between the inmates and their educators, some of whom were always outstanding, such as Repnin in *The Theft* or Father Flanagan, played by Spencer Tracy, in *Boys' Town*.

The better the book, the more cumbersome the task of summarizing it. The latest collection of twelve of Astafyev's stories, published under the title of one of them, *The Tsar Fish*, made me acutely aware of this difficulty. These stories are filled with intensely powerful descriptions of the wild and lonely taiga, northern Siberia's eternal forest, and of its equally wild and lonely few inhabitants.

"The Tsar Fish" is a Siberian version of Hemingway's *Old Man and the Sea*. But the Siberian fisherman has no companion. All alone, he fights his life-and-death struggle with a giant sturgeon whom he holds with many hooks and who in turn, in a tremendous fight lasting many hours, entwines and pulls him to the ground. Only when the man is almost ready to give up does the fish escape and free the man. Masterfully as the details of this battle are related, they are not the essence of what the writer wishes to convey: the fight between man and nature. Soon, the fisherman realizes that what he has caught and what has caught him is not an ordinary fish but the mythical tsar fish that people have been talking about for ages and that only rarely appears to the human eye.

Though gripped by the fear of death, he also reflects on his past life and the sins he has committed. The worst of these is the dreadful humiliation he inflicted on a village girl whom he had loved but who fell for a short-time visitor, a wounded lieutenant. The dashing young man in uniform had been sent to their village for a brief period of rest and recreation. After his rival's departure, the fisherman revenged himself, breaking the girl's pride and future in the torments of his jealousy. She never forgave him for her unhappiness. Was the tsar fish revenging her by slowly killing him? Should he, just in case, have hung an icon in his home, as his grandfather had always urged him to do, perhaps in a kitchen corner where no one would see it and where he could always excuse himself by calling it a memorial gift from his deceased mother if someone did? When the fish finally departs, he feels more than just physical relief. Apparently the long tortures at death's door freed him of some of his guilt.

In "Pominki" (Memorial Feast), Akim, a native from the Lower Yenisey, takes his friend, a newcomer unfamiliar with the life of the taiga, hunting. Akim spots an elk. While he crawls nearer to the beast to get a good shot, his mate falls back and is suddenly attacked and killed by a bear. The elk escapes, but the bear approaches Akim, who shoots him to death. After Akim and his other friends have buried the newcomer's corpse, they feast on the bear's meat and the customary memorial vodka. Then they move on.

"Karga," which means "hag" or "witch," is the Yenisey fisherman's word for certain underwater rocks covered by fish-attracting growth. A poacher who knows every detail about water and fish along that stretch of the Yenisey takes his boat to the Golden Hag. On the way he is spotted by the river police who try to catch him. A wild Jesse James–style chase follows. By clever maneuvering, the poacher, who is far more experienced, leads the police boat to a sand bank where it becomes stuck. The delighted fisherman now dreams about more pleasant things, the most pleasant of all being his fifteen-year-old daughter, his pride and joy as well as the justification for his poaching and his other misdeeds. Now she is attending the school's commencement exercises, so he muses; soon he will send her to a higher school, and she will make a career for herself and maybe marry an important man; from time to time he will visit her. But when he returns to the village, she is dead, killed in all her loveliness on her way home from the ceremony by a drunken truck driver. Maybe it would never have happened had he accompanied her to school that day instead of poaching and having his fun with the fumbling river police.

The more Astafyev wrote, the more he became aware that his beloved Siberia was being destroyed by the actions of man. In the last story, "Net mne otveta" (I Know No Answer), he describes a commercial flight across the parts of Siberia he knows so well; suddenly he sees the changes wrought during his lifetime. He dislikes the crude structures of the factories below him and the houses of Akademgorodok, the country's pride, the settlement of scholars and academicians in the midst of Siberia, "shining in its newness, naked, unhomelike (*nepriyutny*), and strange." He is saddened to see that a river, the playground of his childhood, has stopped flowing and, in contrast to his fellow travelers, he cannot enjoy the view of the new hydroelectric power station that has so cruelly changed the landscape. "We have tortured not only nature but ourselves," writes Astafyev toward the end of this book, which he concludes with the Old Testament's antitheses: "There is a time to every purpose under heaven, a time to be born, and a time to die . . ."

Vasily Ivanovich Belov

Zorin, the same age as Belov and probably his alter ego, holds together the 22 individual *Carpenter's Tales*. The other binding element is the construction of a *banya* (bathhouse), the most important building next to home and barn for every peasant. Zorin became a city dweller the hard way. To obtain permission to enter a technical school, shortly after the war and at the age of fourteen, he had to march on foot from his village to the county seat, a distance of 80 kilometers. The woman "with a wart on her fat cheek" in charge of such applications did not pay the slightest attention to him for quite a while and did not look up when he addressed her. Finally she snapped at him to write his curriculum vitae. He complied, though he had little to say about the few years of his life. After some time she deigned to look at the sheet he had turned in. "Don't you know how to do this?" she snarled. Thrice he had to rewrite it. After returning from her lunch, she demanded one more document that he did not have with him. So he marched 80 kilometers home to his village and back again to the county seat. This time the woman kept him waiting for an hour and a half. Then she requested yet another document, but when he produced it, having marched for the third time 80 plus 80 kilometers, she refused the permission he had come for. "Even today," Zorin (and that probably means Belov) writes, "I turn crimson at the thought of this humiliation." Somehow or other he made his way in town without the technical school training, and now, after many years, he returns to his old village for a visit. In his nostalgia he finds everything wonderful and convinces an old carpenter to fix up the dilapidated *banya*.

The book consists mainly of the tales the carpenter and other villagers have in store for their native son, many dealing with the "dekulakization" of the years around 1930. Everybody who was not considered a kulak himself has some guilty feelings about being involved in sending fellow peasants off to Siberia because they happened to be just a little bit less poor than the others. (One was sent away for having two samovars instead of one.) But gradually Zorin finds that the village is not for him either; he is neither of the town nor of the village, like so many.

Equally random and equally poignant are the stories in the collection *The Dawns Are Kissing*. Belov inexhaustibly recounts the details of stories taken from everyday life: the experiences of a truck driver, for example, and his conversations with the passengers he picks up on the way or the yearly visits of one of those colorful vagabonds whose appearance is eagerly awaited in the village by the children for his funny tricks and jokes and by the womenfolk for his skill at mending old samovars and buckets, although his repairs do not usually last long. Belov always prefers to let the people themselves talk; he just reports what they say and then adds what he thinks they might be thinking.

The conflict between the city smart alecks and the country yokels is an archetypal story. Belov favors stories about misunderstandings between villagers and city folk. In "Manikyur" (Manicure), a village woman has been invited to the city by her brother, who takes her to a beauty salon. With embarrassed horror and cries of "My God" and "Queen of Heaven" she describes her adventures. "Men in white smocks were all over the women, like attendants in a hospital. All kinds of little bonnets, little boxes . . . ; half a day wasted," she thinks, when her brother says: "Now the manicure." "Okay, I think, if it has to be, let's have the manicure. I won't live through it anyway. So they take me to another room . . . " They work on her nails so long that she starts weeping, thinking about her cows who need milking. Everyone comes running, even the boss of the establishment, to enquire after the source of her dissatisfaction. But all she can say is: "For Christ's sake let me go home." Even when poking fun at this village woman, Belov's heart is with her.

Russian readers familiar with the old-fashioned village language, as most still are, read these stories, including the sad ones, with an amused smile because of their pithy vocabulary and wealth of parables and popular wisdom. Many expressions cannot be found in dictionaries; you must guess at their meaning from the content or from their similarity with more familiar words. Rather than being merely exotic or original, these tales are meant to express some of the authentic flavor and folksy depth of old village life, and it is this feature that draws the Russian reader to Belov, not the plot of his stories, which is usually quite simple.

Here and there modern Soviet life reaches into Belov's tales: one lives a collectivized life; one has to consider the local party cell and the country's communist administration. But in essence the peasants, especially the older ones, have changed far less since the Revolution than the city folk and the intelligentsia have; they are more or less the way we know them from the Russian classics (or the way I knew them from my childhood in Rastorguyevo, the village south of Moscow where we spent our winter and summer vacations). Belov is read particularly often by city dwellers who still have their roots in the country and who can turn to him (or to Shukshin or, for that matter, to Pushkin) if they wish to relax or to get away from their daily drudgery.

An example of Belov's critical realism is *My Life.* Tanya, the heroine, born in 1932 (as was Belov), writes the story of her life at age 40. Hers is a very simple biography, not pretty and without any poses. She describes the siege of Leningrad and the accompanying starvation without any heroic undertones; the evacuation to a village; her childhood as an orphan with various aunts, the most positive characters of the story; the hardships in a children's home; school; early love affairs; her first marriage; the birth of a daughter; the divorce from her husband, who cannot forgive her brief adulterous affair with a friend from her youth (with that same Zorin who appears time and again in Belov's tales); a second marriage with a man whom she took into her bed after her girlfriend with whom she shared a room in a laborers' dormitory threw him out of hers; another child; marital tensions because she refuses to allow his mother to move in with them; her husband's drunkenness; a complete break when she gets an abortion although he wants her to bear the child; a second divorce. Her husband goes to Siberia, marries again, and sends her 800 rubles, a lot of money. Her comment: "Finally I understood what a scoundrel he is. I convinced myself again that you should never trust men. They are all the same. So I promised myself, never, never to marry again." Now she has a friend, a quiet man "who almost never drinks," who always comes with a gift, some flowers or a bottle of champagne. When her daughter who dislikes him once threw his flowers out the window, she gave her a sound spanking. A few lines further on the manuscript ends in the middle of a word, . . . almost like *True Confessions.*

Belov's most controversial story, *Commonplace Affair,* appeared during the heated discussions about village literature. The curiously exotic name of its hero, Ivan Afrikanovich, which contrasted strikingly with his trivial village fate, almost became a password in that dispute. Ivan Afrikanovich is a war veteran with a loving, hardworking wife, a brood of children, and very little to eat. When he quietly steals grass at night for their starving cow, his "crime" is discovered, and when he tries to find a job in the nearest town, he has no luck. Back in the village, he finds that his wife has died. First he thinks of suicide, then he pulls himself together and decides to live on without hope for the future but with the boundless capacity for suffering characteristic of the Russian peasant—an impressive symbol, not of strength, but of endurance.

Millions of Russians draw strength from such Belov characters, and they are grateful to him for quietly creating such powerfully moving personalities.

Yury Vasilyevich Bondarev

Four synopses of Bondarev's works follow: two war novels, a postwar story, and *The Shore*, which is part-war, part-today.

The Last Shots is a war story from the first line to the last and describes an episode from the Carpathian battle against the slowly retreating, heavily fighting Germans. The war is nearing its end, but death still stalks each soldier; most of those we read about in this book die in the course of the story. The hero, a 22-year-old artillery lieutenant, yesterday still a boy, has grown into an excellent officer who loves his men and knows his weapons. Lena is the battalion's nurse. After first resisting their mutual attraction, the two young people throw themselves into each other's arms in a dugout shortly before the book ends, a few hours before the lieutenant's death. The two raging storms, of battle and of passion, are welded together, of course with the usual Russian restraint:

> He took her in his arms. She did not raise herself. [She is wounded; he is not.] From below, she flung her arms around his neck and pulled him toward her. His heart skipped a beat, when he felt the softness of her breasts under her tunic; her breath gently touched his chin; her slender fingers passionately caressed the hair on his neck and slid over his shoulders. "Do not spare me [she said], do not spare me. Do with me what you will. Do you not understand that tomorrow I shall no longer be with you?" [Several blank lines follow.] Then she continues: "Now you can let them take me to the hospital. . . . Whatever happens, you are mine." There she lay, warm, weakened, tired, and he kissed her gently.

Then he hurries outside. The German panzers are coming. From the dugout Lena can see that he is killed. She is taken to the field hospital. The war goes on. The last shots have not yet been fired.

The *Hot Snow* is the snow of Stalingrad, hot with blood, tears, and exploding grenades. December 1942 saw heavy battles against the attacking German divisions as they try to break through the encirclement to the beleaguered Paulus army. (Somewhere out there my youngest brother died.) Again a young officer and a nurse are the hero and heroine, but the roles are reversed: she dies and he remains alive.

In *Snow* we also meet some high officers, including the general in command of the army and his political deputy. The two are not fond of each other. The general feels hampered by his deputy, who knows little of military strategy. His opinion is substantiated when the latter, through his own oversight, is killed by the Germans. But for the general the worst news, which he does not yet know although the high command does, is a German propaganda leaflet showing his son, who was wounded and fell into enemy hands, between two German officers asserting that he is well treated and that the Germans only want to free Russia and destroy bolshevism. Was it just a setup? Was it true? Who could know?

Different types of Russian officers and soldiers are depicted here including some who cannot stand the strain and whose nerves snap. But in general they are shown to be tenacious, death-defying fighters. The Germans are hated and one of their majors is depicted as contemptible, but they are respected as soldiers. "They have conquered almost all of Europe; they fight in Africa and carry the war into our land."

Bondarev was now asked to write the script for one of the biggest and most expensive Soviet films, the five-part *Liberation*. (I saw two parts in Moscow.) This is the story of the victors, who fought their way under incredible hardships from the Volga to the Elbe. It is a tribute to Bondarev and to the makers of the film that they show the Germans as formidable and serious foes. Generals Manstein and Krebs are not caricatures, and even Hitler is not a ridiculous Charlie Chaplin look-alike. In the film one of the heroes, my schoolmate Colonel Claus von Stauffenberg, when shot after his attempt to assassinate Hitler failed, dies uttering the words: "Germany will not forget our names." Bondarev understands that a victory only counts and that the hardships involved in fighting the enemy are only plausible if he is a real and a believable foe.

I saw the film *Silence* before I read the novel. One of Moscow's largest cinemas, Rossiya, was filled to the last seat and long lines waited outside for the following showing. During the film you could scarcely hear a breath. When the lights were turned on, I saw stony faces. Silently the people stepped out into the light of Pushkin Square. Part of the crowd turned left on Gorky Street as I did, and only near the Gastronom no. 1, which many Muscovites still call Yelisseyev after its prerevolutionary owner, did I notice that people were conversing again.

Never before had the Russians seen a film that depicted the early post-war years as grimly as did *Silence*. And the novel, which I then borrowed from a friend (it was sold out, of course), was even grimmer.

The scene is Moscow in 1945–46, 1949, and 1953. Two war veterans, Sergey and Kostya, are the only survivors from their entire school class. While Kostya manages to get by with joking, flirting, and a little cheating, Sergey, who lives with his father and sister Asya, cannot adjust to the bleak postwar life. The three men and Asya, whose name and manner remind the reader of one of Turgenev's heroines, are surrounded by unsavory characters. Some of them are wicked, especially a former army officer whose cowardice in the Carpathian battles was responsible for the destruction of Sergey's battery and the death of many of his men. Having successfully concealed his secret, he wants to get the witness Sergey out of the way. Sergey's father is denounced and arrested in the middle of the night, a gruesome scene in the movie, while Sergey is expelled from the party and from the institute in which he has been studying. Kostya also gets into deep trouble; his questioning by a slick and overfriendly man from the secret service reminded me of Raskolnikov's questioning in Dostoyevsky's *Crime and Punishment*. Also depressing is the arrival of a warden from the camp where Sergey's father is being detained. He wants to stay with Sergey and Asya while shopping in Moscow and naively expresses his hatred of the political prisoners who are constantly brought in: "Many of them are traitors who want to kill the genius and leader, Comrade Stalin. There are so many Fascists in the cities! One hardly finds a place to spit. And they are brought to us, brought to us, day and night, although there is no space left. No sleep or rest for us. May they all drop dead."

The entire era comes to life through many nuances: in the anxious question, "Does Stalin know of this?"; in the halfhearted toast to the great leader in whose name one has fought; in the denunciation of "cosmopolitan painters" who betray the fatherland with their nonpolitical paintings; in the frequent repetition of Stalin's favorite phrase, "Facts are stubborn things"; through the novel's sinister characters. Overstated yet grandiose and macabre is the chapter with the fearful gathering of huge masses of people flooding the center of the capital at the news of Stalin's death; even a tough veteran like Kostya barely manages to escape unharmed.

Silence, read and seen by millions, was an important step in the Russians' attempt to cope with their recent past. When I asked Bondarev how he had intended the book's title to be understood he answered without hesitation: "Ironically."

The Shore is also of interest to Western readers, especially to the

Germans. A Soviet author by the name of Nikitin whose novels have also been published abroad (one can't help but think of Bondarev himself) is invited by his German publisher and the Literary Society in Hamburg to participate in a round-table discussion. Nikitin accepts and arrives with another Russian, his friend and guardian. The head of the Society, a well-to-do lady and the owner of a bookstore, Mrs. Emma Herbert, had taken care of all the arrangements in Hamburg. On the first night Nikitin correctly observes some signs of degeneration in Hamburg, but what else would you expect along the Reeperbahn, the red-light district where the two Russians wander. Nikitin, however, also remembers a night in Moscow when he lost much more money, was beaten up, and ended up in a police station: unsavory characters inhabit places other than Hamburg, too.

Mrs. Herbert, now a widow of 44 with a married daughter, had been a girl of 18 when, during the very last days of the war in May 1945, a young Russian lieutenant with an artillery unit stationed in the village of Koenigsdorf near Berlin was quartered in her parent's house after they had fled. This lieutenant, named Nikitin, is an idealist who had never had a woman before. He saves Emma from a sergeant's unwanted attentions. She falls madly in love with him, soul and body. At first he accepts her advances with hesitation, then with deep emotion. His best friend, another young Russian officer, sacrifices his life in an attempt to rescue some German boys recruited by the SS to stop the Russians at the last moment. All this may not constitute a true-to-life picture of those last days of the war; we know all too well that other events were also taking place, but it is important that Bondarev is entirely on the side of Nikitin and his friend.

After five days, the artillery regiment moves on. The Koenigsdorf romance is over, forever, so it seems. But this is not the case. Emma Herbert recognizes Nikitin as the author of the Russian translations she sells in her store and organizes his visit. And so they meet. Nothing that has happened to Emma since has ever equalled those five days at war's end. For Nikitin too, a married man now, whose only son died some years ago, the romance returns powerfully to life. He is deeply disturbed; the foundation of his well-to-do and quiet life is shaken. Urged by his compatriot who thinks he smells a foul intrigue aimed at keeping Nikitin in the capitalist West, the writer decides to fly back to the USSR sooner than planned. In the plane on the way home he dies of a heart attack.

"Wasn't that an all too easy way out?" I asked Bondarev. "I would have liked to know what became of your Nikitin. Much to his surprise he had discovered that the brief episode in Koenigsdorf had been a high point in his life, a unique and never-to-be-repeated union: war's end, a friend's death, spring, and a first love. And now a beloved wife at home, closer to him than ever since their son's death. So I ask the same question that your fans have posed: Why did you allow him to die instead of forcing him to cope with his fate?"

Yes, Bondarev said (or perhaps I should call him Bondarev/ Nikitin?), he had received fan mail of this kind, some had even written: Nikitin should have gone back to his first love, to Emma! "Sure," he added, "I could have written a continuation, a second volume perhaps, could, for example, have described how Nikitin's friend and travel companion had denounced him for falling into a trap and cooperating with some mysterious anti-Soviet organization in Hamburg. But that did not interest me. Nikitin faced an insoluble dilemma: his love for Emma and for his wife. There was no way out, and since writers take everything more to heart than other people do, his very heart broke under the strain. This was the end and not just an easy way out for me."

The importance of *The Shore* lies not in its ending but in Bondarev's brave plea for reconciliation with the bitter enemy of yesterday. One of the two friends in the novel dies in 1945 trying to save some misguided German teenagers, the other in 1971 because he loves a German woman.

Vasil Uladzimiravich Bykau

Among Bykau's books about the actual fighting in World War II the best known is *His Battalion*. It recounts the fate of an infantry battalion from one evening to the next at the end of the winter of 1942–43. In a desperate situation, the battalion's young commander, a captain, also from Vitebsk and hence in a way the author himself, is ordered to attack the heavily entrenched Hill 65 on the following morning. Only 76 men are left in his battalion; they are worn out and have little ammunition, and the commander is deeply worried about "his" men with whom he has fought almost since the start of the war. His mood worsens after unpleasant quarrels with two mean superiors; one of them, a general, lectures him on Stalin's words and even takes the captain's beloved dog, Jim, with him.

Next morning's attack encounters murderous German fire. The losses are so heavy that the captain orders his men to withdraw to their original positions. He is promptly demoted. In the second storm of Hill 65 he participates as a machine gunner. This time the hill is taken, but only a handful of the men survive.

Readers who volunteered their reasons for liking the novel mentioned the interesting tension caused by the clash of personalities. The sympathies of all of them were with the battalion's commander; they approved of his withdrawing his men because he feared for their lives. His superior ridiculed him for precisely this sentiment: "So you feel sorry for them! You weakling!"

All ideological phraseology in the novel falls from the mouths of the superiors. The battlefield details are described almost with the professional coolness of a report on a boxing match between equally strong opponents. The Germans are dangerous invaders and must be killed or driven out, but they are brave and skilled soldiers. One of the "Fritzes" (the Russian equivalent of the "Ivans," as the Germans called them), though himself wounded, saves a Soviet soldier's life by dressing his wound. The novel arouses less hostility toward the enemies on Hill 65 than toward the captain's superiors.

The earliest of Bykau's novels dealing with the human problems of Russians (or Belorussians) behind enemy lines is *Ballad of the Alps*. A Belorussian captured by the Germans and working for them in a factory somewhere in the Austrian Alps, manages to escape when a bomb destroys part of the plant. He flees with a Browning he grabbed from an SS guard. As he heads into the mountains to hide, he finds himself followed by an Italian girl also in prisoner's garb. At first he does not want to be bothered, but eventually they team up. A three-day love story ensues before the guards catch up with them. She escapes; the Russian is killed. Years later the Italian woman, now the mother of the Russian's son, writes to the people of his village, which she has located with considerable difficulty, to thank them for having reared such a brave and wonderful man.

This story strikes me as more artificial than real. But the importance of the *Ballad* lies neither in its literary nor in its stylistic value but rather in the fact that it is one of the first stories to make a hero of a man, who, as far as most Soviet literature was concerned, had no business even existing: a Russian prisoner of war. No Soviet soldier was supposed to be taken into captivity; he was expected to fight to his last breath or, if necessary, shoot himself rather than surrender. We have already met a former prisoner of war in Bondarev's *Choice*. But the *Ballad* was written some fifteen years earlier, which is, I suppose, the main reason why it aroused so much interest among Russian readers. This is understandable in view of the large numbers of Russians who had been defamed long after the war was over for falling into German hands.

The word *obelisk* evokes in the postrevolutionary Russian mind not the image of those grandiose and simple creations of the ancient Egyptians but of a similarly shaped but much smaller monument, usually a war memorial, that has replaced the Christian cross. The *Obelisk* that served as the title for one of Bykau's novels stands in the Belorussian countryside, near a small bridge. Until 1939 the area fell within Poland's frontiers; after the Hitler-Stalin Pact it came to the USSR. From 1941 to 1944 it was occupied by the Germans. The event immortalized by the obelisk occurred in 1942. The obelisk itself is made of concrete, stands less than two meters high, and bears a metal plate engraved with five male names, obviously those of resistance heroes under the German occupation. Lately someone added a sixth name, Maros.

The narrator, perhaps Bykau himself, hears by chance about the controversy surrounding that sixth name. Maros was the village schoolteacher; the other five were his pupils. Eventually the narrator learns that during the occupation the village school, surprisingly, kept the same teacher, Maros, as its director. In 1942, the Germans killed five of the pupils for damaging an automobile bridge that the Germans used (one German soldier lost his life); the teacher was executed with them.

After the war, the boys were considered martyred heroes. They got their obelisk. Not so the teacher. The mere fact that he continued to teach during the occupation made him seem like a collaborator.

Only gradually did the narrator uncover the facts—this was not an easy task. Nobody liked to discuss the touchy and controversial subject: the village people were far too confused and frightened to defend the old teacher's honor; they had other, more immediate worries. And the party and state organs accepted his guilt as a given. It proved easier "to connect the rivers Volga and Don than to get at the truth."

But finally the narrator does learn the truth: the teacher had remained under the German occupation because of his pupils. By staying he enjoyed a certain immunity from the Germans and thus could help his neighbors and even have a small radio receiver to get Soviet news. He had not known about the boys' sabotage plot and had managed to flee and take shelter with a local group of Red guerrillas. The Germans searched for him unsuccessfully. But when he heard that his pupils were about to be executed, he gave himself up, hoping thus to save them. Instead, he was hanged with them. Only one boy managed to escape and devoted his life after the war to rehabilitating his dead teacher. But to no avail; eventually he dies too. The stigma of collaborator and traitor remained on Maros. Now the narrator himself, a journalist, has decided to rehabilitate Maros. He too encounters hostility. People find it much easier to live with a generally accepted lie than to correct it. Why bother? Maros is dead anyway.

Obelisk is not so much about the war as about the occupation. It appeals to the reader because it offers a rare glimpse of someone fighting to restore the reputation of a small village teacher in the face of petty prejudice and bureaucratic apathy. In 1974 Bykau received the State Prize for this novel.

Bykau's most frequently mentioned novel is *Sotnikov*. Although it takes place during the war, the Germans are rarely mentioned. Instead, it concerns the bitter conflict between the guerrillas, called *partizany* by the Russians, and the *politsay*, the police formed by the Germans from anti-Soviet elements. Helplessly between the two stand the majority of the population, practically only women, children, and elderly people. The others are either dead, prisoners, Red Army soldiers somewhere far away, or *partizany*.

The heroes are two partisans foraging for food for their hidden comrades. One is Sotnikov, an unfortunate fellow, sick, and also wounded in the leg, a burden for his partner. The other, younger and sturdier, might have been more successful had he been alone, but he has to take care of Sotnikov.

The peasants are represented by a woman and a decent old man to whom the Germans have given the thankless job of village spokesman. (The former party secretary himself persuaded him to assume this position because otherwise some scoundrel might have taken over.) The two partisans break into his house, call him a collaborator, and take one of his sheep. The old man is arrested because he did not report the matter to the *politsay*. The peasant woman (her husband is a soldier, perhaps dead by now) is also arrested for giving the two exhausted men something to eat. All four—the old peasant, the woman, and the two *partizany*—are locked up and interrogated. The two villagers say nothing because they do not know anything about the local *partizany* group. Sotnikov does not divulge anything despite being tortured. But his younger comrade reveals the partisans' hiding place in a swampy area, assuming that the police know this anyway. He even avows his willingness to join the *politsay*, hoping later to escape and return to his band. The clear conscience with which he acted disappears when his three companions are hanged while he is accepted into the police force. His attempted suicide fails.

This is not one of the black-and-white, hero-and-scoundrel stories that were written in the first decade or so after the war. Of the four main characters only Sotnikov is a hero. The younger partisan is clearly not, nor is the old man. But Bykau does not condemn them either; he shows understanding and even some sympathy for their motives and behavior. The peasant woman, of course, is a totally innocent victim of dreadful circumstances.

All this seems very tame to the West, where war literature frequently debunks and deheroizes war. But for the USSR the road traveled within barely two decades from the 100-percent heroes of the early postwar period to Bykau's true-to-life heroes is worthy of note.

Aleksandr Borisovich Chakovsky

In Chakovsky's case it was easy to select his most popular books: his two multivolume novels about the blockade of Leningrad from 1941 to 1943 and about the Potsdam Conference in 1945. *That Was in Leningrad*, written and published during the war and mentioned previously, was a forerunner to *Blockade*.

First, however, a few words about *The Light of a Distant Star*, for two reasons: it is available in English (in a Soviet translation), and it is Chakovsky's attempt to come to grips with Stalinism. He does this in a polemical way that is directed, in the words of Chakovsky's biographer Ivan Kozlov, "against the Western bourgeois ideologues who are ready to nag at any blot on the sun in order to smear the sun itself." The novel's polemics were probably the reason for its publication in English (1965).

Apart from flashbacks, the story takes place in 1957, a year of great confusion due to Khrushchev's denunciation of Stalin the year before. The hero was severely wronged during the Stalin period; yet he has never lost his loyalty and devotion to the party and in long conversations he tries to win over his young nephew who believes that everything was wrong during that time and that it is up to the younger generation to put the country on the right track. The cards are stacked inasmuch as the hero is a knight in shining armor while the nephew is no good (among other wicked things he fathered a child but refuses to marry the mother). Even Chakovsky's benevolent biographer takes issue with the "superfluous agitatedness (*izlishnaya agitatsionnost*) of the hero's monologues"; they culminate in the thesis that "the cult of personality" was regrettable but overshadowed by the people's tremendous achievements during its duration.

Blockade is, with its 1,640 pages, one of the longest novels discussed in this study. But it covers about two years (from June 1941 to mid-January 1943) and includes no family histories. Instead it offers a panorama such as the one in Sebastopol commemorating the battle of the Crimean War of 1856 that fascinated me as a child. The visitor stands in the middle of the circuslike building while the celebrated events are shown all around him in pictures as well as life-size figures. In his book Chakovsky depicts the panorama of the siege of Leningrad as well as of some other places that bear on it, including the German and Soviet headquarters. The panorama has three tiers: on the top are the political leaders such as Stalin and Hitler, on the next tier are the marshals and generals of both armies, and on the lowest level are the ordinary people—officers, soldiers, and civilians.

The higher the level of the panorama, the greater, I found, is the reader's interest. Stalin is the towering figure, whether in the Kremlin or in his dacha west of Moscow. The Western political leaders who visit Stalin (such as the British foreign minister Eden or the United States emissary Harriman) are shown to be far inferior to Stalin in their political acumen (which they were), and Churchill, who does not appear in person, is portrayed as a great Englishman but a hater of bolshevism (which of course he was). In the novel, Churchill supports the Soviet Union just enough to keep the Germans busy but prefers a mutual German-Russian butchery to a Soviet victory (which was, essentially, true).

Hitler's image comes close to a caricature at times; he is just as hysterical in jubilation as in despair, a maniac who hates his generals because they wickedly ruin his wonderful campaign plans. (He is not shown biting carpets, however.) Throughout he is egged on by the sinister Himmler, who does his utmost to overthrow the famous Wehrmacht generals in order to replace them with his own stooges.

Zhukov is the leading figure in the Russian high command. He is sent wherever the going is tough and travels to Leningrad several times. His chief opponent for most of the novel is von Leeb, who leads the German armies to the suburbs of Leningrad but can proceed no further partly because he has to relinquish some of his divisions for the unsuccessful push against Moscow.

On the lowest tier only one German is shown to be an individual—a brave officer but an ardent Nazi who falls into Russian hands at the end. On the Russian side are a large number of individuals—officers of many ranks, the Leningrad party bosses, a foreman in the great Kirov plant that now produces and repairs tanks, physicians and nurses in the overcrowded city hospitals—but hardly any are workers. The central figures are a young officer who gradually rises to the rank of lieutenant colonel and participates in many battles and the nurse whom he loves, as well as an old architect representing the loyal old intelligentsia and his good-for-nothing son, the book's token scoundrel, a coward and egotist. With this one exception, all Russians are larger than life, people who think only of Leningrad and never of themselves, legendary heroes rather than mortal men with weaknesses and contradictions. This is why they finally triumph.

By contrast, the Germans are a bunch of poorly led bandits, and some Russian readers might wonder how they ever managed to reach the gates of Leningrad and Moscow. But surely there was a difference between the mood of the Germans, brave as they were, but fighting thousands of kilometers from home in foreign lands, and that of the Russians battling with their backs to the wall for their motherland, though probably not quite as great a difference as Chakovsky makes it appear.

Blockade is a heroic panorama where the Russians are very good and the Germans very, very bad. This, however, did not diminish the readers' interest; the book was mentioned by almost everybody I talked to. Nor could one blame Chakovsky for presenting his material in this way. Leningrad is—next to Stalingrad and more than any other city in Russia—a symbol of the entire war: first defeat, then prolonged suffering and heroic fighting, and finally victory; the very cloth that panoramas and sagas are cut from.

Personally, I find the subtler novels of Bondarev or Bykau more to my liking. But those Russian readers who do not mind that a novel's characters are stereotypes (*the* nurse, *the* political officer, *the* old intellectual) will not complain; the story moves rapidly through its 116 chapters, almost like a film script. Everything that a guidebook through besieged Leningrad might have included occurs—the fighting, the starvation, the freezing to death, the wounds, the falling bombs and exploding shells, the precarious road over the ice of Lake Ladoga.

Chakovsky spent ten years researching and writing, and he has been successful in linking the persons on the top and middle tiers who actually existed with the figures of his imagination on the lowest tier. However, I agree with some Russian reviewers of the book who maintain that the author described the real characters better than the imaginary ones. In a way, Chakovsky himself admitted this when he said to me that it was more interesting for him to write (and for the reader to read) about historical people rather than about imaginary characters; nurse Vera must be introduced at some length by the author, whereas when Stalin or Zhukov appear, everybody already knows a lot about them.

The novel's popularity rests, apart from the attachment Russians feel toward war novels in general, on the semidocumentary, semi-imaginary description of the tremendous drama of the Leningrad story.

If *Blockade* showed a three-tiered panorama, *Victory* consists of three stories in one: the Potsdam Conference in 1945, the Helsinki Conference in 1975, and the three journalists who covered both of them. The three stories are linked by frequent flashbacks. Hardly a Russian I talked to had not read at least one of the novel's three volumes.

Obviously, Chakovsky assumed that his book's appeal would increase if it started with the events of 1975 and then jumped back to 1945. The novel's title also links the two conferences: the 35 signatories at Helsinki confirmed the borders that the "Big Three"—Stalin, Churchill, and Truman—established in Potsdam 30 years earlier. But for the reader, the Helsinki conference with its various "baskets" is rather complicated compared to Potsdam, and the author himself has less to say about it. It is, of course, far more exciting to read about three famous men sitting around a table near the ruins of Berlin than about the practically faceless representatives of 35 governments meeting over several years in different places.

My impression is that the Russian readers' interest is primarily captured by the story of Potsdam, a story so fascinating that it does not even need the supporting cast of three journalists. Their adventures fade into insignificance next to the high drama of the conference itself. Just a word about these journalists. The Russian is upright and patriotic, though somewhat inexperienced, being a newcomer at the game of international journalism; the Englishman is wicked (and becomes even more so by 1975); the American is a back-slapping chap with a small piece of gold hidden somewhere in his heart but otherwise only interested in "bucks" and drinks and uneducated to boot (he has never heard of Shylock).

The reader learns a lot about the setting of the conference; about the small palace of Caecilienhof where the meetings took place; about Potsdam; about Karlshorst, the Soviet headquarters. But throughout the novel, the Big Three stand in the center.

President Truman was very new at his job when he came to Potsdam and therefore especially difficult for Russians to understand. In the book he emerges as a rather unlikable little shopkeeper, a small-time politician who is totally unable to fill the shoes of the man whose vice-president he had been, Franklin D. Roosevelt, whom the Russians glamorize. He is not particularly intelligent, certainly not wise, not even shrewd. He is not very good at his homework and possesses little self-confidence. The one thing he does have is the promise of the bomb, which during the conference is coming closer and closer to reality. The first successful test ("Trinity") was made on July 16, 1945, on the very eve of the conference. But at that moment it was not yet clear whether it could be turned into an actual weapon. Truman decided not to tell Stalin (and Stalin only learned about it after Hiroshima, roughly one month later). Truman is described as a man torn between his fear of Stalin's superior willpower and intellect on the one hand and his own invigorating pride in the soon to be expected possession of the bomb on the other hand. At the very least, in light of his secret power, Truman was sure he could achieve the establishment of a truly democratic and friendly government in Poland that would include pro-Western elements. But he failed even in this aim as Stalin doggedly pushed Poland's western border to the Oder and western Neisse rivers.

Churchill is also shown in a rather negative light as a man who delayed assisting the second front as long as possible and was now horrified by the possibility that the Russians, as the true military victors of the war, might control the whole of continental Europe. Churchill's overwhelming desire at the conference was to push the Soviets as far east in Europe as he could. For this purpose, the reader is told, he even kept a German army of some 30 divisions in the British occupation zone ready to join, if need be, the Western forces in what would have amounted to a Third World War. As if this weren't reason enough for Soviet authors and Soviet readers to dislike Churchill, the Englishman is shown as a human wreck, a talkative and bungling shadow of his old self, spoiling time and again the moves Truman planned out on the Potsdam chessboard. Yet Chakovsky does not withhold the fact that Churchill had reason to be nervous and preoccupied: the upcoming British election. To be confronted everyday at Potsdam by the leader of the opposition, Attlee, who had to be kept completely up-to-date in case he should win was most distasteful for Churchill. The blackest day in Churchill's life was losing that election. Here and there, Chakovsky shows grudging respect for the cigar-smoking, grumpy old man, a respect he probably still retained from the stirring days of the wartime alliance.

But intriguing as it is for Russians to learn about Truman and Churchill as human beings, for them the really exciting element of both novels is the man whose name was on the lips of millions of Russians who fought and died, the leader in charge of the USSR from the late twenties until his death in March 1953, the mysterious one about whom they had known so little although they had read and mentioned his name every day. His picture was particularly exciting for the Russians in the sixties when the first chapters of *Blockade* began to appear and the leader's name was still under a dark cloud.

In the years between Chakovsky's completion of his first and second multivolume novels, the evaluation of Stalin in the USSR clearly changed from the tyrant of Khrushchev's depiction to the outstanding, though somewhat blemished, leader of men. In *Blockade*, Chakovsky still phrased his descriptions of the Supreme Commander cautiously; he made but a few veiled remarks that could be interpreted as hinting at the executions of many of the highest Soviet officers prior to the war. There were also a few lines about Stalin's self-centeredness, his unwillingness to listen to other's advice. In *Victory* on the other hand, Stalin is shown as a great man. True, here and there his mistakes are referred to in passing, but those are the mistakes of the past. At Potsdam he brilliantly plans his one-against-two game; he quickly sees through his opponents' intentions; he skillfully lays his traps for them, and, always patient, he outwits, outsmarts, outmaneuvers them at every point. And whatever the Russian readers may think of those "mistakes," they are as pleased as the author about Stalin's superior performance at Potsdam, which so astonishingly increased the might of the empire.

Much of Chakovsky's account is at variance with what Western historians have to say about these men and events. But this is hardly the place to polemicize with a novelist who can always say that he has written a novel, not a historical monograph.

Nodar Dumbadze

Dumbadze's first book, I found, is still his most popular. It was mentioned to me many times although its title is almost a tongue twister: *I, Granny, Iliko and Illarion.* Frequently it is published in one volume with its two continuations, *I See the Sun* and *Sunny Night,* which is how I read and how I shall describe it.

All stories are told in the first person by a boy who had different names in each volume as he grows up, all of them doubtless incarnations of Dumbadze himself. The boy lives first with his grandmother (as did Dumbadze) and his "uncles" Iliko and Illarion in a mountain village; then, when somewhat older, with his aunt, a 35-year-old schoolteacher; and finally in Tbilisi, the capital of the mountain republic of Georgia, as a university student. The three volumes are not structured novels but collections of stories. Not much happens in them; the death of a dog, accidentally killed by one of the uncles while hunting rabbits, is one of the major events in the first volume. There is much chatting and drinking—Mark Twain might have liked it—and the war is far away.

In later stories the war is felt in the village. Soon after it began several official letters arrived in the village announcing the death of this or that man. Then the dreaded notices stopped coming. During a village meeting, the mailman stands up. He alone, he declares, is guilty of causing all the unhappiness in the village. He accuses himself of having brought the notification of death to the women in the village. The people in the room barely dare to breathe, expecting to hear of some terrible new disaster. The mailman continues:

> "Why must I live, dear neighbors, if you fear my coming? I don't want your vodka [he was traditionally offered a glass of vodka whenever he brought a letter]. I don't want to be a mailman; I don't want to. Do you hear?. . . . God, have mercy upon me! Come and carry the letters thyself if thou art God and canst stand everything. I am only a human being! If thou hast created the world, look after it thyself. Why put everything on my shoulders?" Then he holds the mail bag high above his head. "Do you hear me, God? Say something, God!"

And with that he throws down the bag, scattering the mail from the last several weeks all over the table. Many letters bear typed addresses: death notices. He breaks down on the table, "on this heap of pain and little joy, and weeps."

Amusing, if somewhat macabre, is the tale about a school play performed after the war. Written by one of the students, *The Fall of Berlin* has a cast consisting of Hitler, Goebbels, Goering, General Paulus (the general who surrendered at Stalingrad), Eva Braun, and a Soviet lieutenant in charge of three soldiers. But it is never performed. The parents who attend the dress rehearsal are furious. The father of "Eva Braun" is shocked that his daughter is to play Hitler's mistress and takes her out of school. Another father, stressing that he is an old and respected Communist, is angry that he has to watch his son play Goering. The mother of "Goebbels" feels insulted that her son was chosen to play the man with the clubfoot, and so it goes.

The author's ability to tell tragic events with some humor seems to be one of the reasons for his success. Many Russians find the Georgian's style more relaxing than the usually very serious war stories of their own countrymen.

Successful as he was with this genre, Dumbadze was not satisfied. For ten years, he says, he carried the plan for his *White Flags* around in his head. His problem was that the plot unfolds in a cell of the Tbilisi prison where there is not much room for action. Quite a challenge to a storyteller's talent! The novel concerns the ten men who inhabit the cell, their misfortunes and misdeeds; their conversations, sometimes bitter but always humorous; their dreams, fears, and hopes; their rare meetings with relatives; their interrogations; their stereotypical greeting of a newcomer, "Anybody left outside?"; their comradery and mutual understanding; the jokes they play on each other to while the time away.

With one joke they push one prisoner to the brink of desperation by telling him that the vaccination against typhoid and other diseases he was given when entering the prison was really a drug that causes impotence; a large syringe, they explain with perfectly straight faces, is effective for fifteen years. The nurse's visit causes boundless excitement. She is the only woman they get to see, and her inquiries about their health and her treatment of their various illnesses with Luminal (a preparation of phenobarbital), the one medicine at her disposal, generate an enthusiastic response.

One of the ten is our hero, a young Tbilisian, age twenty, who tells his and his fellow prisoners' stories. He is innocent, he asserts. One man was killed in a brawl in which he did not participate, but the guilty ones jointly testified that he did it. He was arrested and is now awaiting trial.

One by one the prisoners leave cell number 10 on the fifth floor; some are taken to trial; some are granted their freedom; one commits suicide. In the end the young hero is all by himself. "Are the authorities running out of prisoners?" he asks sarcastically. No, but a flu epidemic in the city forces the prison's isolation. Finally, justice triumphs. He, too, is released.

The end is somewhat unexpected: a huge white flag, the emblem of the book's title and "the symbol of goodness, mercy, and love flew above the world." Is this an implied criticism of the red flag, the Soviet Union's official emblem? I don't think so. The reviews were generally kind. Quite likely, the powers that be appreciate the novel's rather friendly description of a Soviet prison and the author's indignation at corruption, for example, his disgust with a cemetery administrator who lines his pockets by reselling cemetery plots. For the Soviet reader, so it seems to me, this volume offers primarily a collection of the adventures of some hilarious rascals plus some insight into human nature.

He called *The Eternity Law* his most ambitious book. Again its hero, a writer born in the late twenties, a deputy to the Supreme Soviet, closely resembles Dumbadze. The scene is a hospital in Tbilisi, or more precisely, a room in the hospital occupied by three heart patients. All three have suffered serious attacks caused by coronary thrombosis. One of them, a cobbler, dies in the course of the story, leaving the writer and the priest of a local church.

We read about the venerable physician, the efficient nurse who is responsible for administering injections, and the rats under the beds, but mainly we learn about the afflicted writer. When he was nine, his parents fell victims to the purge; as a young teenager, he worked as a shepherd in the mountains and shot a bandit; at sixteen he had a touching and innocent love affair with a young waitress who was so beautiful that all the men in the village were crazy over her and, when rebuffed, told wicked lies about her. As a university student he and some of his friends were touched by the death of Crazy Margo. Once a lovely girl, she suffered brain damage during a flood just before her wedding and then lived the withdrawn life of a retarded person, washing other people's clothing for a living. So many mourners came to the funeral of this queer yet beloved character that street traffic stopped for two hours. Crazy Margo's life could easily have been a story in itself; the novel's hero is only marginally touched by her fate.

Eventually, the hero becomes a well-known writer and the editor of a newspaper. In the hospital, his mind wanders back to some of his adventures with corruption and bribery. Even in the hospital an unsavory character involved in some illegal business visits our hero in an attempt to bribe him into agreeing to help. Disgusted, the writer knocks his visitor out with the chamber pot.

The hero also recalls the local party committee meeting at which his request for membership was rejected. His parents' long detention has precluded his admission to the party, although they were granted amnesty long ago and are both dead now. He admits that he still feels resentment: "During all those years we undeservedly suffered so much grief, humiliation, and privation." When asked why he continues to apply for admission, he replies: "I want as many decent people in the party as possible."

The most remarkable chapters, at least for the foreign reader, include the long and almost affectionate conversations between the writer and the priest. They both respect and tease each other; the writer remarks that the priest would make a good party agitator, while the priest suggests that the writer might have a good career in the church. While he sleeps with the help of injections, the writer has a vision of Christ that he does not try to laugh off. Before being released from the hospital, the priest goes down on his knees to pray that God may cure the writer and thus give him a chance to understand Him. But if it is God's will to let the writer die while still in sin, then He should mercifully accept the writer and in turn reject him, the priest, because he was unable to make the writer see the proper road. All this is told without a trace of sarcasm. The church in Georgia is still closely linked to the Georgians' sense of patriotism, as the Orthodox church is to that of the Russians.

In my own view, this novel is not one of the major works of Soviet literature, nor did I get very explicit answers when I asked its fans why they liked it. In addition to the sympathy for sunny Georgia and for its people who are an integral part of the Russian literary tradition, the attraction may lie in the novel's main message, which Dumbadze calls the Eternity Law and formulates as follows: "Man's soul is a hundred times heavier than his body. It is so heavy that one man alone cannot carry it. Therefore, we the people, while we are alive, must try to help one another and to immortalize (*obessmertit*) each other's soul: you, mine; I, the next person's; that one, a third person's, and so on, endlessly." An admirable conclusion to a thoughtful book.

Anatoly Stepanovich Ivanov

Eternal Call is, so I found, the most widely read of the lengthy sagas and hence merits a more detailed description. A true *epopeya,* a term used about half a dozen times in the preface to Ivanov's *Collected Works* (1979), it consists of two parts published six years apart, in 1970 and 1976. One covers the period from the first Russian revolution in 1905 to the beginning of World War II; the second takes over from there, reaching into the early sixties. These more than 50 years filled with highly dramatic and demanding events are projected on a Siberian village in the region of Novosibirsk, called Novonikolayevsk before the Revolution.

Reading the prologue of some 70 pages did not whet my appetite for the remaining 1,400 pages; it contained a black-and-white (or should I say red-and-white?) picture of both the wicked and the noble characters. The story proper turned out to be more subtle and complicated, so complicated, that at times even its characters find it hard to discover rhyme or reason in their personal or political relations.

When I discussed this disparity with Ivanov, he defended himself by saying that the prologue was just a sketch designed to provide the background for the story and its characters. But that's just the problem: a sketch in black and white and a completed painting in many colors are two rather different things, and the sketch might deter some readers from continuing. The prologue, in fact, makes one think that the novel's personages are unchanging statues—some forever wonderful; others forever unredeemably mean.

Some characters indeed do not change. On the one hand, we meet the awesome, mean, drinking, whoring landowner who savagely fights the Reds (and gets killed by them) and his son Makar, an enemy of the Soviet state almost to the end, a thief, and a saboteur with political motives. On the other hand, some of the party members have served as glorious warriors for mankind's bright future ever since they were children. One such person is the man who started as a very young underground fighter in the Revolution and died a hero's death when, early in the war, he managed to prevent a munitions factory from exploding and killing the workers.

But changes and mutations are far more frequent. This quality is shown in the character development of two brothers who were very poor and under the iron rule of that evil landlord at the start of the novel. One brother, a fiery young Red during the Civil War and later a model kolkhoz worker, goes over to the German side early in the war and is killed in their service by his fellow Siberians. The other brother, who had risen in the landlord's grace and even became his bodyguard, eventually joins the Reds and, after many years in prison as punishment for having fought on the White side, becomes a loyal citizen and even a hero of the Soviet Union in World War II. Another man, the son of a tsarist colonel killed by the Red guerillas while pursuing them, defies the Soviet system and suffers many years in prisons and forced labor camps as far away as the Magadan mines, but he performs miracles of heroism during the war as a member of a doomed penal battalion.

A young informer for the tsarist police becomes a guerrilla hero and later an important figure in the village, yet he is not loved much by his co-villagers, although they remain unaware of his activities during the Revolution. A captain of the Red Army, the son of an old Communist, caves in under the strain of his captivity in Germany and turns into a prison supervisor to save his life; after the war he spends many years in Soviet prisons, and when he finally returns to the village as a broken man, even his widowed father refuses to have anything to do with him; he shoots himself with a hunting rifle the father gives him for that purpose.

In personal affairs the whirligig is even more amazing. One village woman accepts, though with unhappiness, that her husband has kept a mistress practically since their marriage; the mistress's husband in turn accepts, decade after decade, his wife's unfaithfulness and even works as her lover's assistant. Although virginity is held at a premium, various unmarried girls are being deflowered, one at the age of fourteen. Some consent, but others are raped, and the perpetrators are other villagers, not in the chaotic days of the Revolution, but two decades and more afterwards. These events are described without lurid details, but the facts are clear.

Personal affairs occupy a remarkably large part of the book even during the war years. At that time, the whole country, including Siberia, was in a state of high tension. Thousands of refugees poured in from the provinces occupied by the Germans, and a large munitions factory was built with machines and workers quickly evacuated from western Russia. Yet, for dozens of pages the reader forgets that the country is in the midst of a terrible war because the fate of individuals becomes the focal point.

Stalin is neither praised nor criticized. Yet, the shadow of the purges is there. Meritorious revolutionaries and innocent people are sentenced to long penal terms—some never to be heard from again—because somebody wanted them out of the way. The return of one of the brothers to the village and to his wife after serving five years in prison for no apparent reason tells the Russian reader more about the suffering of that period than a political treatise on the purges could convey:

> They went to the side of the road and sat down. They had not yet spoken—"So you see, Agata, life goes on," he said softly. . . .
>
> "How did you ever survive?" [Agata asked.]
>
> "A man can take a lot."
>
> "I kept waiting for a letter at first."
>
> "I wasn't allowed to write. Well, tell me how you've been."
>
> "Volodya and Dasha are all right."
>
> "Then—it's a girl?" he said hoarsely and his dry lips trembled.
>
> "Oh, Ivan."
>
> "I kept wondering whether it was a boy or a girl. And whether the child was alive. Not knowing was what made it all so hard. . . . So you named her Dasha?"
>
> "Yes. Don't you like it?"
>
> "Sure I do. Dasha is a fine name. Come, let's go."

(This and later quotations are taken from a translation of the first volume [Moscow, 1979].)

Many unlikable people are portrayed in the novel. A girl refugee who lost her mother (and her papers) during the evacuation after a train was bombed by German planes arrives in the village more dead than alive. Some of the men treat her like war booty; even the militiaman who arrests her tries to molest her. "Sometimes, in despair, she wonders why there weren't any kind, intelligent people left on earth." And she says: "What I can't understand is why there's still so much evil in the world. And where does it come from? I can understand the war. The Fascists want to conquer our land and our cities. . . . But what I want to know is why there's still so much evil in our life?" In our life, she says.

One of the most positive characters in the novel, an ex-guerrilla and later a party official, attempts to give some guidance to a group of confused friends. He twice includes the words that give the novel its title in his speech, which could have been spoken by someone in the West to an audience unsure of its goals and values.

> Luckily, man has been blessed with intelligence. That's why he's a human being. And sooner or later he'll begin thinking about the meaning of life, the life of his fellowmen, of society and his own actions and deeds. A powerful, compelling, eternal call to life, an eternal desire to find his own place in life is what forces him to do this. And I believe that from this moment on a person, no matter what mistakes he may have made, becomes a true member of the society in which he lives, a defender of justice, human dignity and happiness. And so, my friends, let's drink to this noble, eternal call and to each and every one of us being aware of it within ourselves always.

Perhaps another sentence, spoken by the same man, comes closest to the groping of the author's characters: "Actually, every person spends his life trying to understand himself. . . . It's a difficult job." Time and again, especially during and after the purges, the thoughts of the novel's characters turn nostalgically to the days of the Revolution and the Civil War, even to the years served in tsarist prisons: everything was simple then, one knew friend and foe, knew what was right and wrong, "what one was fighting for."

The German attack in June 1941 created a similar situation once again; friend and foe could be clearly discerned. Some of the book's main characters, no longer young, volunteer for service in order to cut through the web of confusing entanglements in which they find themselves caught and thus escape it. One of them, an old NKVD-man (the NKVD was the dreaded Soviet secret police), when told, "You are searching for death," answers, "Probably. I can't do it [i.e., kill] myself. I probably lack the willpower to. But out there . . ."

Ivanov was thirteen when the war started. His descriptions of fighting and of life under occupation, neither of which he experienced, sound less true—and more gruesome—than Bondarev's or Bykau's. And his heroes are more superhuman than theirs. (Some of the battle scenes reminded me of those I had read with excitement as a boy during the First World War when the German soldiers performed fairy-tale feats of courage.)

Part of the horrors described are committed by pro-German Russians (including a former and long-term officer in the NKVD) and by anti-Soviet Ukrainian nationalists (who once sawed a captured Russian political officer [*politruk*] in half). Yet, enough blame is left for the

Germans. Not one of them has any redeeming features; they are fat-assed, have hands covered with red hair, and stink. The only good "German" is a Russian who has written his dissertation on Goethe. Taken prisoner, he finds it hard to believe that Goethe's beloved city of Weimar is close to the concentration camp of Buchenwald. He too is killed by sadistic Germans.

There is a curious explanation of Hitler's invasion. He did not like our system, says a party man to an old peasant without convincing him. Old peasants are traditionally fountainheads of Russian wisdom. This one replies:

"That's not it. What do they care about a system? They've gone and trampled all over Poland and France and all the rest of those other countries, and all of them had capitalism for a system. . . . Man's greedy by nature. Just look at her." And he points to a woman selling some potatoes to poor refugees; she is fat enough, yet she is greedy for more and therefore sells her wares at a profit to the highest bidder.

While the characters Ivanov shows are dissimilar and mostly quite differentiated, his world view is monolithically simple, more so than that of most of the other 23 writers. He puts its essence in the mouth of the badly wounded political officer just before his bestial execution by the Ukrainians.

> A constant battle is being waged, a terrible, cruel, pitiless battle between light and darkness, between truth and deception, between good and evil. . . . This battle continues at all times and in all forms, mostly in secret. Since the summer of 1941 it has been out in the open, man against man. This war is not simple, not just any war. It is not Germany alone that is fighting us. *All the evil and dark forces in the world* decided that their hour had come and threw all their power into battle against us. [Translation and emphasis mine.]

I am not the only one to see Ivanov's political message in this Manichaean division of the world into good and evil. The preface to Ivanov's five-volume *Collected Works* quotes these very words, remarking that Ivanov expresses in them what he considers "the only correct criterion for the evaluation of all important events in the twentieth century."

In the *Eternal Call* there is one notable first: the story of a Soviet penal battalion. Composed of inmates from prisons and forced labor camps, some of them volunteers and others draftees, the battalion enters battle with a simple rule: if you are killed, your problem is solved; if you emerge unscathed, you stay in the penal battalion; if you are wounded, you are, after your recovery in the hospital, assigned to a normal military unit and become an ordinary citizen. In rare cases extremely brave penal soldiers, such as a man from the Siberian village, were allowed to follow the third path. Of another such soldier who had spent half his life in prison camps and who, after fighting bravely, was killed in battle, Ivanov says that he had a "wonderful life." The penal soldiers' battle cry is not the Russian *Urrrrha!* but a selection of the dirtiest and most abusive cusswords in which the Russian language is so very rich. These words are merely alluded to, however.

Throughout his novels, Ivanov wishes to show that the people of Russia and particularly those from that Siberian village were purified by the trials of the war, that all that was once bad and mean in them was extinguished by their hatred of the enemy, their love for mother Russia. Every crime they might have committed before can be forgiven except one: treason against the fatherland.

Among the countless portraits drawn or painted throughout the ages are those liked by the persons portrayed and those disliked. The portraits liked do not necessarily have to be smooth and pretty; they may have plenty of wrinkles and scars as long as they make the person look mature and even heroic; nobody wishes to look mean, wicked, or cockeyed.

Eternal Call is a portrait that satisfies the Russians and more especially the Siberians, who are so prominently depicted. The portrait is not flattering; it has a number of warts, but it is one that most readers can accept with a feeling something akin to this: "It was a terribly hard time, but we carried on and held our own." A portrait one might be more proud of than pleased with.

Vil Vladimirovich Lipatov

Lipatov has always been interested in linking his pedagogic message with an intriguing plot, several times with a detective story. One of his frequently mentioned books is *The Village Detective.* Its hero, Anisin, is not really a detective, just a simple policeman, a *militsioner,* in a village on Lipatov's beloved Ob River. Anisin's job is to solve a mystery: Who stole the beautiful accordion belonging to the man in charge of the village club? With its two keyboards, it is a marvel of an accordion, its owner's pride and joy. After 70 pages, a few days of thinking, and a bit of footwork, Anisin discovers that three young brothers stole the accordion, not for any personal gain, but out of hatred for the club manager. Footprints from unusually large boots, seemingly locked doors that can be opened without keys, and other standard mystery-story paraphernalia keep the reader's interest up and thus expose him, almost without his noticing it, to the author's moral teachings.

Nobody can object to Anisin's principles: thou shalt not steal (not even another's tomatoes, let alone his accordion), thou shalt honor thy father and mother (and adults in general), thou shalt not commit adultery (or fool around with other women), and, the oldest of all commandments since Adam, thou shalt work by the sweat of thy brow. Like Anisin, many members of the older generation, not only in Russia, may feel these venerable rules do not mean as much to today's younger set. ("What is youth coming to?") Decades ago, moral tales were common in the Western world too. Today no self-respecting author would dare dwell on "the moral of the story" for fear of the critics' ridicule.

Anisin's adventures reminded me of some stories I read a decade before Lipatov wrote his. Giovanni Guareschi created an Italian parish priest, Don Camillo, to serve as his village's moral educator. Both Don Camillo and Anisin know what is good and what is evil; both are thoroughly familiar with everything that is going on day and night among their flock. The Italian priest defeats the wicked Communists, and the Soviet policemen the wicked anti-Communists, and both are backed by unquestioned authorities: the one by Christ, the other by Marx and Lenin. Yet they mainly rely on their personal authority. When Anisin speaks, the head of the village soviet, the highest local administrative official, and the party secretary bow their heads. Not even his tremendous belly (he weighs 250 pounds) can endanger his authority.

Lipatov follows the same format in his first full-length novel, *And That's All About Him*, which he might have called, "A Town Detective in the Village." Again the setting is Siberia along the Ob River, in the area near Narym, in a village close to a lumber company.

Traditionally the characters in moralistic novels are either good or wicked. In this novel, among the wicked ones are two tractor drivers. One of them, a former prison inmate, sees the light toward the end; the other remains wicked to the detriment of the (state-owned) company: since more can be earned by hauling big logs, he willfully destroys the smaller trees with his tractor, ruining almost 30 cubic meters of wood in a single day. Not exactly wicked but not up to his job either is the local party secretary.

The good ones are the Young Communists (*Komsomoltsy*) under the leadership of the book's hero, the young worker Stoletov, as well as Stoletov's mother, a widowed doctor. Also good and decent is the man from the police force of the nearest town, a captain in the service of the Ministry of the Interior.

A lumber train engineer notices a young man's corpse next to the tracks, Stoletov's corpse as it turns out. The captain is dispatched to the settlement to discover whether his death was an accident or a homicide, and the reader follows his unhurried investigation. At first the captain suspects the ex-convict (a good reason for the experienced whodunit reader to eliminate him from the list of suspects). He also takes a dim view of the lumber company foreman. The latter is a most unpleasant chap, a Siberian sad to say, who is hard to unmask, because he knows how to be popular with his two bosses as well as with the workers; even the party secretary thinks highly of him. In reality he is an egotist, very versatile at finding unscrupulous ways to make money. His large, two-story house has some glass-mosaic windows and soft carpets in the hall to cushion one's feet; it sits on a lot of two and a half acres. The garage is made of stone; several hothouses for growing vegetables stand in the yard. The garden is filled with dwarf fruit trees, and flowers in flaming colors line the garden path. An electric pump fills the swimming pool with water from an artesian well, and a riding horse is also available. The foreman serves an elaborate lunch on thin, antique china and offers champagne in expensive crystal glasses. "We live simply and modestly," he good-naturedly remarks to the young engineer whom he wants his daughter to marry.

With the help of his cronies in the next higher level of the lumber company and in other organizations, the foreman manages to arrange very low plan figures for his division. As a result he and his men exceed the plan without much effort, which means bonuses for everybody and especially for the foreman himself. Since all workers in Siberia get twice the salary a worker in European Russia receives, his income is unusually high. Nobody ever questioned the foreman's figures because they were useful for all—nobody except young Stoletov, an idealistic *komsomolets*, that is. Stoletov smelled a rat, started digging around, and uncovered the foreman's secret. At a meeting he exposed the great manipulator and demanded his dismissal. Shortly afterwards Stoletov's body was found next to the railroad tracks.

As we know, the foreman did not want young Stoletov for a son-in-law, especially after the young firebrand had exposed his machinations. He preferred the up-and-coming engineer (who even wore a suit from abroad!). But at the conclusion of the novel the captain finds that Stoletov was not murdered; he killed himself accidentally, jumping from the train when he learned that his love, the foreman's daughter, had gone with the young engineer on an evening walk in a nearby grove. So, in the end the captain is left with a corpse but no murderer; we may assume that the wicked foreman will be punished for his machinations, though not for murder.

Stoletov, whose death initiated the investigation, emerges as a knight-errant fighting for truth and honesty, a hero of our time. He reminds the captain of Peter the Great.

The didactic tone, somewhat jarring to our ears, did not seem to bother the Russian readers with whom I spoke. They appeared to be neither annoyed nor enthused by its "be a good *komsomolets*" message and to see the novel primarily as an interesting crime story. And indeed, the yarn is well woven, though a bit cumbersome and slow-moving for the impatient, fast-driving Western reader.

Another book that has made a strong impression on Russian readers, to judge from what I was told, is Lipatov's *Gray Mouse*. I am not a specialist on literature concerning alcoholics, so it may be neither here nor there if I say that I have never before read a story that describes a bunch of drunkards in such detail.

Once again we are in a village on the banks of the Ob. Here we meet four young men engaged in a grandiose drinking bout during just one day, a Sunday, from sunup to midnight. This binge did not originate by chance in connection with a special feast. No, every Sunday morning, these four men arise with the firm determination to get drunk quickly and to stay that way as long as possible. When they run out of money, they borrow or beg and always manage to get enough to keep on drinking.

Lipatov puts a lot of energy into describing the four, each with his own alcoholic history. The most dangerous of them is always looking for a fight, yelling, when he finds an adversary: "And for a pig like you I have spilled my blood in the war!" Actually, he has spilled his blood, and if someone hesitates to believe him, he tears his shirt open to show the hideous scars on his abdomen. These scars also help him get money from people who take pity on him.

Russians like to drink. They are inclined to be tolerant of drunkards, to laugh at their stories, and to enjoy their appearance on the stage. Lipatov's almost clinical description of the four young men's spree is read with so much interest because drunkenness was not supposed to exist in the USSR and any mention of it was frowned upon for a long time; Lipatov was one of the first to break the ice. For millions of women and children, a man's drunkenness is a vital concern, perhaps the worst social evil they have to endure within their own four walls. By bringing it into the open, Lipatov performed an important service.

His last full-length novel appeared in the fall of 1977, only a year and a half before his death. Its title bore the name of the young hero: *Igor Savvovich*. The trouble is, this is not his real name. It should be Igor Sergeyevich because his real father's name was Sergey. Igor's involved genealogy need not concern us here, although it is one of the major threads that helps keep the novel together and the reader's interest alive.

The novel tackles two problems. The first is the dual evil of corruption and favoritism; most of the novel's characters are mixed up in one or the other.

Igor's pretty wife Svetlana, although just an ordinary schoolteacher, can do whatever she pleases because her father is the almighty administrative boss of the province of which Romsk is the capital. For her fine car, she gets as much super gasoline as she wants from the official filling station; she can also create havoc on a heavily traveled road by parking her car in the middle of the roadway. The traffic cop shies away from her because he is under her father's supervision. Then there is the man who uses stolen material to build four garages on a lot that was to become a children's playground and the ambitious actress who needs a garage for a Mercedes obtained in some shady business deal and who clinches the illegal deal by offering one of the four garages to Igor's wife so that nobody will dare to expose the irregularity. The local administrative boss agrees to the construction of the garages to please his superior, Svetlana's father. (In the end, justice triumphs and the smelly garage deal blows up.)

Well, corruption has been castigated for many years in numerous official speeches and also in quite a few novels. Lipatov's second concern is more original and, so it seems to me, of greater immediate interest to many of Lipatov's older readers: What is wrong with the younger generation? What is wrong with Igor?

Igor is extremely unbalanced, as the novel repeatedly illustrates. The source of his troubles lies in a mysterious illness that takes hold of him from time to time, causing dreadful pains in the chest and frantic, although unsubstantiated, fears that make him contemplate suicide. The explanation for Igor's troubles seems to lie—in addition to the mix-up about his father—in his all too easy youth, which has ruined his self-esteem and finally even his health. Igor grew up in a well-to-do home; his mother babied him, the one treasure of her life. While still a student he was given a car (quite an extraordinary occurrence for a young man in Siberia). He passed his state examinations without any of the examiners bothering to listen to what he said, because his parents' high social position made his passing a foregone conclusion. "Everything has been done for me," Igor says, "including choosing a wife" with all her connections and privileges. The result is what some people in the story call infantilism and what approaches a form of mental illness.

No doubt *Igor Savvovich* has contributed to a better understanding among Russians of a phenomenon that the Western countries, with their far greater wealth, experienced one or two decades earlier. Since the campus unrest of the late sixties, many adults from Berkeley to Berlin to Tokyo have come to believe that a hard youth is far better for people than a soft one. Many German parents, proud of the way they rebuilt their country from the ruins of the war, complain bitterly that their children grow up without any sense of obligation, "demanding everything and refusing to accept any responsibility," and now similar complaints are coming out of Russia.

Georgy Mokeyevich Markov

The Strogovs is one of those *epopeya*s of which the Russians are so fond. In fact, this saga of three generations in a Siberian family, from the turn of the century to about 1922, is one of the earliest. The oldest Strogov is a beekeeper who lives alone with his family in the depth of the Siberian forest. The nearest village is Volchi Nory, which in English means "wolf den." Matvey, one of his two sons, is the hero of the second generation, and he in turn has several children. Dozens of other people live between the two covers of the novel—mainly peasants—most of them poor and getting poorer in the course of events but some who have grown into well-to-do bloodsuckers. Quite a few tsarist officials, prison wardens, policemen, soldiers, and, of course, revolutionaries— workers and students—appear in the story as well.

Markov wants to show the gradual growth of political consciousness among Siberian peasants. In the beginning they take the old order for granted, then they become rebellious largely due to the efforts of Russian revolutionaries exiled to Siberia. In the end they fight as guerrillas with the Reds against the Whites, and eventually their leaders, including Matvey, are received by Lenin in Moscow.

All the main events in Russia and outside gradually filter down to the Siberian taiga: the 1903 split into (good) Bolsheviks and (wicked) Mensheviks among the Russian revolutionaries, the Russo-Japanese War, Bloody Sunday in St. Petersburg, the shooting of strikers in the Lena goldfields, the tsar's October Manifesto in 1905, the Stolypin reforms from 1906 to 1911, the First World War, and the Revolution.

All these events, of course, are described according to the version of history that was considered valid at the time the novel was written.

The picture Markov draws of the Siberian village is very black. While the peasants are good at heart, they are also drunkards who give their wicked masters a chance to fool and exploit them. The rich fellows are also drunkards but they are sly; they know how to handle the peasants and are very clever at bribing the officials with generous gifts and drinking bouts. Demyan is one of the worst bloodsuckers you can imagine, an evil person who beats and demeans those dependent on him, driving his first wife to commit suicide by hanging and his second by drowning herself in the river. He and his friends kill some of those who stand in their way, including the old beekeeper, but they are not punished because they know how to manipulate the law.

Two chief bones of contention persist between the rich families and the mass of poor ones: a river, which supposedly carries gold nuggets in its sands and runs through the uninhabitable taiga, and a primeval forest of Siberian cedars, which has belonged to the members of the Wolf Den community since time immemorial and forms an important part of their livelihood. Thanks to the Stolypin reforms, the forest is taken from the peasants and awarded to the wealthy members of the community. But although police and later even soldiers defend the rights of the rich, the peasants, armed with hunting rifles and scythes, stand their ground. The same rich families also try to get prospecting rights on the river, but again they are thwarted by the peasants. In the struggles for their traditional rights, the fundamentally conservative and tsar-loving peasants and the revolutionaries from the cities grow closer together, participating jointly in demonstrations against the tsarist regime and in acts of civil disobedience.

"Revolutionizing Siberia" might well be the subtitle of this book that undoubtedly created the impression among many Russian readers that the Revolution became more and more inevitable from year to year. People probably felt relieved when they reached the point in their reading where the Revolution, like an overdue storm, finally broke.

Siberia covers a much shorter period, from just before the outbreak of World War I to shortly before the revolutionary events of 1917. This is one of the most Siberian of all Siberian novels; 95 percent of the story takes place right there, and rightly so, for this is the milieu that Markov knows best. The briefly mentioned non-Siberian sites, Moscow, St. Petersburg/Petrograd, and Stockholm, remain pale by comparison.

Markov concentrates on his own part of Siberia, the areas of Tomsk and Narym, and on one particular aspect of life in the war-torn country: the *podpolye*. This is the Russian equivalent of the Western political term *underground;* in Soviet history it refers specifically to the Bolshevik underground, both prior to and during the early phase of the Revolution. For the Russians, a *podpolshchik* means approximately the same as a resistance fighter does for the Norwegians or the Dutch. Every Russian child is familiar with the history of the *podpolye,* especially its Siberian variety, for almost all leading Bolsheviks, including Lenin and Stalin, were *podpolshchiki* at one time or another. Usually they were sent as convicts to Siberia from where they soon fled westward, most often to Zurich or London.

The novel's hero, Ivan, is a student from St. Petersburg in his early twenties and a member of the Bolshevik Party. Because of his agitation against the war ("Turn the imperialist war into a revolution against the tsar!"), he was arrested and sent to Siberia, to the area near Narym. The novel begins with Ivan's flight in the depth of a Siberian winter and the manhunt to which the local population has been mobilized by the police. The young man successfully escapes, and the rather efficient Bolshevik *podpolye* takes him to various hiding places in the huge and roadless forests. The leader of the *podpolye* is a selfless and highly respected country physician who holds all the threads in his hand.

For the Russian reader, learning something about this underground network (or should I use the American Civil War term *Underground Railway?*) is undoubtedly quite interesting. The comings and goings of couriers with their secret messages and the hairbreadth escapes are depicted as are some women revolutionaries who have equally exciting adventures—something of *The Scarlet Pimpernel* from the other side.

The novel's roster includes a wide variety of social strata, almost no one has been omitted: farmers, fishermen, hunters, freemen and convicts (or their offspring), merchants and officials, policemen, physicians, students and priests, even a Polish dressmaker, Christians, atheists and members of ancient Russian sects, the Old Believers and the self-maiming *Skoptsy.* Yet, essentially only two types of people are portrayed: the Bolsheviks (plus their sympathizers) and all others.

A great achievement of Soviet literature since the mid-fifties has been the acceptance of human qualities in Soviet heroes; they are allowed to develop, to change, even to fail and to be unhappy. This innovation came as a great relief to authors and readers alike who were tired of the "positive heroes" of the thirties and forties who could do no wrong, who were good once and forevermore, and of their counterparts, mostly "class enemies" or their offspring, who were and remained abominably wicked. In a way, *Siberia* is a throwback to that era.

Markov's is a "party line" book. Anybody who is not poor (or a leftist intellectual) is wicked per se, because his private property instinct, of course, is a curse that destroys all human decency in him. The entrepreneurial talent the Soviet economy has needed so desperately all these decades is never shown to be even potentially good; such a talent is nothing but a horror for everyone around (though the Marxists themselves claimed that well-functioning capitalism was the prerequisite for the transfer of an economy to socialism). Merchants fight each other tooth and nail for the local raw materials; they sell their wares for more than they paid for them (imagine that!); their treatment of family members, servants, and all ordinary people is cruel if not downright criminal; a few bottles of vodka is all the natives receive for an entire boatload of high quality salmon or furs. And, of course, the rich can always count on all the other wicked people in the area to be on their side.

To his credit, Markov is an ardent Siberian patriot. Perhaps in a similar way I am a patriot of my beloved Black Forest in southwestern Germany, where I have my home. The difference, to be sure, is that the Black Forest, apart from lumber, trout, kirsch, and magnificent scenery, has very little to offer, whereas Markov's Siberia is one of the largest and richest treasure troves in the world. At any rate, Siberia's vast expanses and its wealth are the second theme in Markov's novel, after the *podpolye*. For Western readers the book may offer too many details about the flora and fauna, the geology, and even the ancient history of Siberia. But on the whole, the author has woven these two strands of his story together quite well. My guess is that the novel's popularity rests half with its *podpolye* adventures and half with its vision of the Siberian wonderland.

Among the papers of his uncle, a learned specialist on Siberia, Ivan finds this eulogy to Siberians:

> No other nation on earth could have carried out a gigantic feat such as the subjugation of Siberia. To move thousands of miles through unexplored areas and to continue in the face of countless difficulties, more was needed than just manliness, courage, and the cockiness that comes from an overabundance of daring. The main thing needed was an awareness of one's historical role, together with the materialized will of the ages and the determination to increase the glory of the fatherland.

Accepting this statement with a straight face is somewhat difficult for a non-Russian who remembers what happened on other continents during the age of boisterous expansion by other Europeans and their confident trust in their God-given manifest destinies.

Yury Markovich Nagibin

Nagibin's many stories, hitherto scattered in many periodicals and some smaller collections, are now available in a four-volume edition published in 1980–81. ("Available" is an overstatement; the only place I was able to find a set was the *Beriozka* in Moscow.)

Now for the plot of the two stories in *Literaturnaya Moskva* that, as I mentioned before, caused such a stir in 1956. (All four stories told here are included in his *Collected Works*.) The first had a strange title: "Khazarsky ornament" (The Khazarian Ornament). The Khazars, not very prominent in history books, once lived in the area around the Caspian Sea and the Caucasus. They have no connection to the Soviet Union, and their ornaments have even less. Thus the author uses the term *Khazarian ornament* as a synonym for something politically highly irrelevant. If a person studies it, he wants to escape from present-day problems.

The specialist on Khazars in our story is hunting ducks with a friend, our narrator. Extremely cautious in whatever he says, the historian is horrified when a stranger they meet by chance criticizes the situation in the country, especially the dreadful roads. The specialist tries to calm the stranger by saying that one could not do everything at once and that, after all, very much had been built. "Built!" the stranger interrupts angrily, "and how much useless rubbish have we built? All those columns, arches, little balconies, convoluted embellishments, all those wedding-cake palaces! They manage to drag a palm tree into the most miserable little bar, to put a monument in the dirtiest little square. But they didn't think about the road, this artery of life, and they still don't."

Profoundly disturbed by such blasphemy, our Khazar specialist leaves the room. Only now do we learn that years ago he had been a self-assured and confident man and that now he is "scared, once and for all." Everybody understands what that means: in that sinister period of Soviet history, the man had been subjected to some terrible experiences. He is nervous and fearful every time he hears such rash remarks, until he learns that the stranger is the newly appointed local party secretary. "Suddenly he had new eyes, or rather the eyes he had probably had in his youth when in his wildest dreams he had not expected someday to devote all the strength of his living soul to the study of the Khazar ornament."

In the quarter century since this tale was first printed, Soviet readers have seen far braver stories. But in those days such criticism of the preceding era seemed exceedingly bold, especially when it came to its characteristic architecture, the wedding-cake style.

His second contribution to the 1956 almanac was equally courageous. In "Svet v okne" (Light in the Window) we read about a resort in the countryside where, among the buildings used for the vacationers, stands one that nobody is allowed to enter except for the director of the resort and the charwoman, Nastya. In this building are four beautiful and well-furnished rooms, including one for billiards, all empty and always ready for Him—if He ever should come. His name is left open; it might have been Stalin or some local party bigwig. Whoever it was, the house was kept in excellent shape for Him; the floors were cleaned daily; the furniture was often dusted; the flowers were always freshly cut. The existence of this empty apartment disturbs the director of the always overcrowded resort, especially when he has to separate honeymooners for whom a few days in this luxurious suite would be a memory for a lifetime.

One evening as he returns home rather late from a walk, he notices a light in the window of the secret building. Through the window he sees Nastya and some employees sprawled in front of the television set and enjoying themselves at the billiard table. He raises a row and chases them away. But their severe, almost triumphant, faces make him fall silent; he listens to a strange new sensation arising in his heart, a sensation of loathing himself. Thus the story ends. Its title may well hint at the light in the window of the late dictator who, as everybody knew, usually worked well past midnight and thus deprived his subordinates of their sleep.

Critical of another social development is "Slezay, priyekhali" (Get Off, We Are There). An agronomist, just out of school in Moscow, arrives in the countryside to work in a kolkhoz. Because of the deep snow, she must be taken there by a horse-drawn sleigh. The old coachman is enchanted by the young girl and already thinks of her as his daughter. But she is taciturn and obviously not very happy. When she discovers that the kolkhoz to which she has been assigned and which needs her very badly has no proper accommodation for her, she refuses to work there. This, the old coachman thinks, is very plucky of her. The second kolkhoz, which he praises as vastly superior to the first, she does not like either. She gets in touch with her organization and before the day is over she obtains permission to return to Moscow. Now she is jubilant and does not hide her scorn for the backwardness of the area to which she had been assigned. Her arrogance angers the old man, and he changes his opinion of her. When she demands that his tired horse step up his pace to get her to the train station on time, his patience snaps.

Abruptly reigning in the horse, he orders her to get out in the middle of the snowy landscape. Then he turns the sleigh around without giving her another look. The patient, well-meaning peasant and the college-educated city youth represent an age-old conflict in Russia.

A considerable part of Nagibin's oeuvre deals with children. One of the favorites I have already mentioned is "The Echo." The ten-year-old boy who tells the story could be Nagibin himself. But he is not the hero, and, in fact, he comes off rather badly compared to the plain little girl who dominates the scene. She must be about the age of the boy, but we are not told how old she is, only that she always swims in the nude. When he brags about collecting stones and stamps, she surprises him by saying that she collects echoes in the nearby mountains. With their mothers they spend a summer vacation at the Black Sea. On a long hike over steep trails she shows him some of her echoes; all are different—one is sharp as glass; another has a deep and frightening growl. But in her hour of need, when, again naked in the sea, she is insulted by a bunch of boys, he lets her down; he does not want to be known as this funny girl's friend. Eager to better his standing with the boys, he takes them to the echoes. But they are silent. Again he is disgraced.

The girl shows her magnanimity by coming to say good-bye just before she leaves. His mother comments on how pretty and charming she is, and he suddenly notices this. Running after her, he tells her through the window of the departing bus how beautiful his mother thinks she is. The bus gathers speed. She throws a kopek on the road to guarantee her return once again, and he decides to follow her example when he leaves, so that they may meet again. But when he mounts the bus some weeks later, he has forgotten all about it.

Valentin Savvich Pikul

I read all Pikul's novels with keen interest. He does not write the finest Russian prose, but he is a born storyteller and knows how to captivate the reader. Here I shall present some of the historical novels that are so characteristic of his style. But in addition I want to mention another book briefly, although it is not a novel in the proper sense of the word; Pikul calls it a documentary tragedy. It concerns a joint Anglo-American-Soviet wartime enterprise. *Requiem for Convoy PQ-17* is an account of the destruction of the last great British convoy to Russia by the German navy in the summer of 1942. The drama concerns not so much the individual ships and sailors as the convoy as a whole, the same convoy, incidentally, that British author David Irving handles in his *Destruction of Convoy PQ 17* (London, 1968). Although Pikul does not refer to Irving, he probably consulted his book, which came out ten years before he published the third and revised version of his own narrative.

The crucial problem relates to the question of why London recalled the convoy's naval protection on July 4, 1942. This left the merchant ships at the mercy of the Germans, who sank 24 of them together with all their—mostly American—equipment for 50 thousand Soviet soldiers, from tanks to canned food. Pikul assumes that Churchill sacrificed the convoy in order to weaken the Soviet Union, which he hated though he needed it as an ally, and the Russians who were then fighting desperately to repel the German attack on Stalingrad. His opinion may be colored by a personal experience. Many Soviet sailors were sent to Stalingrad as reinforcements, and many died, including his father. Pikul is most severe in his accusations; he calls Britain's First Lord of the Admiralty, Sir Dudley Pound, a *lodyr* and a *trus* (a good-for-nothing and a coward) and labels Churchill's policy a *prestupleniye* (a crime). His verdict: "The Allies betrayed us." Irving does not share his opinion. Navy historians will judge the two versions; Pikul's confirms the Russians' distrust of Churchill.

But even worse than the Englishman Churchill, in Pikul's eyes, are two Prussians, Frederick the Great and Bismarck. In *With Pen and Sword* he denounces Frederick as a wicked man in his youth and in his old age, defeated time and again by the Russians, given to weeping and despair, and finally saved, much to Pikul's anger, by the Russians themselves. In January 1762, when Frederick's fortunes in the Seven Years' War were at their lowest, the good (Russian) Tsarina Elizabeth died and the bad (German) Duke of Holstein-Gottorp, her nephew, became Tsar Peter III. An enthusiastic admirer of Frederick, Peter made peace with him and withdrew the Russian army, paving the way for Frederick's eventual triumph.

The two chancellors who provide the title to another of Pikul's novels (*The Battle of the Two Iron Chancellors*) are Bismarck and Gorchakov. Perhaps Pikul felt uneasy about portraying Frederick as an antihero in *With Pen and Sword* without offering a true Russian hero to oppose him. So he counterbalanced the next Prussian rascal with his Russian opposite, Gorchakov. For Gorchakov and Pikul the tsars' unification (and extension) of Russia was beneficial and in line with the natural course of history, whereas Bismarck's unification of Germany was imperialistic and dangerous. Pikul's rather one-sided account of European international affairs could have been produced by any loyal tsarist historian before the Revolution. He only deals with what the

Germans call *Kabinettspolitik,* politics between governments, without bothering about people or social processes.

Next to the Russians, the people that come out best are the French: they even brew better beer than the Germans! But eventually they too prove to be a disappointment. Their Emperor Napoleon III, the vainglorious fumbler, handed all his trump cards to the wicked but ever so clever Bismarck.

The one friendly word about Bismarck in this novel comes from Lenin. At least one quotation of his should be included in every novel, and the most suitable Pikul could find was this: "Bismarck did something historically progressive; he did it in his own way, *po yunkerski* [in the *Junker* manner, from the German word for a member of the conservative landed aristocracy of Prussia]. The unification of Germany was necessary."

The plot of Pikul's most discussed novel, *At the End of the Line,* is generally familiar to many millions thanks to Robert K. Massie's *Nicholas and Alexandra,* published twelve years before Pikul's book, and to the film adapted from this novel. Western readers may be interested in a somewhat more detailed comparison between these two books than I offered for Pikul's and Irving's *Convoy,* so I will highlight their most salient features.

Pikul's account runs from the 1800s to the end of 1916, Massie's from 1894 to the summer of 1918. In the center of both books stands the same cast of personages: Emperor Nicholas II, Empress Alexandra, and Grigory Rasputin. They are surrounded by a multitude of grand dukes and politicians together with their wives and mistresses.

In contrast to Pikul, however, Massie devotes a good deal of his story to the disease that plagued the imperial heir, Alexey; his own son's hemophilia aroused the writer's interest in the fate of the *tsarevich* and thus in the end of the Romanov dynasty. Massie correctly found that Rasputin's tremendous power over the empress (and through her over the emperor) mainly derived from her belief that he was the boy's savior, the only one who could stop his bleeding. After all, her raison d'être was the crown prince, whom she had finally born after bearing four daughters; his illness was her personal catastrophe and whoever could alleviate it must have been sent by God in answer to her fervent prayers. This important aspect, as well as the description of the imperial daughters, is missing from Pikul's novel, but he does not explain why.

Yet surprisingly, the two books written by authors from such diverse backgrounds show more similarities than differences. Both probably used the same sources, though Pikul does not name them, and Massie offers the reader a bibliography and 54 pages of notes. Both refrain from ideological judgments. Apart from the handful of quotations from Lenin, Pikul's novel could just as easily bear the name of a Western author. He is primarily fascinated by the story as such, understandably as it is one of the most extraordinary of this century. Instead of using the awesome events as the framework for furiously denouncing the feudal and capitalist order and for glorifying the revolutionaries' virtues, Pikul, even more than Massie, dispenses with "the masses" and keeps the reader within the relatively small circle of the court and the political establishment. True, Pikul's exalted characters are rather unpleasant, but so are Massie's, though he shows more sympathy for the tsar's family. But not everyone in Pikul's novel is contemptible: Stolypin, Russia's premier after the 1905 revolution until his assassination in 1911 and hitherto considered anathema by Soviet authors because of his policy of helping the enterprising elements among the peasants, is pictured with respect, and his death is portrayed as the result of secret police conspiracies and right-wing machinations rather than as a glorious deed committed by the Reds.

Pikul attributes, I think correctly, the fall of the tsars' empire to the disintegration of the ruling elite rather than to the success of the revolutionaries. The empire was collapsing of its own accord because it was morally at "the end of the line" and because the terrible losses and defeats of the war were more than it could bear. No one was left to pick up the pieces (except the Left, which is not described). The decline also expressed itself in the erosion of sexual mores, a theme that Pikul emphasizes more than Massie, without becoming explicit, however. He alludes to this development mainly through Rasputin's debaucheries.

One salient feature of Pikul's book is his nationalism. The fall of the Romanovs is the fall of *his* national dynasty, and any victory of the tsarist armies is the victory of *his* armies. He disproportionately extols their initial triumph around Gumbinnen (August 20, 1914), while unduly minimizing their collapse near Tannenberg (93 thousand prisoners fell into German hands). The most curious element of Pikul's Russian nationalism is his description of the role Jews played during the last years of the empire. Instead of praising the many Jews among the revolutionaries (he does not even mention them), Pikul gives a very negative picture of the rich Jews and their demoralizing influence on Russian society and politics. All the Jews he names are unpleasant; they only think of money (they even undermine the Russian war effort, first against Japan then later against Germany, for personal gain) and of power for themselves, hence their antipathy toward the Russian nobleman Stolypin and their treasonable hopes for a German victory. There is more than one hint that the Zionists are pulling the strings behind individual Jews. The Zionists provide Rasputin with unlimited amounts of money and even with a set of false teeth for his appearances at court; one of them gives him lessons in hypnotism. Thus Pikul dislikes the Jews not so much for being Jews but for not being patriots of the empire (they could hardly have been patriotic in view of the way they were treated) and for traditionally siding with the Germans. In a way, they were super-Germans in his eyes.

If Massie's book was a best-seller in the West, Pikul's was a true sensation in Russia. After I had read it, I understood why I had encountered such difficulties in obtaining a copy while in Moscow in 1981 and why out of all the books I had sent home from Moscow by mail this was one of the two that disappeared from one of the parcels, pilfered, no doubt, by an ardent Pikul fan. I also understood why I got another copy in 1982 only by offering in exchange five books not obtainable in Moscow except in the *Beriozka*. Incidentally, this copy was some kind of photocopy of the novel's serialized publication in a literary review in 1979. Only by knowing that such copying machines are a great rarity and their services practically unavailable to ordinary mortals can one understand the high price.

Of course, Pikul ran into trouble. In an article published in *Pravda* on October 8, 1979, Pikul was accused of immersing himself in the gossip and bedroom secrets of the tsarist family and the court camarilla, preferring the description of amusing and farcical situations and superficial adventures to a deep study of the nation's history. This judgment, hardly overstated, did not diminish the readers' interest. For Pikul has given the nation something it has never had before: an exciting fictional account of the end of the tsars, a historical event for the Russians if there ever was one. Until Pikul came along, the Russians mainly knew what their textbooks told them—reports about the wicked and stupid court and glorious chapters about the noble revolutionaries. Pikul, on the contrary, recounted the details, turning the leaders of the ancien régime into human beings and even making the sinister monk Grigory Rasputin seem real. This was fascinating reading. The secret of Pikul's success was his colorful and intense style of presenting events still near enough to be important for the present day yet far enough removed to be read like a fairy tale.

In the early seventies Pikul published one more book on the last years of tsarist Russia, *The Moon Strait*. This novel, however, never acquired either the popularity or the notoriety of *At the End of the Line* probably because it described a sideshow of that period, the naval war between Russia and Germany in the Baltic, in the archipelago outside the Gulf of Riga. When the German navy obtained control over most of the archipelago in 1917, part of the Russian fleet was bottled up in the Gulf of Riga; its only way of escape was the strait between the mainland

and the island of Moon (also called Muhu). Pikul's main objective was to show how Russian patriots moved with relative ease from fighting for the tsar to fighting for Lenin, and he dwells especially on the naval officers who went through this transformation. The final escape through the strait of Moon occurred shortly before the Bolshevik Revolution.

Again the hated enemies are first the Germans (in all seriousness Pikul even comments that their naval officers had special lashes worn out from beating the sailors); then Churchill, who, constantly drinking whisky, refrained from helping the Russian navy in its hour of need because he wanted the Germans to destroy Petrograd, "the heart of the Russian Revolution"; and third, the Jews—in order to evacuate them from Poland, Pikul writes, before the onslaught of the German army, 120 thousand railway cars were withdrawn from servicing the front.

Pikul's latest novel, *The Three Ages of Okini-san*, was, as far as I could ascertain, a disappointment to his fans. It is the story of a Russian naval officer who participates in the 1905 battle of Tsushima, a disastrous engagement for Russia, and in the no less disastrous First World War. During the Revolution he joins the White forces, eventually escapes to Japan, and lives in Nagasaki at the mercy of his former Japanese love, a prostitute and now a poverty-stricken old woman. In the end they both drown, half voluntarily, in the dirty port.

Obviously Pikul wanted to write a story about the sea that he so loves, preferably one about the glory of the Russian navy, but there was no glory in either of those two wars. However, the sad end of Okini-san and her forlorn lover surely will not be the end of Pikul's writing. Russian history offers many more intriguing stories. He gave his credo on the last page of *With Pen and Sword*.

> Never think, reader, that history is only history. The ancient past of our land and our people is linked remarkably with our today. Do not believe those who say: We don't need that—that's history. . . . Ideas have changed; people are different, but the fatherland is still the same, mother Russia. . . . In history there is the voice of blood. May Russia be great even though our names decay! (*Da vosvelichitsya Rossiya, da sginut nashi imena!*)

Pyotr Lukich Proskurin

Proskurin's main work, the one most frequently mentioned to me and most eagerly looked for in libraries, consists of two books, *Fate* and *Thy Name*. This two-part work is a true *epopeya*, covering the period from 1929 to the era of Soviet spaceships. The Russians, as I explained earlier, are not frightened by seventeen hundred pages; they love to read *epopeya*s and to follow the destiny of a family. Here it is the Deryugin family. Zakhar, its head, participated in the Civil War as a young man, played a leading role in the collectivization, and was responsible for exiling the kulaks to the arctic regions. A self-willed and stubborn man, he is respected but not loved by his fellow peasants. He loses his job as head of the kolkhoz because, although married, he has a child by a neighbor's daughter without feeling remorseful about it.

A vast epic involving countless people unfolds, almost exclusively in the village, although the modern age also intrudes in the form of a giant motor works being built in the center of the neighboring county. The real drama, of course, is the war. This village in western Russia, although off the beaten track, is quickly overrun. Zakhar, drafted into the army, is captured and disappears from sight, as does his oldest boy, who is forced to work in Germany. His daughter Yelena joins a guerrilla band and becomes a heroine. His wife burns down her house on purpose, killing the German soldiers quartered there. The Germans are the enemy, of course, and Proskurin shows them committing a truly evil deed: they brutally evacuate a hospital full of Russian soldiers to make room for wounded Germans. He also draws a somewhat hostile picture of a German lieutenant in charge of a prisoners' labor unit and of his interpreter. But the few Germans are episodic; the story occurs almost exclusively among Russians, and its hatred focuses on the Russian collaborators. The novel's number one scoundrel is an ex-villager who was dispossessed during the dekulakization in 1929 and cruelly exiled to the White Sea island of Solovki. Now he gets his revenge by serving—with other Russians under his command—as chief of the village police for the German occupation force. Once, when he is reproached for his anti-fatherland behavior, he shouts back:

> Fatherland! To some it's a mother, to others a stepmother. When I was 25, at the height of my youth, I was exiled to Solovki. For ten years after that I was a homeless dog always on the run, at all kinds of garbage cans, under assumed names and with stolen papers. . . . Now, though late, I too want to take what's mine. From other people's crumbs you don't get your fill. I have come to collect old debts, and I shall drag the last kopek from the past.

Stalin is depicted twice, both times in connection with the provincial party leader who fought together with him in the old days long before the Revolution. This man acts as Stalin's conscience. He is critical of the dictator's unquenchable thirst for glory, of his "cult of personality," as Khrushchev called it in a gross understatement. He also mentions that while the Revolution demands harsh actions, "certain moral norms of human society have existed and are obligatory at all times and for all [social] formations." But even he does not dare to voice these thoughts in Stalin's presence, he merely thinks them.

The village is portrayed as a community that resembles almost a family or a clan. Everybody knows everything about everyone; some people like each other, and others hate each other; strong friendships endure next to old enmities. Two men who have worked closely together, the chairmen of the kolkhoz and of the village soviet, hate each other so intensely that one tries to shoot the other.

The second part of the novel, *Thy Name*, is richer in design and more accomplished. It tells, if I counted correctly, of 126 different people, 44 of whom are of major importance to the story: a famous physicist involved in space exploration, young Deryugin's teacher; a director of a leading machine factory; a painter; a number of kolkhoz chairmen and party secretaries; and many peasants, especially women. (The village is denuded of men; almost 150 did not return from the war.) Many problems of the time in many different spheres are described—on high administrative levels, in the village, in Moscow, in the industrial world, and in academia. The novel presents a microcosm of the USSR between the war's end and our own day.

One of Zakhar Deryugin's sons becomes a high-ranking physicist; one remains in the kolkhoz; one, captured by the Germans and believed dead, dies many years later in France. But we learn the most about Deryugin's daughter, Yelena, who is married to a Soviet VIP by the name of Bryukhanov.

The war does not play a major role in the novel, but it forms the background and its consequences are felt everywhere—in the poverty of the village after the ravages of the war, in the reminiscences of the people, in the hatred of the Russians who collaborated with the occupying power.

The main theme is the postwar restoration, especially in the countryside. The difficulties are enormous, the results rather unsatisfactory. Time and again the peasants complain about their misery. (Only after many years, toward the end of the book, are the villagers shown to be better off.) The young people are attracted to the towns; the new factory sucks the village dry of manpower. Proskurin dwells on the creation of the Soviet atomic bomb and a manned flight into space during which one of Deryugin's sons loses his life.

The Stalin chapters in the second volume are of particular interest. Bryukhanov, a top industrial administrator and Yelena's husband, visits him twice. The dictator is now shown as a great man—calm, well informed, persistent—a leader of men and able to inspire loyalty and obedience. The deathwatch at his coffin and the weeping millions in the streets of Moscow are major scenes in the novel, though not very closely tied into the rest of the book.

The author pays a great deal of attention to human relations in the postwar years. Obviously, the war severely damaged the social fabric of the country, especially in the occupied areas. Relations between men and women are no longer what they used to be. Marriages break up. Deryugin, after leaving his wife who faithfully waited for him and moving far away with the woman who bore him a child at the beginning of the book, returns after her death many years later to his wife and the village without anybody now getting very upset. Deryugin's son, the scientist, brings his girlfriend from Moscow to visit his parents in the village, but not even his mother objects to their sleeping together. Before leaving to serve in the army, the other son is enticed, with the help of a potent drink or two, into a village woman's bed. Yelena, the former guerrilla heroine, leaves her powerful and always busy VIP husband and small daughter because she feels neglected (instead of being grateful for being such an important party leader's wife!); she moves in with a young man with whom she has fallen in love, only to leave him too after a while. A student gets an abortion. These things happened in Russia before, of course, but in novels they were either condemned or omitted. What is still taboo is the explicit description of sex. Only vague allusions of a few lines in length can be found.

The achievements of intellectuals are shown to be exemplary, but not so their personal lives. When they attack their colleagues, they claim that they do it to promote the good of the country, but they are usually thinking primarily of their own careers.

Proskurin enjoys using popular language, especially that of the peasants; the author obviously enjoys putting old-fashioned words and popular wisdom into the mouths of his village characters. Their speech is full of references to God, frequently without any religious significance (such as "For God's sake" or "Thank God," expressions often employed by Khrushchev too). Sometimes their expressions can be associated with religion, such as "buried without a cross and a prayer." More concrete religious traits also appear, including icons and prayers, and the biblical verse *Ne otrin menya vo vremya starosti* (Cast me not off in the time of my old age, Psalm 71:9) furnishes the title for the second part of the first book. Even the traditional Russian figure of a fool appears in the person of a woman who is not quite sane. (A similar *yurodivy* appears in *Boris Godunov*.) These unusual characters were not to be harmed, for they were considered God's children and were noted for sometimes stating truths others would not dare utter.

Surprisingly, references to pre-Christian religions abound: the night before Whitsuntide is important for barren couples who want children; a woman of stone, hewn in Scythian days, is assumed to possess a magic force—a young Communist, very much a child of today, even believes that he experienced an orgastic union with her.

What attracts the Russian readers in the two fat volumes of this novel? Here are my guesses based on the comments I received. People like to read books about themselves and their likes, provided these are written in a lively, interesting way. Proskurin does not "rub it in," and he is not doctrinaire; with rare exceptions he shows human beings, not angels and devils; he lets his people express anger, even despair, at their country's shortcomings, which is, of course, a proven method for allowing the population to let off steam.

But the main reason for the popularity of this novel, I think, is the reader's feeling that here he has found a vast canvas, a true *epopeya* covering half a century of tremendous events that he has either lived through or heard about from his elders. Of all the novels I read, this one most deserves to be called the Russian national epic of our time.

Valentin Grigoryevich Rasputin

Four novels in a decade, and all of them masterpieces. In addition to some stories and plays, this is Rasputin's harvest so far.

The plot of *Money for Maria* is quite simple. Maria, Kuzma's good-natured and simple wife, has been talked into managing the village store. At first she strenuously objects because she feels she cannot handle the job. Several of her predecessors landed in prison because of their lack of experience and the usually chaotic method of accounting for deliveries of goods. When she finally agrees, she repeatedly requests that somebody be sent to take inventory and to show her how she is making out. After one year an inspection turns up a deficit of about one thousand rubles. If the amount is not paid within five days, Maria will go to prison. One thousand rubles! How are Kuzma and Maria to obtain that huge amount with four children at home and their own debt of 750 rubles around their neck?

While Maria weeps, first in despair, then in defeat, Kuzma, who never even questions the justice of his plight, goes from door to door. He soon finds that begging among equally poor people is a terrible chore, and the reader is not spared any of his tribulations and disappointments. Four rubles per household, an amount easily spent on vodka, might save Maria, but fists are tight, always for a good reason, of course. Pettiness is never a pretty sight, and the pettiness of the poor is especially painful. A few peasants have some money but do not want to part with it although Kuzma swears he will repay it; others would like to give but have none. One old woman, on her deathbed, gives him the small savings she had set aside for her funeral in order not to inconvenience her children.

Then the kolkhoz chairman decides to help. He calls a meeting of the kolkhoz staff and suggests that they should all, himself included, loan their next month's salary to Kuzma. They reluctantly agree, but then some of them send their wives to Kuzma with sob stories and renege on their generosity.

Kuzma's last hope is his brother in the city, who is fairly well-off but with whom he has little contact. By bus, train (overnight), and again by bus, Kuzma travels to him. The trip is a character study in itself: Kuzma must buy a second-class ticket because the cheaper ones are sold out, but the second-class passengers resent the presence of a smelly peasant and manage to shove him off into a cheaper car.

Just at the moment when Kuzma reaches his brother's door, the story ends. For Rasputin, evidently, the final result of his hero's endeavors is not important. What is important are the attitudes of a poor peasant's neighbors when he suddenly, without warning and through no fault of his own, must borrow one thousand rubles. The author does not attempt to analyze his characters, but he masterfully portrays them through their own actions in a few, succinct sentences.

Period of Grace has a very simple plot, too. An 80-year-old peasant woman in a Siberian village is dying. Her son Mikhail, with whom she lives, telegraphs his three sisters and one brother, all of whom are advanced in years, to come immediately. They come, save for the youngest in faraway Kiev. When the four assemble at their mother's bedside, it seems that her end is at hand. But bolstered by the arrival of her children, some of whom she has not seen for a long time, the old woman rallies. Although she has been ready for death, she now wants to postpone it to enjoy the company of her children. With surprise and joy the four children watch her recovery and congratulate her on having cheated death. But as one day after another passes, they begin to fret. Having grown apart in the long years since their ways had parted, they do not know what to do with themselves or what to say to one another. To while the time away, the two brothers get a whole case of vodka. They retire to the bathhouse and get gloriously drunk, together with another villager who smells their binge.

When the old woman indicates that she does not intend to die until she has seen her youngest and most beloved child, the one who lives in Kiev, Mikhail lies to his mother. He says that he sent his sister another telegram assuring her that in view of their mother's miraculous recovery the long trip from Kiev was no longer necessary. This information and the departure of the three others on the last riverboat for some time destroy the old woman's will to live. She dies.

Rasputin uses the few days between the children's arrival and their departure to provide matchless descriptions of their characters simply by telling what they do and say, without any interpretation on his part. Throughout, the old woman holds the center of the stage. Her simple yet profound peasant wisdom towers high above her children's. Mikhail, the least intelligent and the one who has stayed in the village, is the most humane. The others are no longer villagers, but neither are they cityfolk. The author writes of the second son: "He looked as if he had lost his own face to somebody else in a game of cards." Rasputin likes none of them; his heart belongs to the dying woman and to her little granddaughter, an intelligent and matter-of-fact child, who, although only six, understands what the adults are up to and knows how to turn her knowledge to her advantage.

In contrast to the somber tone of Rasputin's other three novels, there is a good deal of dry humor here even though dying is the central theme. The drunken scenes in the bathhouse are truly hilarious, and the story the guest drinker tells is a gem: how he outwitted his mother-in-law when she sat with her spinning wheel covering the trapdoor that led to the cellar and to the homemade vodka. And yet, the impression left is one of sadness. Again Rasputin shows the seamy side of life, but his message is not, "People are wicked," but rather, "Such is human nature." Rasputin never moralizes or preaches, he just "tells it like it is."

The novel *Live and Remember*, though the title does not indicate it, is extremely impressive. Some of its dramatic high points are even more so on stage than in the book, therefore I shall describe the production I saw at the Moscow Art Theater in 1981. When the curtain rises on an almost totally dark stage, one sees a Siberian bathhouse and the silhouette of a woman washing herself. Immediately something ominous is in the air, something tragic and erotic. The war is still going on. Nastyona, a young Siberian peasant woman, lives with her parents-in-law in a village on the bank of the Angara River. From some small signals she senses that her husband, Andrey, a peasant but now a soldier, is in hiding nearby, probably a deserter. She heats the bathhouse a little way from the village for them both. He comes, ragged and hungry, hungry also for her. Apart from a few group scenes, the rest of the action involves only the two of them. Their problem is unresolvable, so the drama can only end in tragedy.

In 1941 the young men of the village went to war. Some were killed in action. Andrey, wounded twice and still recovering in a Siberian hospital, is due to be demobilized, but a tough army doctor orders him back to the front. In the general chaos of the last months of war, Andrey manages to escape and to return to the forest near his home village. In a ramshackle hut on the other side of the Angara he survives, aided by his wife who visits him secretly from time to time. Whether he gives himself up or not, they both know he is lost, and she is too because she helped him stay in hiding. When she gets pregnant, Andrey is filled with a wild joy: no matter what happens to him, he will live on through his child. But her situation becomes more and more difficult as the village women and her parents-in-law begin to notice her condition.

The war ends. The surviving men return. What happened to Andrey? No death notice came for him. There are indications, including his wife's pregnancy, that he is nearby. The hunt for him is on. As they are closing in on him, Nastyona drowns herself in the Angara.

The audience sat with bated breath while the tragedy moved toward its final catastrophe. Most had probably read the novel, as I had, and knew what was coming, but now we were seeing it with our own eyes. The power of the play lay, I think, not so much in the plot as such— although there were soldiers in practically every family, few families harbored a deserter. In a way, we could have been witnessing the plight of any fugitive in hiding. Andrey had brought his fate upon himself. Nastyona was totally innocent; she stood by him with a loyalty that was unwavering. She was his wife and that was that, no matter what the consequences.

Again in Siberia and again about death, as so many of Rasputin's stories are, *Farewell to Matyora* concerns the death of an island. The island Matyora is swallowed up by the huge lake formed by the new dams in the Angara River. What Rasputin says about the island's village and its people is taken from the village in which he grew up.

The younger people in the story, less attached to the village and more easily persuaded of the need for the dam, have left the island in good time. For the older ones, the death of their homes and of their island is a catastrophe. They have always accepted people dying at the hand of God or fate, but Matyora's death was decreed by people, by bureaucrats who even demand that the island's age-old cemetery be destroyed because future tourists might be unsettled to see wooden crosses from the graves floating around their excursion boats. Rasputin's heart and soul are with the old islanders who could easily be his grandparents, and as he tells the story, Matyora almost seems to be a holy island.

I am enchanted and moved by Rasputin's four novels. But what is the key to his immense popularity with the Russian reader? All his stories are sad and offer neither a happy ending, nor a positive, uplifting effect, nor even a possible alternative as a reward. The author is pessimistic; what people call progress will win and the old ways, so close to his heart, are doomed. So what is his novels' attraction?

Many of the writer's admirers I spoke to also yearn for the peaceful simplicity of former years; in their hearts they echo Rasputin's nostalgia. They also esteem a writer who is admirably honest and who lives in his native Siberia rather than in one of the capital's modern apartments. In addition they like his wonderful, never artificial-sounding command of the villagers' rich language inherited from generations of hardworking and frugal Siberian pioneers and his vivid descriptions of primeval rivers and forests. And finally, after all those superoptimistic, super-progressive, superheroic tales that were the Russians' standard fare in the thirties and forties, people want to read something that more closely reflects reality and yet is not negative or destructive. Having been spoon-fed on socialist realism, they appreciate what I would like to call humanist realism.

Julian Semyonovich Semyonov

The fame of Semyonov rests on his Stirlitz thrillers, which have already been mentioned and about which more will be said. But he has also written other books, including some of the type the French call *roman policier,* the Germans *Detektivgeschichte* and the Americans, with their passion for snappy words, whodunit. His best known is *Petrovka 38.* The street in the center of Moscow that bears this name, a stone's throw from the Bolshoy Theater, was once famous for its shops, including my (German) grandfather's confectionary, Einem. Now, number 38 houses the headquarters of the municipal police. The main criminal in *Petrovka 38* is neither an American nor a Chinese; he is a Russian, but one with a wicked past: he has fought under General Vlasov, who had gone over to the German side and fought against the Soviet army, and now lives in quiet secrecy near Moscow devising criminal plots, including murder and robbery, that his young accomplice, named Squire, has to execute. Squire was the son of a high secret service official who killed "many honest Communists" in the years of the purges. As the son of a VIP, the young man led a very pleasant life. He had a chauffeur who drove him out of town with his girl friends, caviar, expensive brandies, the best tailors, and of course money. Squire used to dream of the time when his father would die and he would be left with the car, the country house, and his father's secretary. But his father did not just die; he was shot together with Beria. After his father's death, Squire led a wild and aimless life, thinking: "What if there's a war with hydrogen bombs, rockets, and all that? What's the use of thinking about tomorrow?" It was then that he met the former Vlasovite and tried drugs for the first time. In the end, of course, Squire and his boss get caught.

A detective-plus-spy thriller by Semyonov was being made into a movie while I was in Moscow in 1982: *TASS* [the Soviet news agency] *Is Entitled to Declare*. It concerns an African country called Nagonia. In the struggle between the CIA and the Soviet counterintelligence within the KGB, the Russians win as expected but with great difficulties. Prior to the opening of the story, the CIA (which the Russians render as TsRU) had gotten the better of the Russians by recruiting a Russian in Moscow. Smarty, his code name, is very smart indeed; even minutes before he is finally caught, he outsmarts his pursuers once again by taking poison. But at least his American contact, who works at the U.S. Embassy in Moscow, is caught red-handed and later exchanged for a Soviet agent.

There is, in addition to the story's thrilling quality, another reason for the popularity *TASS* enjoys with Soviet readers: the novel describes in unusual detail the functioning of the organization about which Russians hear so much and know so little—the KGB. That the fine human qualities of all the KGB agents in the novel are what so fascinates the reader one may perhaps doubt; after all, this group of people is more feared than loved. (Still, the author should be praised for holding up noble characters for emulation.) Instead, it is the description of the KGB's day-to-day activities that captivates the readers. For one thing, there seems to be no lack of agents nor of cars for them. Nagonia is not exactly the hub of the world, and one spy who supplies the CIA with (unspecified) information from an institute on African affairs can hardly disrupt Soviet foreign policy. But Smarty is searched for high and low as if the future of the Black Continent depended on finding him. When one of the suspects flies to the Black Sea, off goes an agent on his tail. When another goes jogging in a Moscow park, at least three agents watch the park's exits, and, when he is driving, two or three KGB cars take up the chase, reporting his every move to headquarters by car phone. By the end of the story, I had learned more about the work of the KGB than I have ever read about that of Scotland Yard.

One important but delicate question is left untouched. How does a Soviet citizen become a CIA agent? How can a person who has lived on the side of the angels turn traitor and work for the deadly enemy? The author leaves this question open. Of course, there is some money involved, but we never really find out why Smarty needs it so badly. A woman also plays a part, but Smarty's feelings for her do not prevent him from poisoning her the moment he learns that she begins to suspect him. In the end we are left with the verdict supplied by a KGB general: "Treason is a pathological category, unusual for a normal person." That's too simple and too easy an answer. Nowhere is there any indication that Smarty may have gone astray because he disagreed with the Kremlin's foreign or domestic policy. Political theories are never mentioned, nor are political leaders or the scriptures of the ideological fathers.

In some of his books Semyonov has tried to create a second Stirlitz in the person of a young Russian foreign correspondent by the name of Stepanov who might be Semyonov himself. His activities are similar to those of Stirlitz, except that they are not clandestine. In a story that I saw in 1981 on the stage of Moscow's Sovremennik Theater, *Search 827*, Semyonov's Stepanov helps some good Germans locate art treasures in order to return them to Russia. A special unit of the Rosenberg ministry stole many treasures from Russian churches and palaces during World War II. But Stepanov still has a long way to go before he can match the fame of Stirlitz.

Now to some of the Stirlitz thrillers themselves. Table 5 lists the eight in existence so far, in chronological order according to the events they describe. (They were not written in this order.) Stirlitz makes his earliest appearance in *Diamonds for the Dictatorship of the Proletariat* still using his real name, Maksim Maksimovitsch Isayev. As an officer in the *Cheka*, the secret police of the early postrevolutionary days, he is involved in collecting and selling abroad some of the treasures of the tsars and the vanquished aristocracy. Moscow and Reval, capital of the then independent Estonia, are the places of action. (Some of the tsarist diamonds were used to finance grain imports for the starving country.) Around the diamond trade Semyonov weaves the story of the New Economic Policy, the NEP, created by Lenin in March 1921 partly in response to the famines sweeping across the country.

During the NEP, thousands of formerly persecuted specialists, many of bourgeois origin, were reinstated because of their expertise,

Table 5

The Stirlitz Novels

Title	Time of Action	Place of Action	Time of Writing
Diamonds for the Dictatorship of the Proletariat	1921	Moscow, Estonia	1963–64
No Password Needed	1921–1923	Asia	1970–71
The Alternative	1941, spring	Yugoslavia	1973
The Third Card	1941, summer	Ukraine	1973–74
Major Wikhr	1944–1945	Poland	1965–66
Seventeen Moments of a Spring	1945	Germany	1968–69
Your Order: To Survive	1945	Germany	1982
A Bomb for the Chairman	1967	Germany, Hong Kong	1970–71

even in the diamond and gold trades. The NEP was a feverish era, and Semyonov describes its atmosphere with a suitably hectic breathlessness. At times, the style is as chaotic as the period, and it is not always easy to figure out whether people are "White" or "Red"; some of them are both, and some have no loyalties except to themselves. Even Isayev had been temporarily with the (White) Kolchak army, thus remaining an object of suspicion to some Communists.

The Alternative and *The Third Card* treat the events surrounding the German occupation of Yugoslavia and Hitler's attack on the Soviet Union during the spring and summer of 1941. Isayev is now Stirlitz, a high-ranking SS officer, in reality, Moscow's master spy.

With his sure sense for drama, Semyonov chose brief time spans of high tension for both novels. *The Alternative* covers just twelve days. On March 25 the Royal Government of Yugoslavia joined the Axis. Two days later it was toppled by a military putsch. On April 5 the new government concluded a treaty of friendship and nonaggression with the USSR. On the following morning, the German invasion began. (Eleven days later the blitzkrieg was over, but this is not part of the novel.)

The Alternative is a swiftly moving story, a rich tapestry of events and ideas. Here for the first time and in very readable form, Russians found the story of the twelve days that delayed the German attack on the USSR and thus perhaps prevented the capture of Moscow.

The main scenes are set in Yugoslavia, in Belgrade of course but primarily in Zagreb, the capital of Croatia, as well as in Berlin and Moscow. Semyonov colorfully describes everyone's intrigues against everyone else—intrigues between supporters and foes of Germany, between Serbs and Croats, between pro-German and pro-Italian factions—in addition to Hitler and Mussolini's quarrel over Yugoslavia's future and, of course, the infighting in Berlin among Heydrich and Schellenberg of the State Security Forces; Ribbentrop, the foreign minister; and his rival Rosenberg, head of the Nazi Party's Foreign Policy Office, all of whom had their own representatives in Yugoslavia stepping on each others toes. One of these representatives was Veesenmayer, who had done well to bring Slovakia into the German fold in 1938 without force of arms and who was expected to do the same with Yugoslavia because Hitler did not want a Balkan war. And then of course there was Stirlitz, working closely with Veesenmayer, while at the same time supplying Moscow with urgent messages, even predicting exactly when Hitler would start his attack on Yugoslavia.

As in Semyonov's other novels, there is an amazing lack of antipathy toward the Germans. They are depicted as efficient, loyal, hardworking patriots doing their best to create favorable conditions for close cooperation between their country and Yugoslavia, similar to the cooperation they enjoyed with Slovakia or Hungary, under German hegemony, of course. Field Marshal List, the leader of the main invasion force, is described without animosity as a father figure for his soldiers and disdainful of Hitler, which was typical for many of the older Wehrmacht officers. During the night before the attack, he listens to a young air force officer read his poetry.

Veesenmayer, Stirlitz's secret adversary, is a likable fellow: good-looking, tall, intelligent, remarkably broad-minded; when a young Nazi calls the Russians pigs, he says that one must esteem and love even the enemy. And he repeats: "Yes, love." Stirlitz too, despite his life-and-death struggle against Hitler, does not hate the Germans. To another Soviet agent who calls every German a Fascist, Stirlitz answers: "If this were so, I would ask Moscow to relieve me of my assignment." Throughout the novel Semyonov grapples with the German-Russian problem, perhaps the most persistent theme in all his writings. *The Alternative* is, in my opinion, the most serious of the Stirlitz novels. Here Semyonov analyzes his hero's main conflict: how to combine working for a good cause with working in the headquarters of the devil. "Collaboration in a crime, even in the name of good, is immoral," Stirlitz realizes, but he never quite succeeds in finding the solution to this dilemma. And there is none, as there was none for a man I knew, Richard Sorge, the master spy in Tokyo during the Second World War. Day in and day out he lived under the weight of betraying Ott, his closest friend, the German ambassador in Tokyo, by transmitting what he learned from him to Moscow, including the date of the German attack on the USSR, just six weeks after that on Yugoslavia. Stirlitz is in some ways a brother to Sorge.

The Third Card covers the brief period between June 11 and June 24, 1941, the days immediately before and after the Wehrmacht attack on the USSR. This time the areas around the city of Krakow, occupied by the Germans owing to their deal with Stalin in 1939, play the role of Zagreb and the anti-Russian Ukrainians that of the anti-Serbian Croats. Some of the Germans who worked with the Croats now operate among the Ukrainians, and the names of two German specialists on Eastern Europe who actually existed and whom I know make an appearance, Theodor Oberländer and Hans Koch. Finally, there is, of course, the ubiquitous Stirlitz. This time a German group of anti-Hitler and pro-Soviet conspirators helps him. Among them is a blond countess named Ingrid, whose description reminded me of Mrs. Harnack, an American woman whom I met in the early thirties when she came to Germany as a student. Later, with her German husband, she worked for the Russians and was eventually executed. If the parallel between Ingrid and Mrs. Harnack is intentional, the undercover group Semyonov had in mind is the *Rote Kapelle*.

Just like the Croats, the Ukrainians are split into hostile groups, each with its own leaders, Stephan Bandera being the best known among them. Bandera collaborates with the famous intelligence chief of the German army, Canaris, while his rival, Melnik, works with the Gestapo. On the eve of the invasion and during its first days, the pro-Nazi Ukrainians are united in their desire to drive the Soviets from their homeland. In the novel, they are described as the devil's own devils.

The ambiguity of Stirlitz's position as a Soviet agent high in the Nazi hierarchy becomes especially evident in this novel. Many examples of the secret messages he sends to Moscow are given, but none provides very valuable information except—here again he is another Dr. Sorge— the date of the Wehrmacht attack, June 22, 1941. We see him essentially as an observer of the events around him. A Swedish journalist or a Red Cross agent, had they been in the area at that time, might have felt and reacted quite like he does: he is appalled by Hitler's attack on a country with which he had only recently signed a nonaggression pact and horrified by his murderous treatment of the conquered nations. Semyonov might not have been correct in every detail of the atrocities he describes, but Stirlitz's appraisal of Hitler's *Ostpolitik* coincided with that of many Germans, including myself in faraway Shanghai, where I spent the last years of the war. Hitler did not actually want the friendship the anti-

Soviet and anti-Russian Ukrainians offered in the beginning; on the contrary, he wanted their land and their slave labor for the benefit of the German farmers who were to move into these areas.

Semyonov uses the novel for thoughtful though one-sided portraits of some leading figures of the time who had never before been presented as individuals to Russian readers. He describes Bandera and his boss Oberländer, then in charge of the Ukrainian Nightingale Battalion; the old Hetman of the Ukraine, Skoropadsky; Canaris; and one man who especially impressed me when I visited him at his church residence in Lvov in 1934, the Galician Metropolitan Count Andrew Sheptytsky.

Seventeen Moments of a Spring, my first introduction to Semyonov, is still his most popular work. Here Stirlitz rubs elbows with some of the leaders of the Third Reich, including Himmler, Goering, Goebbels, Kaltenbrunner, and Gestapo-Müller. During his hair-raising adventures he obtains information that he then radios to Moscow; he also prevents a Soviet nightmare from coming true: the last-minute alliance between the Americans and the defeated but still strong German Wehrmacht against the Soviet Union. (It is in this connection that Allen Dulles shows up.)

Whenever I asked Russians why they found this novel and the film made from it so especially fascinating, I was usually given three reasons. First, the story as such is exciting. (Not everybody in the West will agree. For our taste it appears too long-winded and lacks the compressed tension so characteristic of our thrillers. But the Russians have always liked epic breadth.) Next, it is interesting to find out more about life in the West. (This too might not hold true for a Western audience. The Swiss cabaret offering a hint of a striptease, for example, would hardly arouse us, but for the Russians it provides a peek into a forbidden and exciting world.) Finally, and most importantly, Semyonov gives an idea of what the Third Reich was like during its final months. Much of what is available in the USSR on the Third Reich is too abstract and lifeless. Semyonov's story is much more informative and plausible because it shows the Nazi leaders not as Frankensteins or caricatures; they too have their personal ambitions and intrigues and even Gestapo-Müller must cope with private problems. There are also decent Germans in the book, a pastor, for example, (possibly patterned after Niemöller) and some ordinary soldiers.

Of *Your Order: To Survive*, the sequel to *The Seventeen Moments*, I have as yet seen only some extracts.

A Bomb for the Chairman deals almost exclusively with West Germany during the first two decades after the end of the war. I shall mention only one episode that might also be of interest to non-German readers. The novel's hero, an important German industrialist, rebuilds and enlarges his economic empire. He hates Hitler for ruining Germany, but because he hopes for Germany's greatness, he dreams of a united Europe with a powerful Germany at its center. For this scheme he wants the support of Mao (the chairman of the book's title) to serve as a counterweight to Brezhnev. For this support, he is willing to help China get a nuclear bomb. In other words, the industrialist envisions a super-Rapallo (though this word does not appear in the novel), where China would assume the role that Russia played at Rapallo in 1922 after the German defeat in World War I. Here Semyonov touches on another Soviet nightmare: an alliance between the West and China against the USSR. (Fortunately for Russia, things go awry in the novel.)

I have dwelled at some length on Semyonov's novels because his enormous success with the Russian masses says something about their present mood. Their fascination with novels dealing with contemporary world history is also clearly apparent in the popularity of Chakovsky's novels, but it is even more pronounced with Semyonov. A few possible reasons for this will be suggested in the Conclusions.

Vasily Makarovich Shukshin

Translating the title of Shukshin's best-known story (and movie) *Kalina krasnaya* caused headaches for Western editors, unnecessary headaches I think. However *Kalina* is translated (snowball or guelder rose in English, *Schneeballstrauch* or *Wasserholunder* in German, *Viberum opulus* in botanical Latin), it is still the name of a bush commonly found in Russian villages, beloved by the people as a symbol of peasant life and praised in many folk songs, the most famous being "Kalinka, Kalinka, Kalinka moya." *Krasnaya*, of course, means red, and red are the berries of the *kalina* in the late summer.

The *kalina* is almost as close to the Russians' heart as the *beryoza*, or birch tree. In the story, *kalina* as such plays no role; the word has a sentimental rather than a descriptive value. A German author might create a similar feeling by calling a story the *Lindenbaum*, a tree that stands next to a well at the town gate, according to a popular song, and an American author from the South might mention the magnolia.

After spending his childhood in an orphanage, Yegor, a young village boy, comes to town. Completely lost in the unaccustomed surroundings, he is taken in by a gang of criminals, gets caught in a robbery, and spends five months behind bars. Having regained his freedom, he tries to go straight with the help of Lyuba, a young woman with whom he corresponded while in prison. But his old cronies catch up with him.

When he refuses to cooperate, the gangsters kill him in a birch copse. Lyuba's brother pursues them in the kolkhoz truck, and when their car gets stuck in the mud, he smashes into it, demolishing their car and killing them. Thus, the town criminals who killed a decent peasant lad were killed by another villager, an event that is met with thunderous applause in the movie.

The story, or better, the novella, should be read or be seen as a movie if its deeper meaning is to be clearly understood. Shukshin depicts more than just the antipathy between village and town, the struggle between the gang and its victim, and the complicated love affair between Yegor and Lyuba. *Kalina*'s value, as that of most of Shukshin's stories, lies in its careful psychological descriptions of the Revolution and collectivization in the countryside, of the urbanization of countless millions of Russians, of the labor camps and the endless migrations as a result of the war. Though very much an individual, Yegor at the same time represents the shattered village; the reader is left with the nostalgic memory of a common bush with red berries and the lovable character of the common people. Shukshin's people may be forlorn, confused, desperate, criminal, mean, yet they are lovable. They belong to the grand tradition of Russian literature; for Shukshin good and bad are not ideological categories.

Yegor stands for many characters in Shukshin's stories. He and the hundreds of others who appear across the pages form a mosaic of the *pays réel* as the French call it, of the country as it has existed since those tremendous upheavals that brought about the collapse of the traditional order. They are all groping about for an elusive new identity, but when they tire of this, they often dream of the red berries of yore. They feel a void where their *dusha* (soul—one of Shukshin's key words) once was and try to fill the emptiness with dreams and schemes, often imaginary and irrelevant ones but necessary substitutes for the missing soul.

It is awkward to pick examples from the wealth of Shukshin stories, because one is as good as the next. But here are a few.

In "Klassny voditel" (A First-Class Driver) Pavel, a truck driver, gets a temporary job in a village. Confident of himself and happy-go-lucky, he goes to the village dance on his first evening there and immediately falls in love in Nastya, the village belle. He enrages the other young men by flirting outrageously with her; climbs into her room at night, although he knows she is engaged to an engineer; and gets his face slapped by her, which doesn't bother him because he senses that the engineer does not mean too much to her and believes himself close to the fulfillment of his desire. But when she tells him that the engineer is about to leave her out of jealousy over him and sees her pitiful tears, his heart melts. He puts her in his truck, takes her to her engineer for an immediate reconciliation, and leaves the village for good, a victor who relinquishes his victory out of compassion all in a single night.

Then there is Bronislav Pupkov. All his life he has suffered from his silly name. The Polish Bronislav was bad enough in a Russian village, but on top of that he was saddled with Pupkov, from *pup*, meaning "navel"! But during the hunting season when hunters came out from town, he was a different man. Knowing the forests in and out, he was highly valued by them. His greatest hour was always the last evening. Then he told the visiting hunters his whopper—how he almost freed the world of Hitler. This is what happened, so he said, on July 25, 1943: The Germans sent a scout across the front line to obtain a very important document and bring it personally to Hitler, who happened to be close by during those days. When the Russians caught the scout, they saw that he looked very much like the soldier Bronislav Pupkov. Pupkov was given the German's uniform and a different document and sent across the line to kill Hitler.

The hunters listen breathlessly and every so often urge him on with another glass of vodka. At last Pupkov entered the Führer's bunker. German generals were everywhere. When one of them wanted to take the document from him, he refused: he insisted on giving it to Hitler himself and said in what he thought was his best German, "Mille pardons, madame." Hitler came out. "I shot." At this moment Pupkov falls silent. His head sinks down and he weeps. His face streaked with tears, he confesses: "I missed."

All are deeply moved and fill one more glass for him. Pupkov leaves the group to sit alone in the grass. For two days he goes on a drinking binge. When the other villagers make fun of him, as they do every year, he threatens to beat the daylights out of anybody who comes too close. He expects them to understand and to forgive his weakness. "Mille pardons, madame." (This is also the story's title.)

In "Styopka" the hero escapes from prison although barely three months remain of his term. Spring is here, and he wants to see his family and friends. Yet he knows full well that when they catch him he will be confined for another two years. After his arrest, on his way back to prison, he explains to the policeman that he has recharged himself. "Spring is beautiful around here, isn't it?"

A sovkhoz sends a group of men to work in the forest for several weeks. One of them is put in charge. His first leadership position goes to his head, and he becomes a real dictator. His fellow workers must be punctual to the minute (of course they are not); they must renounce vodka (they do no such thing); and so it goes. When he tries to punish a worker who talks back, the others turn on him. And although he now wants to console them by explaining that he did not really mean to sound so harsh but just spoke in an *oratorsky priyom*, a rhetorical manner (this is also the title of the story), they beat him soundly and he runs away.

In "Mikroskop" (The Microscope), too, only a few words would have to be changed to accord with Chekhov's time. A husband returns from work with a long face and tells his wife that he has lost 120 rubles. (In reality he has saved the money to fulfill his dream of buying a microscope.) She gets very angry. In order to make up for the loss, he now works an additional half-shift every day; his wife calms down. One day he comes home with a microscope. It is a reward, he explains, for his exemplary work. (His wife, of course, would have preferred a vacuum cleaner.) He is very happy now, and with his son, a school-age child, he begins looking for microbes. And lo and behold, he finds them everywhere—in water, in blood, and even in sweat. Microbes, and more microbes! Shocked and frightened by this discovery, he begins devising ways of getting rid of them, by using electricity perhaps? But just at that moment one of his fellow workers comes to visit and spills the beans: no microscope had been awarded to his pal. The structure of lies collapses, and the poor man drowns his remorse in vodka for two days. Returning home, he learns that his wife has gone to a secondhand shop to sell the microscope in order to make some sorely needed purchases. (With Shukshin the wives are usually practical, the husbands dreamers.)

The author's heart beats more for the villagers than for the townspeople, especially if these feel superior to the peasants. In "Srezal" (Cut Down to Size) he tells of the peasant Gleb Kapustin (from kapusta, meaning "cabbage"), who has his fun every time some VIP visits the village. As soon as the high-and-mighty visitor arrives, the peasants gather at Gleb's house, then together they head toward the house where the guest is staying. They greet him, get a glass of vodka, and watch Gleb go to work. They are never disappointed. The knowledge Gleb has gleaned from the media plus his natural peasant's slyness enable him to make the highfalutin guest sound ridiculous and ignorant. For example, he trounces a colonel by asking him who started the Moscow fire in 1812. The colonel thinks and thinks and finally comes up with Rasputin, but of course that is nonsense. On another occasion, he confuses a proud young scholar working toward his doctorate by asking how mankind was prepared to communicate with creatures from outer space. While Gleb makes some concrete though amateurish suggestions, the learned visitor sits there dumbfounded and visibly shaken. When the peasants leave to go home, they are highly pleased. *"Srezal ty yego,"* they tell Gleb, "you cut him down to size."

Most of Shukshin's heroes have impossible dreams. Yegor, broken by a bad childhood and criminal company, wants to be what he was born for, a peasant, but he cannot, he does not even know how to milk a cow. Bronislav Pupkov lives on the phony glory of having almost killed Hitler. Styopka wants to smell the meadow and freedom for a few hours, although he must pay for this whiff with more years behind bars. The man in the fish market wants simple justice to prevail, nothing more, and almost loses his will to live when this is denied him. And the desire for a microscope and Gleb's ability to cut the smart alecks from the city down to size are dreams to fill the huge void caused by the decay of the ancient order and the traditional customs.

Can religion satisfy this great need? In "Na kladbishche" (At the Graveyard) an old woman tells a man whom she meets by chance at a graveyard about an odd occurrence: a soldier on night duty at the gate of his barracks hears weeping in a nearby cemetery no longer in use. He reports to his officer. Another soldier, dispatched with a lamp, finds a woman and asks why she is weeping. "I am the Mother of God," she answers, "and I feel sorry for you people." Somewhat shaken, he explains that he is a member of the Komsomol, the (atheist) communist youth organization. But before he can turn away, the woman touches him softly. Back in the barracks nobody believes him, but on his tunic he finds the woman's picture as large as her palm.

Another of Shukshin's key words is *volya*, a Russian expression for freedom, free will, or liberty, but wilder, more anarchic, sometimes also more brutal than our terms. In Shukshin's early novel *Lyubaviny* (The Lyubavins, 1965), *volya* is on the minds of the Altai villagers who, in 1920, are peasants, bandits, and freedom fighters all in one. His novel about the peasant rebel Stenka Razin is even called *Ya prishol dat vam volyu* (I Have Come to Bring You Freedom, 1971).

Of the Shukshin comedies, I saw *Energetic People* in Moscow's Mayakovsky Theater. Compared to the subtleness of his stories (my brief summaries can give but a vague idea of this quality), I found this play flat. A corrupt director of a government store and some of his employees embezzle large sums of money. They have a clear conscience: the state economy, so they say, could not function without them, and since the government does not properly compensate them for their important work, they have to help themselves. This they do. All this is presented in a rather farcical way. Still, the audience laughed heartily all along, and the police arrive just before the final curtain falls.

Toward the end of his life, Shukshin groped for a new style. He wrote some satires, one in the form of a fairy tale. They were hits with his intellectual admirers, who understood their insider's humor, but too allegorical and sophisticated for the general public. Anyway, they were not popular with the fans to whom I spoke. His last piece, "Denunciation," published after his death, is really more an outcry than a story. It is an outcry against inhumanity in general based on a somewhat minor affront the author suffered while in the hospital: his relatives and friends who came to visit him were rudely treated at the gate.

Many of Shukshin's writings are outcries against wrongs committed in his country. In the last line of "Denunciation" he asks, "What is wrong with us?" And in "Grievance" the man unjustly accused while shopping with his little daughter at the fish market wonders all the time: "What's wrong with these people?" In a manuscript later used for a play, the intellectual hero who has been apprehended for his involvement in a drunken brawl explains the anger that brought him to this point: "I told myself, life makes no sense. . . I distinctly felt that the world is being destroyed; that this is the end. . . . And that from now on I would just pretend to live, to feel, to work. . . . It makes me sick to talk about it."

I am inclined to think that Shukshin was not a crusader, just a great writer, perhaps even a poet, who wrote almost naively what he felt he had to write. Of course, he wanted to improve the lot of his fellow man. But his critical view of the social order that he took for granted was a by-product of his compassion for mankind. What he worried about was not so much the *condition sociale* as the *condition humaine*.

Konstantin Mikhailovich Simonov

The Living and the Dead, the first part of Simonov's first war trilogy, was mentioned most frequently to me. It deals almost exclusively with the fighting on the German-Soviet front from June 22, 1941, to the beginning of the Russian counteroffensive near Moscow in December of that same year. Sintsov, the central figure, worked for a Red Army newspaper in the city of Grodno before the war. As a result of the Hitler-Stalin Pact of August 1939, the USSR took over Grodno from Poland. Early in the summer of 1941, he and his wife travel to the Crimea for a vacation. When the war breaks out, his wife returns to Moscow while he tries to get back to his newspaper and his colleagues. But Grodno has been overrun by the Germans. He becomes a political officer (*politruk*), joins other units that are then surrounded by the enemy, and survives some incredible adventures. Barely escaping from one pocket of intense fighting, he finds himself in another and experiences the war at its cruelest. Most people in the novel are killed in action. Not all are heroes.

Sintsov is wounded, loses consciousness, and is captured by the Germans but manages to escape. In the end, after fighting his way out of one encirclement after the other, he reaches Moscow. But his troubles do not end there; he has no documents and "without documents you are not a human being," as the novel points out. Even at the height of danger, Moscow's bureaucratic apparatus is intact, as Sintsov finds out on his desperate odyssey in quest of new documents. So he decides to return to the front without them. For his bravery he is given a military decoration but not his party card. And when the novel ends, he still does not have it.

Apart from the novel's very last pages, it tells of nothing but terrible defeats and losses. The question of why the USSR was caught unaware bothers everybody. An old Muscovite puts it this way: "You can hear a party next door," he says, "so how was it possible for an entire German army to gather just across the border without our noticing it?"

The purges of 1937 also come up. One of the novel's heroes fought with honor as a regimental commander in the Civil War and later worked as an instructor at a military college. In 1937 he was arrested because he took his duties seriously enough to study the German language and German military doctrine. Very suspicious indeed! Off with him to the easternmost end of Siberia! Freed after the start of the war, he fights heroic battles together with Sintsov. But because of his past, every little *politruk* thinks he can cast suspicion on him. While in the hospital recovering from a wound, he asks himself what many others also wondered about: "How was what happened to the army in 1937 and 1938 possible? Who needed it? And how could Stalin have permitted it?" He is full of "soul-wrenching, conflicting feelings about Stalin."

The turning point, of course, was the year 1956 when Khrushchev delivered his famous speech about Stalin. I spent several months in the USSR that year and vividly remember how the nation reacted to this change: with utter bewilderment. Every day something new could be observed and discussed: the removal of Stalin's birthday presents from the Museum of the Revolution, an event that I witnessed; the disappearance of Stalin's pictures from the walls of offices and of Stalin's name from the mausoleum on Red Square. While the dictator's death brought a feeling of relief, it made millions of Russians wonder how the Soviet Union could proceed without the "wise father of the people" and what the Stalin period was really like. Among the topics avoided hitherto was the execution of top army leaders in the midthirties and the humiliating military unpreparedness in the war.

Having worked as a war correspondent, Simonov was tempted to write about his activity at that time. This he did by publishing, in addition to his war diaries and at considerable intervals, a trilogy, *The So-Called Private Life: From the Notes of Lopatin.*

One would assume that the hero Lopatin is Simonov. But the author denies this in his preface; Lopatin, he says, is about twenty years his senior. However, the difference in age is not decisive in the life of war correspondents, and I assume that much of the book is based on Simonov's own experiences in one way or another. This would account for its rather loose structure and uneven quality. The first part consists of war episodes held together merely by Lopatin's presence. We simply follow him wherever he is sent by his editor-in-chief. One story within the story tells of a peasant woman whose family was deprived of its possessions during the collectivization and sent to Siberia. She leads a miserable life, is overrun by the Germans, and caught by the Russians while helping the German troops decide whether a severely damaged bridge can still be used. Some Russians want to shoot her right away, but in the end she is sent back to the local headquarters for questioning. We never learn what becomes of her. Then there is the young woman, a hospital assistant, who is driving a horse-drawn buggy when a grenade tears the horse to pieces and nearly kills her. After the initial shock, her spirits quickly rise when she discovers that a small bottle of shampoo that she recently purchased in town did not suffer in the incident. Finally we meet the officer who had once fought bravely in the Civil War as a young man but then went through the hell of the bloody purge machinery and remained a broken man even after his innocence was proven and he was released. In a crucial moment during a German attack he loses his nerve. The thought that he might once again have to endure endless interrogations before a war tribunal makes him shoot himself.

Simonov is quite discreet about the purges, yet more outspoken than some of his colleagues. In connection with the officer's suicide he says: "This was that same wave of arrests in 1937 that we all thought about now, in the middle of the war, whether we wanted to or not. . . . Almost anyone who thought about it felt in his soul that all these arrests, taken as a whole, could not have been justified."

At the end of the first part of the trilogy we learn about the breakup of Lopatin's marriage. This entire book is not exactly uplifting: we read of almost nothing but defeats and of human characters full of inner problems and contradictions.

The second part starts with Lopatin's five-day stay in Tashkent in Soviet Central Asia, a long way from the front and from its horrors. He goes there because a Tashkent studio is making one of his war stories into a movie. The director has never seen the war and makes a mess of the film. Lopatin tries to salvage it. While in Tashkent, Lopatin, now separated from his wife who lives with another man, falls in love with a woman seventeen years his junior. But he must return to Moscow before their relationship has a chance to develop very far. Will they ever see each other again? On his way back Lopatin stops in Tbilisi to see some Georgian friends. A very moving chapter covers his visit with them and with other Georgian parents whose boys went to war. Some of them have been killed during a headlong flight through open fields that Lopatin himself witnessed. When his host pours the last drops of his very last bottle of wine on a piece of bread in memory of the boys, Lopatin is reminded of the bread and wine in the New Testament. That sacred tradition, he muses, commemorates Christ's sacrificing himself for others, as these boys have done by giving their lives for their country. And long-forgotten words come to his mind such as "Bear your cross" and "Resurrection."

The last part of Simonov's final trilogy has been widely read, especially since its publication in *Roman gazeta*; it brings the story close to the war's end. Lopatin is sent by his *Red Star* editor to the northwest front, which is advancing toward East Prussia. He narrowly escapes from a harrowing experience: the tank group to which he is attached is destroyed by the Germans. His friend, also a reporter for the *Red Star*, is killed together with three soldiers when he insists on being the first to set foot on German soil.

An illuminating discussion takes place between Lopatin and the commander of an entire army, who tries to explain to him the reasons for the terrific Soviet losses in manpower. They are attributable to the inability of many Soviet officers and to their disregard for tactical lessons.

> Our soldier lies in a valley, the German on a hill; ours in front of a village, the German inside the village; ours in a swamp, the German at the edge of a forest. Why? Because of geography? Why are we not on the hill and the Germans in the swamp? . . . When we expel the Germans from a hill or a village they do not stay in the valley or in the swamp; they withdraw a kilometer or two until they find a hill overlooking the area. And we? Once they withdraw, we follow until we can't go any further. As a result, they are on the hill, and we are in the swamp. What good can a kilometer of swamp do?"

The slogan, often used by Stalin, "No step back" has been abused, the general feels. It has often needlessly cost men their lives—men who are now needed. He grows furious thinking of an officer who forced his men to hold an unfavorable position instead of withdrawing to a reasonable place. "Perhaps he managed to hang on to his position by the bones of his men and even by his own bones. And yet one should call him a son of a bitch."

This third part is better known and better liked than some of Simonov's other novels because it is only one part war and two parts Moscow. The readers I talked to preferred the Moscow portions, including Lopatin's private problems: his divorce under the unpleasant circumstances arising from their enervatingly poor and cramped living conditions, his love affair with the young woman he met in Tashkent, and his lively teenage daughter. Perhaps this is a sign that by the end of the seventies the Russians had gradually begun to tire of the battle descriptions that Simonov wrote so well.

Vladimir Alekseyevich Soloukhin

Whichever prose style Soloukhin uses, all his words carry essentially one and the same message: the beauty of Russia, her culture as well as her landscape, must be preserved.

In *Byroads of Vladimir*, Soloukhin describes a 40-day hike in diary form ("First Day," "Second Day," and so on) through the villages and towns of his home province. He praises the lovely harmony of nature and architecture, the wisdom and self-assuredness of the people. He wonders how some Russians can rave about southern palm trees—is not Russia's beloved birch far more beautiful? But he also sees many distressing signs of decline. Thus he tells of the worthy ancient Russian horn players who were discovered by a smart impresario and taken to the capital for appearances on radio and television. After spending all their pay on vodka in the big city, they return home shamefacedly.

He deplores the fate of the once famous artistic needlepoint studios of Mstera. After they are subordinated to an Organization for Industrial Products, they are forced to increase their production year after year according to the plan. He thinks it is as ridiculous to demand needlepoint artists to step up their output as it would be to require a great painter to create a certain percentage more pictures each year.

In *Dewdrop*, which the author wrote in 1959, he depicts his home village, combining childhood memories with later impressions, practically going from house to house describing the present and former occupants. By the time we have read the novel's 200 pages we know everyone in the village's 36 households.

Soloukhin's visits to one of the museums in Leningrad produced a number of essays in the form of letters to an unknown person, probably to the Russian reader in general, that were published in book form as *Letters from the Russian Museum*. The museum is housed in a structure built under Tsar Alexander I and converted, around the turn of the century, into a museum devoted primarily to Russian art. He uses the *Letters* to sharply attack many violations of Russian historical values, especially the desecration of ancient churches. After quoting the great Norwegian writer Knut Hamsun, who praised Moscow as a fairy-tale city with its incredibly beautiful view from the Kremlin over the cupolas and towers of countless churches, Soloukhin lists some of the most famous Moscow churches, adding each time with laconic terseness its fate after the Revolution: "Demolished. Empty place with stalls." "Torn down. Parking lot." In place of the Strastnoy Monastery, the "cheerless facade" of a movie theater now stands. He deplores the renaming of ancient Russian cities such as Vyatka, Tver, Samara, and Vladikavkas after leaders of the Revolution (he refrains from including Leningrad in his list). Sarcastically he compares what has been destroyed with what has been put in its place: a swimming pool on the Moskva River where the grandiose cathedral of Christ the Savior once stood. And approvingly he quotes the French poet Saint-Exupéry: "You only need to listen to a folk song from the fifteenth century to understand how low we have fallen."

In *Black Boards*, Soloukhin tells how some years ago he was seized with the passion for collecting ancient icons, especially the "black" icons that had become dark from old age. He recounts his search for them and his exploration of the countryside around his home village. With each icon he has a story to tell of people, churches, and villages, just as Turgenev in his *Sportsman's Sketches* speaks more about the people he met on his hunting expeditions than about the hunts themselves. And just as Turgenev's book helped to bring about social changes, so the *Black Boards* have contributed to halting iconoclasm in Russian churches.

Soloukhin writes about the icons' senseless destruction, about their beauty (and value!) with such convincing grief that collecting icons became a veritable fad. The news that icons are valuable and should no longer be destroyed or left to rot traveled down into the villages. In his younger years, Soloukhin confesses he participated in antireligious campaigns and made rafts from icons for use on the village pond, but now he implores people to do the opposite, to preserve them. He never mentions what, if any, religious significance icons have for him; he defends them as national treasures and points out that in the eyes of the West they are celebrated and valuable. He writes: "If you are a Russian, you must know about Pushkin, the epic *O polku Igoreve*, Dostoyevsky, the battle on the field of Kulikovo [against the Mongols], Pokrov na Nerli [a church], the Tretyakov Gallery, Rublev's Trinity, and the Mother of God of Vladimir." (The last two are ancient icons.) Courageously the author speaks of the Mother of God as if she were a figure from Russian history, and the people whose conversations he describes are more often believers than atheists. A peasant woman complains:

> All right, so they closed the churches. All right, so they dismantled the iconostasis, probably a good thing, what good is it in a storage room? [The church was converted into a storehouse.] All right, so they put the icons somewhere. But why, of all things, make mangers of them? You take feed to the horses, bend down over the manger, and jump back. It's awful! From the depth of the manger Christ or the Mother of God looks up at you. The features are severe, the eyes large. It's frightening.

When the church in his own village was converted to other uses, Soloukhin notes: "Our fathers, grandfathers, great-grandfathers married within these walls. Doesn't the place that is ritually connected with the burial of our parents and forefathers deserve better treatment? From this point there is only one more step to the desecration of their graves."

Those who do not appreciate his observations should read about other things, Soloukhin suggests, "about the building of a gas pipeline, about the heroic deeds of scouts [known as spies in the West], about the kolkhoz machine and tractor depot."

Soloukhin's pan-Slavic heart beats vigorously in his *Slavic Copybook*, published after a visit to Bulgaria. For him that country is not just an ally of the USSR, it is first and foremost a land inhabited by Slavs who were liberated from the Turkish yoke by Russian soldiers and generals about one hundred years ago. Soloukhin mentions three wars that were "the most popular, the best understood by the people, and the most holy" in the eyes of the Russians: the battles against the Mongols, against Napoleon, and against the Turks. (Curiously, he omits those against Hitler.)

While hiking with a knapsack through royal Bulgaria in the twenties, I found many monuments and memorials erected to the tsar's generals and soldiers who fought in 1877–78. These men are still greatly respected in communist Bulgaria. Ironically, the gratitude the Russians would like to hear expressed by the Rumanians and Hungarians, by the Slovaks, Czechs, and Poles for their recent destruction of Hitler's armies is continually accorded them for their victory over the Turks a century ago by the same Bulgarians who, in the Second World War, fought until five minutes to twelve on the German side.

Any country should be happy to have a writer of the first order clamoring for the preservation and restoration of cultural sites. In the Soviet Union it takes more than just good judgment, it takes courage to do so, especially when the cultural monuments have religious or feudal-conservative associations. As he has shown time and again, Soloukhin has this courage. In his most recent book mentioned by his admirers, *A Time to Gather Stones Together*, a collection of five essays, with a title taken from the Old Testament, Soloukhin calls attention to various cultural sites that have fallen into decay and need to be restored. He presents his case by describing his visits to these sites and by employing, as the Bible suggests, the cunning of a serpent. He pleads for the restoration of a dilapidated monastery called Optina Pustyn by elaborating on the influence it once had on Gogol, who frequently stayed there; on Dostoyevsky, who took the idea for the saintly Zosima, a central figure in his *Brothers Karamazov*, from one of its monks; and on Tolstoy, who visited the monastery six times, the last time just before his death. Soloukhin also cleverly points out that American capitalists, if they found out about the monastery, might quickly buy what is left of it, with all its icons and books, carry it away, and rebuild it somewhere in the United States.

After a good deal of research into the history of the monastery and its famous visitors, Soloukhin uses his experienced pen to advance his cause. To make his plea more convincing, he furnishes much, often exciting, information not readily available from other sources. He even argues convincingly that, once restored and properly maintained, Optina Pustyn would earn money as a tourist attraction. But he also frankly states what truly motivates him: "Beauty does not need the excuse of being useful. After all, this is the beauty of our land, a measure of how civilized we are."

Sergey Aksakov (1791–1859), a landowning conservative and a lover of the old-fashioned Russian life-style, is not among the authors studied by young Russians in Soviet schools; and his name was mentioned only once when I asked Russians about their favorite classical authors. Yet he and his son Konstantin were among the seminal Russian minds of the nineteenth century, and his writings contributed much to Russian thought and culture. In *Aksakovskiye mesta* (Aksakov Places), Soloukhin launched a one-man campaign for the restoration of Aksakov's native village. To be sure, some attempts had been made earlier, but they came to naught, and in 1960 the family's manor house was torn down. Now the village looks, Soloukhin writes, the way Moscow would without the Kremlin. A school, like thousands of others in the USSR, occupies the place where the manor house once stood. The square looks like any square in front of a factory or a railway station. No trace remains of the church: the hole in the ground that was once the crypt is now being used for garbage.

The chairman of the kolkhoz to which the village belongs, a hardworking manager with important decorations on his breast, is proud of the new school and the square and has not the slightest understanding of Soloukhin's concern. The chairman's thoughts are thus interpreted by Soloukhin: "Everything is fine [in the kolkhoz]; the higher-ups praise me and give me decorations and laudatory documents. My only trouble is that fellow Aksakov. Of course, there were landlords and gentlemen, but do we really have to pray for them? And the tourists! In the summertime they come in large groups and have nothing to do. They ought to be sent to the kolkhoz to dig potatoes . . ."

It is a deeply saddened Soloukhin who, after leaving Aksakovo, looks through the train window to the changed *Landschaft* (he likes to use the German word for landscape because Russian lacks an equivalent). He strikes up a conversation with a stranger, who tells him of two swans who came to the neglected lake in the old Aksakov park some years ago but left again soon. When Soloukhin asks him why they did not stay he replies: "They laid two eggs. But when they started to hatch, somebody removed them. . . . So they flew away immediately and never returned. This is a pity."

Soloukhin mentions rumors that in Germany "swans just swim on the lakes. People are around them, but they just swim with their little ones." And the stranger responds: "I tell you something: it's our own fault. With our behavior we are obviously not worthy of having swans living among us. We don't deserve it. Swans, brother, you must be worthy of." And Soloukhin, an Aksakov of the late twentieth century in his own way, divulges his ultimate and principal aim: "In every new generation, the young people must be taught patriotic sentiments."

Seventy-five thousand copies of the book came out while I was in Moscow in 1981. They were sold out immediately. I obtained the last one at the *Beriozka* bookshop, where it was only available for dollars.

Arkady and Boris Natanovich Strugatsky

Since 1959, the Strugatsky brothers have published about two dozen science fiction novels. Seventeen of them—and this must be a record—have also appeared in either English or German or both. They are the most popular Soviet writers in this field, both at home and abroad. I have summarized novels from four different creative periods: 1963, 1968, 1972, and 1977. The summaries can be brief because Western fans of the Strugatskys can read their books in good translations; in English, Macmillan has done the most for them.

Far Rainbow concerns a distant planet somewhere. We are not told where, and it makes no difference since it does not exist anyway. Because of the continuing increase in human population, there are settlements on many planets. Rainbow has been turned into a gigantic laboratory in which scientists of many nationalities work together (in an unnamed language). Rainbow itself is very sparsely settled; there seem to be not more than five hundred scientists and their families, and we meet about two dozen of them. Life on Rainbow is quite pleasant when suddenly two gigantic waves, perhaps brought on by the scientists' experiments, engulf the entire planet; their impact annihilates everything near the scientists' town. By chance a spaceship happens to be on Rainbow as the catastrophe is about to hit. Naturally each scientist wants to get on it or at least to evacuate some of the priceless results of his research. But the captain of the spaceship, a Russian, decides that only the children can come aboard. They are saved while the adults are drowned by the waves.

An American reviewer wrote that one of the two books that brought tears to his eyes in his adult life was *Far Rainbow*. Perhaps the novel did not cause me to shed tears because its heroes, though human beings of a relatively near future, appear bloodless and abstract. Even the two doomed lovers—Tanya, a Russian schoolteacher, and Robert, her friend about whom we learn very little, not even what he is doing on the planet—suffer from these liabilities, as do a mother (remaining) and her son (departing). How incomparably more alive and filled with character are the people in almost any other novel discussed here.

If all the Strugatskys' books were like *Far Rainbow*, I would find it very difficult to understand the Russians' love for them. But the brothers are very versatile. If one might call *Rainbow* sentimental, then the *Second Invasion of the Martians* is bitterly satirical: an entire city (which might represent an entire country or an entire planet) is captured by unknowns or rather by the fear they arouse. But even "arouse" is too strong a word. The unknowns do not have to do anything; the mere rumors about them, contradictory as they are, create dread, even panic, and the desire hastily to submit.

Cleverly the brothers tell the story through the diary of a retired schoolteacher, a latter-day Babbitt who needs nothing but his stamp collection, his cronies in his and their habitual haunt, and most of all his peace and quiet. From his diary we gather that his fellow citizens are just like him—the chief of police, the bartender, the druggist, and others—all are only too willing to recognize and obey the new masters, although they know nothing about them. They call them Martians although they have learned in school that no life can exist on Mars. One of the men, a one-legged veteran of the war (which war?), organizes a little resistance, but he too has nothing more to offer than strong but mostly senseless talk.

The people's willingness to submit is illustrated through an absurd example: it is said that the Martians pay cash for gastric acid, which they suck out by means of tubes, and that this acid will soon replace money altogether. The teacher's pension, too, so it is said, will be paid in gastric acid. The conversation about this strange measure is no less grotesque than the rumored measure itself. The Martians, some say, are able to make gold from it; no, others guess, atomic power; and so it goes. Anyway, the citizens are quite willing to swallow the tubes and part with their acid.

The matter-of-fact way in which foreign rule is accepted by them without any force being applied is the truly terrifying feature of this story, more frightening, I found, than even Orwell's *1984*. By calling their book *The Second Invasion*, so Arkady Strugatsky told me, they wanted to refer to H. G. Wells, who had the Martians conquer the earth by force of arms. In our day, the brothers say, the force of rumors does it.

The pleasant title *Picnic on the Roadside* is deceptive. The picnic was a grim event—if it ever took place. The year is 19—, the place a town by the name of Harmont, perhaps somewhere in the United States, situated on the edge of the mysterious and forbidden Zone. In all there are six such Zones on our planet, apparently all possessing invisible and horrifying forces for which new terms had to be invented, such as flycatchers (they squash everything that gets close to them) or thundering napkins (I didn't find out what havoc they could create). The Zones are also full of all kinds of strange paraphernalia: the Empty Zero, the Full Zero, the Tickler, the Sponge, the Silver Cobweb, the Witches' Brine. The children of people in contact with the Zone are furry, animal-like creatures, and those who move to some other place bring misfortune to their new neighbors: hurricanes, an increasing death rate, and more frequent accidents on the road. Some dead people even arise from their graves and visit their relatives.

There are many theories concerning the origin of the Zones: they were targets for shots from outer space, proof of attempts by other creatures to establish contact with earthlings, or—this hypothesis gave the book its title—they were the sites where cosmic creatures on an interplanetary flight had stopped for a picnic and left a lot of trash behind in true picnickers' fashion. Even the International Institute for the Study of Extraterrestrial Cultures, established in Harmont to conduct research on these disturbing phenomena, has nothing but wild guesses to offer although twenty years have passed since The Visit.

If there actually was a visit from outer space and if it did have a meaning or message, mankind has not grasped it and has gone on living as if nothing had happened. The people of Harmont have turned their town into a profitable place for treasure hunters, an attraction for sightseers who come by the busloads, and a temptation for poachers who risk their lives in order to get some of the Zone's strange objects to sell to the highest bidders. Thus the people of Harmont "who work hectically during the day and spend their evenings in front of the television set" have turned their town into a paradise for smugglers and profiteers instead of using the unique opportunity of The Visit to increase their knowledge and wisdom.

The reader should not be misled by the huge number in the title *More Than a Billion Years to the End of the World.* This story takes place in the Leningrad of today, in some of the large apartment houses in which scientists live. We meet several of them, friends though they work in totally different fields. We become more familiar with an astronomer studying problems of outer space and with his wife. The others we meet include a rocket specialist, a biochemist, a mathematician, and even an orientologist. They have one thing in common: all are on the verge of exciting new discoveries. Up to the time when our story begins, they have led normal scholars' lives and have kept busy with their thoughts and research.

Then strange things begin to happen. Inexplicable distractions constantly interrupt the astronomer in his thoughts. First a big box of food and liquor from a delicatessen is delivered to him. Although he never ordered or paid for it, he is pleased to receive such a delicious gift. Next, an alluring young woman moves in with him, supposedly a friend of his vacationing wife's, preventing him from pursuing the train of his thought just when he is close to an intellectual breakthrough. The biochemist is haunted by a red-headed gnome who demands that he stop his research. The rocket specialist shoots himself in the head—or did somebody else do him in?

Soon there is no question left in the reader's mind. Some queer powers are at work and are determined to disrupt the scientific work of these scholars and, we might infer from this, that of other scholars too. Why? Gradually we begin to understand: progress has become a danger to mankind and even to the universe.

But who are the forces bent on interrupting that dangerous research? This question is heatedly debated by the scholars. Some suggest that a highly advanced extraterrestrial supercivilization has learned of the earthlings' perilous doings. Others believe that mother earth itself, having reached that same conclusion, has set these interfering forces into operation. In the end both explanations produce the same conclusion: research must stop.

At first the scholars are not only frightened but also outraged and inclined to go ahead with their work anyway. But they run into barriers. The astronomer cannot recreate that happy moment of almost-discovery, he can only putter around with the manuscripts he has already written. While he is still uncertain about what to do, his wife returns. She finds a bra left by that strange young woman who had given her husband a letter of introduction from her that she had never written. To appease her anger, the astronomer tells her the entire horrid story. Loving confidence is restored. To save both of them and their son, the astronomer decides to surrender. After wrapping up all his research papers in a bundle, he takes them to the mathematician who is the one least willing to give up. There he learns that the others have also brought their findings and abandoned their research.

The mathematician is determined to fight on. He intends to move to the high Pamir mountains (in the USSR) in order to continue his work and to preserve that of his less courageous friends. But he realizes that the forces, whoever they are, will find him there and probably kill him.

Here the story ends. To judge from its title, the book seems to offer hope that our world will go on for more than a billion years—because science has been stopped or because the mathematician continued his and his friends' studies? This question is not answered. Obviously the Brothers Strugatsky are more interested in questions than in answers.

When I asked people why they were Strugatsky fans, I did not get very clear answers, perhaps because I did not ask the right questions due to my own distance from this literary genre. I shall try to give, as best I can, an explanation in the Conclusions.

Yury Valentinovich Trifonov

I read Trifonov's *The Exchange* in the early seventies and saw it on the stage of Moscow's Taganka Theater in 1976, when its production was finally permitted after a drawn-out struggle between the theater's famous director, Yury Lyubimov, and the cultural department of the capital.

The plot is simple and macabre: Viktor, a 37-year-old employee, lives in Moscow with his wife, Lena, and their young daughter in one room of an apartment that also houses a number of other families, with just one bathroom and one kitchen for all. (In the midthirties my wife and I lived like this in Moscow, and many Muscovites still do today.) Viktor's mother lives in Moscow, too; she also has one room in an apartment with others, but on the other side of town. Terminally ill with cancer, she does not want to admit that her end is near. At this juncture, Lena suggests that the family and the mother exchange their two separate rooms for two rooms that are together. Thus, she says, she can take better care of the old woman.

This sounds quite sensible and commendably decent to a Westerner. But any Muscovite immediately sees through Lena: if Viktor's mother dies in the room she has now, it is lost, but if she and her son's family have two rooms together, the family will keep her room after her death and will be able to spread from one room into two—an almost unbelievable improvement in their life-style. Viktor, a softer character than his wife, is at first horrified by her cold-blooded scheme, but he soon realizes how reasonable her plan is. The problem is that, at the moment, his mother is in the country, and she has the key to her room. This key plays a "key role" in the plot, since Lena needs it to show the room to people interested in the exchange. (Usually couples getting a divorce are on the lookout for two rooms as far apart as possible.) Finally Viktor summons his courage and, while visiting his mother, asks for the key. She too immediately understands: her son wants to profit from her death, which he expects soon. She refuses to accept this death sentence at first, but after Viktor has left, she reconsiders the situation. She realizes that she will die soon anyway and might do her son this last service. She phones him to say that she agrees to the exchange, adding that he should hurry.

A number of other people are involved, two of whom are unforgettable. The wheeler-dealer who arranges the exchange is one of them. With thirteen partners involved, his exchange is a true work of art; should one partner withdraw, the entire edifice would collapse. (This character presents a wonderful opportunity for an actor.) The other important character is Tanya, Viktor's mistress, one of those patient, quietly suffering, almost angelic figures that emerge from time to time from Russian literature. Her husband abandoned her because of Viktor, yet she knows that there is really nothing left between her and her weak lover. She might have been a better wife to him than Lena, he muses, and he is sorry that things turned out the way they did. But what can you do? He even takes the 200 rubles she had saved to buy herself a new coat.

But apart from this one angelic ray and the tortured love of a dying mother, the picture is grim and sad. The constant struggle against a thousand large and small adversities—including the battle to gain a few additional square feet of space—have made Trifonov's people cold, calculating, and emotionally impoverished. The readers of the book and the viewers of the play know as well as foreign readers that many Russians do not resemble Trifonov's traumatized people, although the living conditions he describes are true to life. So why, instead of resenting the book and the play, do they pay black-market prices for the book and the tickets? Not even my dollars or marks could get me a ticket, and in the end I only got in because I knew somebody who knew somebody who . . .

A year after *The Exchange* came the next of Trifonov's Moscow novellas, the *Preliminary Balance Sheet*. The story is again told by a man who has not been very successful in life, Gennady, a translator in this case. After a quarrel with his wife, he leaves Moscow to live, at least temporarily, in a small settlement in Soviet Central Asia. While working there on his current translation, his thoughts wander back over his life. These memories are rather melancholy, and the reader gets the impression that the people Gennady had to deal with were actually as pitiful and self-centered in their lives as they appear in his memories, petty careerists who get ahead by taking advantage of all kinds of little irregularities, black-market deals, minor corruption, and, above all, the inevitable assistance of the proper "connections."

In Gennady's circle of acquaintances there is only one decent person: Nyura, the deformed, deaf, sickly housemaid who, taken for granted as a dog would be, lives like a saint in the unpleasant and constantly quarreling family. Gennady at last realizes her invaluable contribution toward maintaining relative peace when she is taken away to an asylum for schizophrenics. (The author's hint that only a schizophrenic can be a good person in today's world?)

The depth of human depravity is embodied in Gennady's son. A representative of his ruthless student generation, he was nursed and loved by Nyura all his life, yet he deprives her of her one prized possession, an old icon she inherited. She loves the icon not for its material value, of which she is unaware, but for its soul-healing religious quality. Without a pang of conscience, the young man sells the icon and buys himself a motorbike.

Did Trifonov mean to say that the Soviet people are like this, 60 years after the Revolution that was supposed to open a bright new chapter in the history of mankind? In view of his father's fate, one might assume this. But I am inclined to think that Trifonov was holding up a mirror to reflect, not Homo sovieticus specifically, but rather contemporary Homo sapiens in general, although under the specific conditions of the Soviet state.

It is Trifonov's deeply probing seriousness and his persistent search for truth that explains, I think, the reverence Russians feel for him. In his works, they do not expect a happy ending but a story of substance, and that story, more often than not, is sad, calling for commiseration rather than for a smile.

When *The Other Life* appeared, the author still had another six years to live. But death repeatedly enters the story, and it may well be that the title has a double meaning. Yet, we learn about the novel's events through the thoughts of a woman who stands with her feet firmly on the ground, Olga, the head of a biological laboratory. Her husband died two years ago, and she now lives in a small apartment of only a few square feet with her sixteen-year-old daughter and her mother-in-law. In sleepless nights and intense dreams, Olga relives important phases of her life. Her husband was a historian working forever on his dissertation and leaving it unfinished at his death. Yet (such is the academic bureaucracy in Russia), his salary continues to be paid.

Of special interest to Russian readers normally incognizant of such things is the world of the occult into which the husband had been drawn. The reader learns the names of famous prerevolutionary spiritualists, usually women, and the titles of books about spiritualism of that period. Olga, the hard-bitten and matter-of-fact woman, disdains this hocus-pocus and thinks it ridiculous that her husband believed he could communicate with a Swiss monk of the sixteenth century by the name of Arnulf.

But, as always in Trifonov's novels, the main value of *The Other Life* lies in the excellent and convincing characterization of the people involved. One can easily understand why the guardians of the Soviet Union's cheery, optimistic image are unhappy with the characters Trifonov depicts, since they are so far removed from the desired portraits. Trifonov's heroes, mostly members of the capital's middle-class and intelligentsia, are not very different from their counterparts in the West whom we might meet in contemporary American or German novels or even in real life. They certainly have not surpassed them morally in the 65 years since the Revolution promised to create the New Man. Were one to substitute Western names for the cumbersome Russian ones and to replace the old-fashioned Russian household tools with modern equipment, the story could be located in New York or Frankfurt.

Yet one circumstance of life in Moscow intensifies all ordinary human conflicts among Russians: the heavy and incessant burden of day-to-day existence, especially standing in line in the shops and living in extremely limited space, often with other people in the same apartment. Take the strained relationship between Olga and her daughter, for example. They live in a state of perpetual enmity relieved by occasional armistices. While she washes her daughter's underwear in a tub,

Olga thinks: "Again this devil hasn't washed any of her things. Well I would just have to rewash them anyway; when she washes, she merely moves the dirt around."

What we hear about life in Soviet academia is also rather dreary. Plenty of intrigues and personal grudges permeate this community, too; they managed to prevent the husband's trip to Parisian archives. Even Olga does not emerge as a pleasant person, although we read the story through her thoughts and memories; she is frequently edgy and irritated by the hardship of her daily life, and she takes this out on those closest to her.

The writer's next two books attempt to come to terms with the communist past. *The House on the Embankment* is not only of first-rate literary quality, it demonstrates high moral courage. Although the story is revealed through flashbacks to the thirties and early postwar years in the novel, I will tell it chronologically here.

Glebov, the hero, comes from an average Moscow family. Together with a half dozen other families, they live in one apartment in an old Russian house that stands—in a double sense—in the shadow of that ugly, gray mountain of a house on the embankment of the Moskva River. Built during the First Five-Year Plan for the VIPs, it was considered a model of communist modernism at that time. Glebov's classmate Lyova, a child of the new upper class, is the object of awe and jealousy because he lives in the big house and has an all-powerful father. When some of his schoolmates plan to play a humiliating prank on him to vent their feelings of envy, their families disappear from the school district. Glebov's only and very small influence lay in his ability to obtain tickets to a cinema where his mother worked as cashier. He even got his first kiss from a girl at school for getting her a ticket to the *Blue Express*. But Lyova spoiled it all by inviting his classmates to his parents' roomy apartment to show them that very film on their home projector.

The difference between the inhabitants of the big house and the rest of the children is revealed in many minor incidents. Glebov is immensely impressed when Lyova's mother sends a fancy cake that had made his mouth water back to the kitchen because it was "not fresh," and he is convinced that a dog that *lives* in the big house has nothing but contempt for him, the boy who only *visits* there.

The war is barely mentioned, and afterwards Glebov is again drawn into the orbit of the house on the embankment: his professor of literature, once a hero of the Civil War, lives there with his daughter Sonya, who eventually becomes Glebov's devoted mistress. During the purge of the late forties when a witch-hunt starts against the professor, Glebov does not defend him, an act for which he is promoted at the institute and awarded a special stipend of 30 rubles a month.

The final paragraphs of the book bring us up to the present, to 1974. We learn that Glebov has continued to rise in his academic field, the old professor has been rehabilitated, Sonya has died, and Lyova has gone downhill but is still around.

Trifonov does not show much interest in external events. Layer by layer he bares his characters' innermost thoughts and feelings and, even more important, their consciences. This novel is to me an example of *apolitichnost* (nonpoliticalness), the exact opposite of the *politichnost* demanded by the party, and in this respect it corresponds to many readers' attitudes. It is one of the unexpected paradoxes of Soviet life that this novel was published and that its dramatized version is being shown at the Taganka Theater, sold out long in advance.

The most artful of Trifonov's novels is *Starik*; it is also the most demanding because its various time frames are less clearly distinguishable than in *The House on the Embankment*. There are really two stories, and it seems that originally the author intended to write two separate novels. One story takes place in 1973, involves an old man who lives with the younger generations of his family, and concerns a small dacha near Moscow. The person who lived in the dacha has recently died, and the young people hope to get it by playing on the fame of the old man, a revolutionary hero in the Civil War. But he is much more interested in a letter he received from a woman whom he loved more than half a century ago. And this, in turn, leads to the second story, that faraway time that is of no interest to those around him. The problem plaguing the old man is: Was he morally right when, on that Civil War front along the Don, he refrained from doing his utmost to save one of the most colorful figures of that era, the Red cossack general Migulin, who was suspected of betraying the communist cause? (The novel's Migulin is patterned after a historical figure, Filipp Mironov.) We never find out whether Migulin had contemplated treason and what the old man's role was in the general's fall. Again Trifonov is primarily interested in posing painful questions instead of offering cut-and-dried statements; again he forces his heroes to judge their right and wrong by their conscience rather than by the party's (varying) judgments, to engage in that *samokopaniye,* that self-searching, I mentioned before.

Trifonov completed the manuscript of his last published novel, *Time and Place*, in December 1980, a few months before his death. His widow put it into final shape. To start with the two parts of the novel's title, the time covers more than four decades, from 1938 to 1979; the place is almost exclusively Moscow. Countless people come and go; some go forever; others reappear. The thirteen chapters are loosely linked by the novel's hero, Antipov, whom we first meet in 1938 as an eleven-year-old boy at the moment when both his parents disappear. Later in life he wants to become a writer. This he does, but with little success.

The numerous episodes the author has woven into his novel are mostly sad. Because of his poor eyesight, young Antipov cannot join the army. Instead, during the war, he works in an airplane factory in Moscow. The foreman sends him to a nearby black market to exchange a head of cabbage for some stolen tobacco; due to his lack of experience in such matters, he is caught red-handed, arrested, locked up, and nearly sentenced to prison. For another foreman, he transports a 100-pound sack of potatoes of somewhat suspicious origin on an overcrowded electric train from the outskirts of Moscow to the foreman's abode. When the sack breaks, a lot of the potatoes are trampled under foot by the crowd. He tries to sell the pitifully few remaining ones in the street because he now has nothing to carry them in. In the end, he must sell his most prized possession, a fur cap he inherited from his father, to buy another sack of potatoes on the black market for the foreman. Another boy finds a note at the door of his and his mother's room when he returns from school: "Careful, I am hanging here." She had written the note before committing suicide.

Trifonov's world remains sad even when it is sometimes lit by rays of human decency. After eight years in Siberia, Antipov's mother returns to Moscow without a permit for entering the capital. On the train, she tries to make herself as small and inconspicuous as possible. By mistake she pulls the emergency brake. The train guard rushes from one compartment to the next in search of the culprit. If she is found out, she will be sentenced to at least a year in prison. Fortunately for her, a man in uniform in her car, realizing that she was the one, shields her by telling the guard that nothing happened in their section of the train. In Moscow, she lives in one room with her remaining family, terrified year in year out that somebody will tell on her and that she will be exiled from the city and punished in addition for living in Moscow without a permit. "I am a scared crow," she says of herself, adding that others are even ten times more scared than she is. Indeed, everyone is scared of something or somebody most of the time. Trifonov's heart goes out to them all, although he does not say so explicitly. And so he takes us through fistfights and love stories, marriages and divorces (or simply disappearances of one of the partners), endless tensions and irritations caused by the cramped living conditions, the unhappiness of children pushed hither and thither, hatreds and reconciliations, intrigues, frame-ups, and sudden bursts of helpfulness. In this world, Antipov remains inoffensive, good-natured, naively trusting, and therefore in needless trouble time and again.

Trifonov has no message and offers no consolation. He never says that everything will be better after the war is over, nor does he say that one should change the system. He simply says: that's the way it is. Yet people read his books avidly, and there are never enough of them. I found the reason for Trifonov's popularity expressed most concisely as I was leaving a performance of the dramatization of his *Exchange* in the Taganka Theater. As I was waiting in line with hundreds of others to get my coat from the theater's overcrowded checkroom, I heard a woman in front of me, probably in her thirties, say to her female companion: "Let's stick together for a while. If I go home now, I shall go to bed and weep. What we just saw on the stage is not a play. It's our life."

Arkady and Georgy Aleksandrovich Vainer

The two novels to be summarized here had a curious history of publication. *Visit to Minotaur* first appeared in 150 thousand copies in the periodical *Iskatel* (The Searcher), a supplement to *Vokrug sveta* (Around the World), a journal read mainly by young people; next in a review published especially for the police; and finally as a book with a print run of 150 thousand copies. That, of course, proved to be far too few. For reasons I will explain shortly, the brothers fared even worse with *Medicine for Nesmeyana*. This, however, has not diminished their broad appeal.

The *Visit to Minotaur* moves on two historical levels that are far apart in time, space, and atmosphere: the Italian city of Cremona in the early eighteenth century and Moscow in 1970; violin makers and monks in Italy, and detectives and criminals in the USSR. Each of the seventeen chapters begins with a page or two in Italy and then switches to the Soviet capital.

The home of Russia's greatest violinist, whom the Vainers called Polyakov, was burglarized. Many valuable items were stolen, but only one loss really matters: a priceless violin, one of the finest in existence, built in 1722 by Antonio Stradivari of Cremona and loaned to Polyakov by the Soviet government. Among those who search for the stolen Stradivarius (and in the end, of course, find it), is the Vainers' favorite detective, the narrator Tikhonov.

The search is made difficult because, in addition to professional criminals, there are a large number of suspects, including two other great violinists, Polyakov's potential rivals. One is even more talented than Polyakov, but he has no perseverance (he eventually commits suicide); the other, once a rising star, slipped into crime because a broken arm ruined his career. Some suspects are just there to lead the reader astray: for example, Polyakov's next-door neighbor whose wife has a key to Polyakov's apartment because she looks after it in his absence. True enough, the neighbor's fingerprints are found on a glass in the violinist's home. But, as it turns out later, he was there simply to help himself to some of Polyakov's liquor. (In Western mystery stories, I believe, it is against the author's ethical code to use red herrings totally unrelated to the crime.)

Now and then the reader is allowed a glimpse of the secrets of Soviet detective work. One of the as yet unidentified suspects had a tin of marinated mushrooms. (My mouth watered, if I may interject, these being a Russian delicacy.) A policewoman working on the theft finds twelve figures and characters stamped on the tin, and we learn how she identifies the store that sold it and eventually the man who turns out to be the criminal mastermind.

I have read better detective stories; the flow of events is not as crystal clear and transparent as in those of Agatha Christie or Simenon, but this genre is still relatively new in Russia, and the reader's taste not too discriminating as yet. In addition to the hunt for the criminal, he gets something that Western whodunits do not offer: the story of Antonio Stradivari and his colleagues or rivals. The Brothers Vainer have done a lot of research in order to depict the Cremona of the early eighteenth century. They skillfully describe the greatness and rivalry of the three dynasties of violin makers—Guarneri, Amati, and Stradivari. In dark contrast to them, they picture the fanatical priests and monks with their obscurantist mentality, especially those of the Jesuit order for whom all nonreligious music is of the devil. But apart from the fact that the stolen violin is a Stradivarius, the connection between the two levels of the novel is not very clear. If the seventeen bits of the Cremona story were cut out, no one interested in the detective story would notice. Nevertheless the Cremona angle adds color and an additional dimension that the Soviet reader, to his credit, seems to appreciate.

One might say that there is yet a third level: the story of Minotaur. Half-man and half-bull, this dreadful monster who dwelled in the dark labyrinth of Crete was fed seven girls and seven boys from Athens each year. Finally Theseus killed him and returned to the light of day with the help of the thread furnished by lovely Ariadne. The symbolism of the Minotaur myth is tenuous; after all, one might call every detective's work a visit to Minotaur's labyrinth.

As in so many other Soviet detective stories the origin of crime as such is not identified. In an aside in one case we learn that the father of one of the criminals was an Orthodox priest, but the theme of the thief's sinister "social origin" is not developed. No connection is established between the father's former profession and the son's criminal activities half a century after the Revolution. Envious rivalry or a broken arm are somewhat more convincing causes of aberrant behavior but again not quite sufficient to explain crime in supposedly near-ideal surroundings. But a whodunit needs criminals and detectives; where the criminals come from isn't necessarily the author's concern. This is understandable. And in the USSR as elsewhere, the reader wants a detective story, not a treatise on the origin of crime.

During the years since the *Minotaur* was published, the brothers have developed and refined their pens' work. *Medicine for Nesmeyana* was, in my opinion, rightly named by Vainer fans as their best book. First, a word about the title: *Nesmeyana*, literally "the not-laughing one," is a tsar's daughter in a well-known Russian fairy tale. By wicked magic she has been forced to lead a life of deep sorrow, and only from the beloved hero of Russian fairy tales, the Tsarevich Ivan, can she learn to laugh and be happy. Thus one might translate the title as "Medicine for the Sad Princess."

This is not a whodunit that you read breathlessly and without a pause. The Vainers have taken great pains with the description of their characters, and these are not the usual clever murderer, dumb prosecutor, beautiful woman, and quick-witted detective. There is not even a corpse.

The plot revolves around an as yet nonexistent medicine that scientists all over the world are trying to develop, a medicine to cure what the Vainers consider mankind's most serious affliction today: the worldwide spiritual depression caused by fear and anxiety. Such a medicine is thought to be so urgently needed that its discoverer is likely to be awarded the Nobel Prize.

While investigating a crime committed in Moscow, Detective Tikhonov, the Vainer brothers' Maigret, stumbles into various "labyrinths" that eventually lead him to top secret chemical laboratories where research on the medicine is being conducted. He learns that two scientists in Moscow are working on the problem and have advanced far beyond chemists in other countries. Once they were friends, but then they parted company. The always successful one becomes head of a large laboratory with many assistants; he disparages his former friend Volodya, a luckless fellow but the real genius of the two, and tries to push him out of scientific work. He cannot prevent Volodya, however, from continuing his research with very limited means. In the end Volodya discovers the formula.

Thus the story's real conflict is not so much between a young criminal (a playboy type) and the detective but between the two scientists. On the one hand stands the gifted but corrupt egotist, who has taken the hedonistic Latin *carpe diem* for his motto, who laughs at the humanitarian *yerunda* (nonsense) his rival believes in, and who wishes to use the secret formula for his own purposes. On the other hand there is Volodya, who wants to help mankind and to whom the medicine would be more than just a chemical process to be manipulated at will.

To make this point clear, the brothers introduce a second historical level, sixteenth-century Germany. Volodya's ideal, the person he strives to model himself after and the man he identifies with, is Paracelsus, who was called von Hohenheim after a place near Stuttgart and, incidentally, not far from my home. The Vainers call the German-Swiss physician, a contemporary of Luther's, the "Luther of Medicine," and he becomes at times almost the central figure of the novel. The roughly twenty passages devoted to him, printed in a different typeface than the rest of the story, fill almost a sixth of the book and are a song of praise for this selfless idealist who was hated and persecuted by the contemporary medical establishment because he refused to adhere to their useless dogmas and devoted his life instead to the study of the true nature of man. The great Erasmus of Rotterdam advised him to compromise, to make his peace with the quacks of his time in order to be left in peace, and then to do what he thought was right. Paracelsus spurned the advice and died in poverty.

One can easily see many parallels between the great Paracelsus, portrayed almost as a saint, and the young scientist Volodya, who, fighting the career-oriented dogmatists of his day, falls into poverty and disgrace. One might say that the Paracelsus passages could be cut without the crime story as such losing anything, but the connection between the two historical levels is far more subtle and convincing than in *Minotaur.*

Finally there is one more level, a story around the story. Some present-day dogmatists did not like the manuscript for two reasons. First, they objected to its original title, *Medicine Against Fear.* Anxiety is not supposed to exist in the optimistic communist world, so the title had to be changed to *Medicine for Nesmeyana.* Second, they looked with a jaundiced eye on the figure of Paracelsus and wanted him removed, most likely because they felt that some Russian readers might draw the undesirable conclusion that in the USSR true scholars and humanists are suppressed and pushed into poverty. The Vainers refused to cut out

Paracelsus, offering to waive their honorarium if the Paracelsus parts were left in. They finally obtained permission to go ahead but were given paper for only 15 thousand copies instead of the 150 or 300 thousand that would have sold easily.

Minotaur was given to me by Arkady Vainer; I found *Nesmeyana* in a library in California.

Boris Lvovich Vasilyev

Vasilyev, as we have seen, was a late starter, his first novella, *Dawns Are Quiet Here*, only came out in 1969. It covers fewer than 40 magazine pages and part of this space is used for illustrations. When Russians mentioned the story to me, they usually called it "the one with the sergeant and his girls."

It is May 1942, somewhere on the northern front. Most of the fighting is occurring further south, around Leningrad and in the Ukraine, so it is quiet here. A sergeant and two dozen soldiers man some antiaircraft weapons. Because there is very little to do, the men drink heavily of the vodka prepared by the lonely and eager women in the small village nearby. The sergeant, a conservative peasant boy, is deeply upset by their unbecoming behavior. Urgently he asks for replacement troops; he wants soldiers who neither drink nor womanize. He gets them: a group of girls in uniform.

The next few scenes seem like a situation comedy, even the setting is just right: one sergeant, a platoon of girls, and a village full of lonely women. The sergeant is soon completely at sea: panties dry in the breeze, naked young women sunbathe, and a lot of smart back talk wounds his ears. He only finished four grades of elementary school, so most of these new soldiers are better educated than he is and have no compunctions about seeming impudent. But then the war reaches them. A German patrol invades their forest. The sergeant and five of his soldiers go to search for them. He returns alone. None of the girls is left: four died bravely, one cowardly. But together they wiped out most of the Germans.

Vasilyev has a keen eye for topics that are not only gripping and memorable but also unusual. In *His Name Was Not Listed*, the singular setting is an overrun fortress and a cast of essentially two people.

The scene is the old fortress on the edge of the city of Brest on the newly established Soviet-German frontier. Border and town were overrun in the first hours of the blitzkrieg in June 1941. But while the German juggernaut rolled along toward Moscow, some members of the

Brest garrison survived in the winding catacombs and cellars of the fortress, believing that within a short while the Red Army would return and liberate them. One by one they were killed or captured by the Germans.

In the end, only two people are left in the catacombs, Mirra, a crippled young Jewess who happened to be in the fortress when the Germans attacked (she had been working in the kitchen), and Vasilyev's protagonist, Nikolay. After graduating a few weeks earlier from a military academy near Moscow with the rank of lieutenant, he arrived in Brest a few hours before the German attack. He had not yet registered with his new unit when the bombs began to fall and thus never had a chance to be listed (hence the novel's title). Instead of surrendering, he lives—first alone, then with Mirra—in the ruined underground world, mainly on crackers and tins that he found in a bombed storage room. Month after month goes by, all hope of relief fades. Love develops between the two young people. When Mirra gets pregnant and tries to escape to save their child, she is killed by German guards.

Now the young lieutenant is alone. From time to time he appears above ground, kills a few Germans, and always manages to hide again. But in the end he runs out of ammunition and of food. In this dire situation he gets a message from the Germans to give himself up, and he does so.

As he emerges from the cellar in the final scene, a German army ambulance with a doctor awaits him.

> "They were all silent. The [German] soldiers and officers were, and so was the general. The women who were working nearby were silent, as were their guards. And everybody was looking at him as he stood severe and motionless like a monument. The general spoke in a low voice, and it was translated to him: "Give me your rank and name."
>
> "I am a Russian soldier," he answered. . . .
>
> Stern and straight, he now walked seeing nothing and orienting himself by the sound of the ambulance motor. And all the people stood in their places. But he walked along, moving his swollen, frozen feet with great difficulty. And suddenly a German lieutenant clicked his heels and threw his hand to his cap. The soldiers snapped to attention and stood like statues. And he walked and walked, walked proudly and straight, the way he had lived, and he only fell when he reached the car.

A powerful end to a powerful novel. Its fascination for the Russians, I found, is twofold. One lies in the name of Brest. In those first disastrous weeks of the war, when the entire front went to pieces and countless Soviet soldiers disappeared in prison camps, Brest was a symbol of brave resistance. The ruins of the fortress are now a national shrine visited by millions, and the young lieutenant who continued the war for ten months has become a legend.

Western readers might object that Nikolay's portrait possesses too little psychological depth, that in spite of the many hours they spend with the young lieutenant they do not learn very much about him. Vasilyev is no Dostoyevsky, yet he has succeeded in creating a figure of epic dimensions.

Nikolay told the German general: "I am a Russian soldier." He did not say "I am a Soviet soldier" or "a communist soldier." Nikolay withstood the supreme test of a soldier, and he is a Russian who fought and died for his Russian fatherland. It was the non-Russian Stalin himself who, at the end of the war, paid special homage to the Russian people for their part in the Soviet victory. Vasilyev will certainly quarrel with me, but to my mind Nikolay is not a soldier who could only be Russian. Schweik could only have been a Czech soldier; Nikolay transcends national boundaries.

The novel with the strange title *Do Not Shoot the White Swans* is far removed from the world of war. The word *shoot* has no connection with the war. Indeed the war is barely mentioned, almost as if it had never occurred, and political slogans are just as absent as are the names of political leaders. The place is a small settlement established for lumber exploitation once upon a time in the northern Russian forests; the reader learns neither its approximate location and size nor the time the novel's events occur (probably somewhere around 1970). All such information seems irrelevant to the author, and indeed it is for his story.

Vasilyev has a message: a plea for ecology. During the last few years ecological awareness has grown rapidly among the Russians. When there were no more trees to fell, the settlement lost its purpose. Its inhabitants hope to improve the local economy by offering recreation facilities to townspeople eager for a glimpse of mother nature. But to attract tourists, they must have something to offer. Thus the little river is dammed, pleasure boats are built for rowing on the new lake, places for picnics and parties are fashioned. Good ideas, no doubt, and for a worthy cause. And the settlement has one more feature to show for itself: a still untouched area of reserved forest located around what is known as the Black Lake.

Yet, more important is the novel's other aspect. Vasilyev delights in describing Russian characters, and he obviously loves them, almost all of them anyway. His greatest sympathy belongs to a rather unusual hero who at first sight seems more like an antihero if not a village idiot. His name is Yegor. His willingness to do the right thing is unbounded. But, no matter how much he tries, everything he does goes wrong, and as a result he never keeps a job very long.

When Yegor is told to dig a straight ditch in which pipes are to be laid, he works so hard that in one day he accomplishes what he had been expected to finish in three. The foreman is ready to praise him until he notices that at one point the ditch suddenly deviates from its otherwise beautifully straight course. The odd detour was made because of an anthill that Yegor could not bear to destroy. While he is grieved by the foreman's furious wrath, he still feels that he did the right thing. In his next job he is ordered to paint numbers on the bows of the rowboats. He works long hours and even overtime, but again he earns anger rather than thanks. Instead of numbers, which he considered unattractive, he painted the boats with different symbols: a pig, a dog, a duck, and so on. Now he must destroy his artistic endeavors and replace them with boring figures.

This then is the kind of man Yegor is: the laughingstock of the neighborhood, a pain in the neck to his wife, penniless, and an embarrassment to his school-age son who is endlessly teased by the other children because of his father's eccentricities. But gradually the reader understands that Yegor is more the village saint than the village fool. He never becomes angry, not even at people who deliberately hurt him, and he is always willing to help; blissfully naive and trusting, he never suspects any dirty tricks and barely even notices them.

The author says of his hero:

> He acted not from deliberation, not with a purpose, nor for praise from above, but according to his own conscience. . . . He had a simple rule: never force anything on anybody. . . . He lived quietly and shyly, always radiated contentment, never bothered anybody, . . . was never underfoot. . . . For all this one ought to have thanked him from one's whole soul. But nobody did thank him. Nobody.

Yegor's brother-in-law is just his opposite in every way—a wheeler-dealer, a practical man who knows which side his bread is buttered on, always on the lookout for his and his family's interests and, if need be, ready to make shady deals. But then, who is not? When he saw that lumbering was coming to an end, he made sure he was put in charge of the forest reserve, a nice, steady job, with a lot of wood for his own use or for peddling on the black market. Unfortunately for him, this job ends abruptly. A new forester smells corruption and theft and, having taken a fancy to that queer but unusually honest and conscientious Yegor, makes him the new forest warden. He could not have made a better choice. Yegor works from dawn to dusk and begins to get the forest in good shape, he even cleans up the garbage the tourists left behind, a task his predecessor had never bothered about.

The new forester is another one of the main characters, as is the young woman who was recently sent from the city to teach school in this neck of the woods, a shy virgin who, having fallen in love with the forester, summons all her courage to visit him and ask him for a kiss, the first in her life. When he hesitates to go further, she runs away, taking this as proof that he does not love her. In fact, he loves her too. His trouble is that he does not know whether he is married or not. Some years ago he had a one-night affair with a student; on the following day, he dutifully registered their marriage, thinking that this was the way it was done, but she soon disappeared never to be seen again.

The reader meets all kinds of memorable individuals, most of them quite far removed from what many people expect the standardized Soviet man to be. Yet Yegor remains in the center. His greatest ambition as forest warden is to change the lake's dreadful name. It became black because its once pure water became polluted; it used to be called the Lake of the Swans. But where to get swans in a planned economy? When he is sent to Moscow to attend a meeting of forest workers, he pesters the people in the zoo there until, impressed by his naive insistence (and to get rid of him), they actually sell him two pairs of their white swans for his own money. He brings them safely home by camping with them in a freight car.

Now Yegor is a truly happy man (in contrast to his wife who did not get a present from Moscow because he spent all his money on the swans). But he does not remain happy for long. One night he hears shots. Rushing to the lake, he finds a gruesome scene: some men have shot his beloved swans and are about to grill them at their drunken party. When he asks them to follow him to the police, they kick and beat him so brutally that he dies a few days later in the hospital. He does not reveal the identity of his attackers to the police investigators as would have been his duty; he has settled the matter by forgiving them: "With a smile he thought very simply and quietly that he had had a good life, that he had never hurt anybody, and that to die would be easy. Quite easy, like falling asleep."

Well, what is that? A pious story from a Salvation Army weekly? No, a novel by one of the most popular Soviet writers on World War II. Vasilyev calls his book a novel (*roman*). We would probably rather speak of a collection of character stories held together by a few people living at the same time and place. Its unobtrusive quietness and lack of wartime drama as compared with his earlier books puts it into an entirely different category of literature. It amazes me and speaks well for the Russian reader's loyalty that people, when naming Vasilyev as one of their favorite authors, mentioned the *Swans* in the same breath as his war novels.

So much for the readers. But what might be the view of those—and, of course, they too exist—who think not primarily of entertainment and literature but of political aspects when looking at books? I have already mentioned that one is hard put to find something even remotely connected with the official ideology of the party. Ecology, of course, is well and good and maybe quite acceptable to the Kremlin though, as we know in the West, very expensive.

And what about Yegor, the semisaint? Well, he teaches a lesson useful in the eyes of political leaders: fulfill your duty (in this case, that of a forest warden) without a thought for your life and limb and go, if need be, unarmed against a bunch of drunkards who have guns and knives because that's your duty. That is okay, but we have seen how personally Yegor views his duties. His real master is nobody except his own and very private conscience.

Ivan Antonovich Yefremov

Yefremov's first and last major triumphs will be summarized, and then we will take a brief look at some of his other books.

The Andromeda Nebula initiated the second Soviet science fiction wave; the first one mainly included Alexey Tolstoy's *Aëlita* and Belyayev's *Amphibian Man*. Yefremov the scientist does not simply give free reign to his imagination but is motivated by the desire to project our present scientific knowledge into the future.

The earth's population at the time he has in view—around A.D. 2500—is politically united and has coalesced into one big nation. Hence the crew members of the spaceship *Tantra*, the main theater of events, are not defined by their national origin. They are still humans, though almost perfect ones, of sterling character and great beauty. Their love is lofty and almost Victorian. Nisa, the dark-auburn-haired navigator of *Tantra*, has been with Erg, the spaceship's commander, for five years before she dares to touch his hand, and, for all we know, she is still a virgin when both return from space after a total of thirteen years. Yet when Erg sets out on a new journey that will last 84 years, she follows him once more, hoping to bear him a son on board who might navigate the ship back to earth. The author describes women's bodies and their relations to men quite freely for Soviet literature of that era though never in an explicit way.

Only one person's background is even briefly discussed: Darr Veter, the retiring director of the Outer Stations, mentions his Russian background a few times and his respect for the Russians as the "people who took the first steps toward building the new social order and toward the conquest of the cosmos."

If the book had a dedication, it might read: "To mankind's brighter future." Yefremov is an idealist who wants to improve life on earth by turning our present hopes into future realities and by describing them as if they were facts. Only two of the characters in his novel are shown in an unfavorable light, and one is only half-bad and the other mends his evil ways in the end. The author is also a Russian intellectual in the European tradition. His aims for the future are those of many liberals in the West; even his praise of collective leadership does not fundamentally contradict Western democratic ideas. Whom is he criticizing when he emphatically voices his disapproval of some planets suffering from the "arbitrary action of small groups of people, oligarchies, that emerged suddenly and cunningly in the most diverse forms, . . . where the highest achievements of science were used for intimidation, for torture and punishment, for mind reading, and for turning the masses into obedient semi-idiots, ever ready to fulfill the most monstrous orders?" Or when he says that there are limits even where the means to a desirable end are concerned, meaning that one cannot justify every misdeed by saying that it is being done for a good cause?

We cannot ask him. The Western reader is free to think, as some have suggested, that these and similar criticisms are directed solely against the *kapstrany* (Russian word, short for capitalist states). But there is no evidence to support this position apart from the ritual remarks that every Soviet writer has to make if he wants to be published. Rather I think Yefremov wanted to describe the ideal world of the future in a way many, probably most, Russians would like to see it.

A liberal Western writer might have written a story with more or less the same words and visions, the main difference would have been that he would have omitted the word *communist,* which comes up a few times in the course of the book. Yefremov, like many utopian writers before him, chose to project this happy, idyllic life into the future because he could not find it in the society around him. His book was published in 1957, memorable not only because this was the year of the Sputnik but also because of the party leadership's relatively generous attitude toward the arts.

Questioning people a quarter of a century after its publication, I found it somewhat difficult to obtain a clear picture of the reasons behind *Andromeda*'s popularity. However, it seems to me that it provided an answer for the Russians then, and to a lesser degree still does today, similar to the answer the millennium has offered Christians since time immemorial: life may be hard now, but someday, perhaps only in the distant future, we will be in paradise.

Yefremov describes his paradise far more concretely than the Bible describes the Christian paradise. In fact, my main quarrel with this book is the overabundance of semiscientific, futurological glimpses on too many levels. The novel covers not only the thirteen-year-long flight of the *Tantra*, which almost comes to an untimely end when the spaceship runs into an "iron star," but also the archeological discoveries at the bottom of the Mediterranean and in the Gobi, the sounds of new music in the Thirteenth Blue Cosmic Symphony in F-Minor, and the new principles for better schools for the young.

A Western reader might feel that he is getting more scientific information in this work of science fiction than he bargained for; the information takes up so much space in the novel that its characters, who, after all, are still supposed to be human beings, are not very real. (In this respect they resemble the Strugatskys' *Far Rainbow*.) Throughout the novel, the present-day scientist cum future-day idealist prevails over the novelist cum realist.

Yefremov's main interest, he once explained, lies in the periods of great change, and the Alexandrian age was such a period, with its new view of political power, geography, and religion. But he did not live to see his novel dealing with this period, *Thais of Athens*, as a published volume.

His heroine is a historical figure, the beautiful and clever hetaera and the beloved of Ptolemy, Alexander the Great's comrade-in-arms. She participates in the Macedonian's fantastic campaigns and, as Ptolemy's wife, eventually becomes queen of Egypt after Alexander's death. An emancipated woman, a student of philosophers and sages, an initiate to the Orphic cult, and a keen observer of her time, she represents an extraordinary age, embodying what was humanistic and cosmopolitan as a result of her extensive travels. In India, Yefremov even lets her meet a wandering sage from China in order to bring that ancient civilization into the picture. But he also shows Thais as an impulsive and barbaric force by describing how she persuaded Alexander to destroy the glory of Persepolis as an act of revenge for the Persians' earlier attack on Athens.

With extraordinary enthusiasm, Yefremov delved into the history of ancient Greece, and he wrote his book as if he wanted to turn all Russians into experts on that period. Technical details and terms relating to Greek life in antiquity fill the first chapters, and Yefremov also included several pages of information on the Greek calendar, Greek weights and measures, and even various words they used for greeting each other.

At the age of 40, Thais hears of a city of light and brotherhood built by visionary Greeks on the shores of Asia Minor. She rushes there and disappears from sight, as does the mysterious city, that all too early utopia, overrun by wild tribes representing the spirit of that wild time— and of our time too, the author might have wanted to add.

Hardly a writer interested in history has not been tempted to write a book about the great Alexander and his age sooner or later. Yefremov, too, succumbed to that impulse. He wrote in an elevated style not normally used in Soviet novels, with a careful choice of noble words and an obvious delight in his work. The Russians who spoke to me about *Thais* had a happy and romantic gleam in their eyes. I too read the novel with pleasure. After countless books on Soviet villages and World War II battles, it was a welcome change of pace to read something about the age of the great Macedonian by focusing on one of history's famous beauties.

Among his other books that are also always *na rukakh* is *The Great Arc*, a collection of separate stories. The one about ancient Egypt depicts the struggle between power, as personified by the conservative Pharoah, and mind, as embodied in his treasurer, an inquisitive and almost modern man who brings wondrous and exciting information from his travels to distant lands. Another story deals with the confrontation between power and beauty, the latter represented by a young Greek sculptor who turns into the leader of an insurrection.

The four parts of *Razor's Edge* are barely connected and not consecutive. The author lets his imagination and his erudition roam unchecked in all directions, from the present day back to the time of Alexander the Great. Alexander's crown, supposedly lost after his death during an expedition along the southwest coast of Africa, is found by a group of present-day Italians on a pleasure cruise through distant oceans on their yacht. The Italians are mysteriously affected by their find. The book has scenes set in contemporary Russia that are quite lifelike and appealing and others that take place in faraway countries where the characters are not taken from the author's experience.

Western readers, historically more sophisticated, may be less captivated by these somewhat disjointed stories than the Russians who enjoy reading lively and undogmatic descriptions of scenes such as those in a lama monastery in Tibet or of historical episodes such as a medieval witch-hunt. The link between the witch-hunt and the rest of the chapter is somewhat tenuous: in Moscow's Lenin Library, the hero shows his beloved a copy of the *Malleus maleficarum*, the infamous handbook on extorting confessions from supposed witches.

Throughout, Yefremov proclaims the noble message of humanism, decency, love, brotherhood, and compassion that he wishes to bring home to his readers in the form of usually well researched historical parables. He uses the story about the witch-hunt, for example, to castigate the blindness of bigotry in general as well as the oppression of women throughout the ages. Here and there I am somewhat irritated by Yefremov's implication that these values are potentially better attended to in the Soviet Union than anywhere outside the communist orbit. Soviet authors who wish to raise their voices in favor of humanism often adopt this approach. They may even believe in their thesis on the assumption that what is *still* bad in the USSR is potentially better than what is *still* good in the West, an assumption that is called scientific by Communists but that is in my opinion only an unprovable hypothesis.

IV
Conclusions

14
Some Thoughts

So far only the *objective* facts have been reported—the methods I used to learn the names of the most popular writers, the titles of the most favored fiction, the Russians' reaction to their reading, as well as a brief run-down of the authors' lives and of the novels' plots and characters. Now I must plead guilty to basing the concluding part on *subjective* assumptions. Others will reach other conclusions, of course. Quite a few points are likely to have led me, the non-Russian, into misinterpretations; obviously my conclusions are not final and are open to discussion.

The conclusions are based, as are the other parts of this book, only on the 24 most popular authors among Russians today and on 111 of their most popular works. I did not set out to prove anything about the Russians; nor did I pick these authors and novels; they were given to me by the people I questioned. Before I started my search for the most popular Soviet writers, some of the names of the 24 writers did not mean much to me. Although my own list, were I to draw one up now, would include a number of the 24, its composition would be somewhat different, with four men at the top: Aitmatov, Rasputin, Semyonov, and Trifonov.

As I examine the results of my endeavors, I find several surprises. One of the two topics appearing most persistently in the Russians' favorite works of fiction is almost never found on Western best-seller lists, and the other only very rarely: the village and the Second World War. This is strange. The USSR is one of the most industrialized countries in the world; why then is the factory proletariat not the central hero of popular Soviet fiction? And is not the Second World War just as far removed in history for the Russian people as it is for the other nations? Only one of the 24 writers uses Moscow as the scene of action in his novels; for others this city is just the background, many do not even mention it. Siberia, of all places, is instead the locale for a large portion of the prose examined. Science and scientists, the core of the much vaunted "scientific-technical revolution," rarely hold center stage in our novels; we meet them mainly in science fiction.

Villages, Villages, Where Are the Factories?

In many ways the village is better off today than it was before the Revolution. Most villages have a store and electricity, radios and television sets; there are schools in the village, hospitals for man and beast, and libraries and cinemas in the neighborhood; the roads are better, and one has a chance to visit the nearby town and perhaps even Moscow. Yet for decades the Soviet media have railed against young people who abandon the village. Markov, in one of his stories not discussed here, specifically praises a village girl and sets her up as an example for others, for turning her back on the city and going home to her village.

In addition to complaints about those deserting the village, one frequently reads reports about people assigned to villages who are unwilling to go there—teachers, mechanics, doctors, accountants, and other professionals. The American farm in the Midwest rarely belonged to a village; from the start it was something of a kingdom run by one family and admirably suited for modernization. Not so the Russian village that, until a few decades ago, was still medieval. Modernization has made it neither fish nor fowl: side by side are hoes and tractors, huts and apartment houses, perhaps even factories; compared to the old village, it is usually a restless and strenuous place to live, with most of the ablebodied gone or commuting.

From all this it seems safe to assume that it cannot be the reality of today's village that attracts the readers, that on the contrary many of them dislike it, and that, as a rule, they prefer almost any other place of work to the village. Then why this desire to read novels and to see movies depicting village life?

I suggest several explanations. The first is the most obvious. Few among the present urban adult population had grandparents who lived in the city; most are first- or second-generation "immigrants" from the village who had—and many still have—difficulties in adjusting to the pace of town and factory and who are still torn between the city's alluring conveniences and its harsh and enervating demands. (According to Soviet statistics, in 1917, the year of the Revolution, the ratio of village to town dwellers was 82 to 18; in 1981 only 24 percent of the Soviet population was engaged in agricultural work.) As a result, even those who for several decades lived in a town or a factory settlement may still harbor in their hearts the lingering dream of the ancestral village amidst birches and fields, of the quiet peace of mind they once had—or now think they had—in the shadow of its simple, well-known church, even though to many city dwellers the cross is today less a symbol of organized orthodoxy than of the comfort religion offers in general.

Every reader of classical Russian literature is familiar with the great importance of the dacha, the house in the country, where city families spent their vacations. Summers were eagerly awaited and greatly enjoyed although life in the dacha was about as primitive as that of the neighboring peasants, with smoking kerosene lamps and water drawn from the village well. To have a dacha, to spend the summer in the bosom (*lono*) of nature is to this day considered the best of all possible vacations. Consequently, even the traditional city dweller surrounded by the tension and hectic pace of his urban life has a warm feeling when he thinks of the country.

Nostalgia, then, for the hard but simple life of the peasant of yore is, so it seems to me, the main attraction of village prose. Were one to ask its admirers whether they wanted to go back to the old village with its poverty and illiteracy, tough landlords, lack of electricity and all other facilities, and aching backs caused by stoop labor in the field, they would, of course, furiously deny it; this aspect of the old days is not what engenders nostalgia. Rather it is the romantic image of the village as a refuge offering stability, an unhurried pace, and security, the dream of a closely knit, loving, and dependable family with babushka and *dedushka* around the samovar, father working in the fields or in the barn, mother spinning or tending the cow and the tomato patch, children playing in the birch copse along the clean brook in summer or on the ice of the village pond in winter, summer evenings filled with accordion music, flirtations, laughter, and songs, with Easter and other church holidays forming the happily celebrated high points of the year. This may not quite have been the real village, but it is the village as it appears today in the imagination of many Russians and in my own memory, that of a German boy in the Russia of pre–World War I.

The reader will have noticed that none of the village novels discussed in this book takes place in the rich Black Earth region in the south, with its endless and much more easily modernized farmlands, nor in the vast cotton plantations of Central Asia. What the authors usually describe are the non–Black Earth areas in northern Russia or Siberia, with their relatively small farmlands and big forests, regions that are much more difficult to modernize. In fact, I have heard Russians say that these areas should no longer be cultivated but should be turned into vast recreation areas or national parks. Because of their climate and geography, not even immense investments could convert them into modern high-yield agricultural regions.

People have an inborn desire to identify with something (that much we certainly learned in the sixties from Erik H. Erikson). Unquestionably, Russians identify with the collectives they work in and the various circles to which they belong (sports, theater and chess groups, and literary clubs). But millions of Russians still find it easier to identify with the village they came from (or, for that matter, with the Moscow Kremlin and the city of Peter, the two capitals of what had once been essentially a rural Russia) than with the miles of prefabricated apartment blocks in the cities or the smokestacks of the highly eulogized giants of industry. Like many people in the West, the Russians have begun to feel that human values are being sacrificed on the altar of progress, that modern cities are by no means better than the old-fashioned villages, that, in fact, preindustrial life possessed many advantages. Progress, it now appears, is harmful to nature. Ecology came late to Russia, but this movement can now be felt there, and the "back to nature" it propounds also means "back to the village" and even "back to Siberia." Belov, one of the 24 and a leading village author, wrote recently: "Our technical forces are now so great that within some three or four years we can destroy or severely damage what nature created in billions of years. There obviously is a limit to man's global interference with nature."

In the twenties and thirties, novels about the village dealt in an orthodox way with collectivization, dekulakization, mechanization, and other changes. But that kind of literature had run its course when the war started and other topics took over. A new phase of village prose began with a writer not presented in this study, Valentin Ovechkin, who, in 1952, published a series of stories with the rather nondescript title *Rayonnye budni* (Every Day in a County, or perhaps better: in the country). Bravely he criticized the agricultural policy, an act for which he was severely castigated. But he had broken the ice, and soon a new type of village literature emerged; the early Abramov took up the cause.

But today's most popular village authors are less reformers, like Ovechkin, than chroniclers. Men like Rasputin or Shukshin take the structure of Soviet agriculture for granted and describe how people live and act within this framework. Neither they nor their readers, so it seems, want to hear about the mode of payment for rural work, the system of grain deliveries, the joys of driving a tractor, and similar issues of organization. These concerns took up much space in earlier village novels but are rarely and only marginally mentioned now. Nor do the writers appear to be particularly interested in the question of how collectivized agriculture functions. Not even the issue of the inability of today's highly mechanized village to feed the Soviet population is being raised. (Instead, Western sovietologists discuss it furiously.) What primarily concerns both writers and readers are the personal interrelationships, the human aspects of the village.

Part of the beloved old village flavor is its language. For a nation raised on the prose of political declarations, reading the traditional peasant language produces an almost physical delight; so rich and colorful are its sound, syntax, and texture. One can hardly call it a dialect because that term suggests a local, if not a tribal, version of the national tongue, such as the dialects of Saxony or Bavaria in Germany. Apart from some local shadings, the Russian peasant language is similar from Smolensk to the Pacific. The narrative portion of these village stories is, of course, written in normal literary Russian, but the conversations often employ the old speech, which is a joy to read, especially if presented by masters such as Belov and Rasputin. If written in a literary tongue, Lipatov's *Gray Mouse*, for example, would be nothing but the story of a painful and abhorrent drunken orgy. But it becomes bearable without losing its impact because it elicits laughter through its wonderful, strong, and colorful, though not indecent, dialogues in a vocabulary not to be found in normal dictionaries. In the West our leading writers are usually city-bred intellectuals who frequently have no direct contact with rural life. This kind of hillbilly talk, as one might characterize it, can seldom be found in Western works of fiction, and, indeed about the only variations from standard American English are some traces of black slang or occasional eruptions of a vogueish short-lived idiom such as that of the New Left in the late sixties or of the California "valley girls" in 1982.

The love of village novels contrasts sharply with the lack of interest in novels about industry. The absence, in the prose discussed here, of what was called the production or industrial novel in the twenties and thirties is the second surprising result of this study. To be sure, books and stories of this kind are being published, but they were never included among the readers' favorites; in the most popular novels, factories are either not mentioned at all or only in passing. They may be "near the village," or they may appear as places that lure the labor force away from the kolkhoz or as one of several backgrounds for one of the heroes' personal problems. Not once do they assume center stage, however. Not a single book among the 111 favorites deals with life and work in a factory. This seems to be a topic that the more popular and established writers do not wish to touch upon for more than a few pages—not even those who have had some experience in factory work. (The theater is a different story. Plays about industry are frequently shown on Soviet stages. To check the degree of their popularity would require a special investigation, however.)

None of the founding fathers of Marxism ever lived and worked in a village. (Mao Tse-tung did, but was he really a Marxist?) Ever since Communists equated human progress with industrialization, the proletariat of the factories was to accomplish the revolution; the proletarians of the world were to unite as mankind's vanguard. In the twenties and thirties, novels extolled the romance of industrialization; the ironworks of Magnitogorsk or the Gorky automobile plant were some of the shining symbols. The village was only described in its process of heroic transformation from the old and backward individual ways to modern collective forms. The new collectivized village had to produce grain, meat, and milk like a factory, while the differences between it and the city were to disappear in favor of the city, the sooner the better.

That sounded fine, but it did not work for people with a stubborn peasant mentality. The endless stream of decrees and resolutions issued since the collectivization in the late twenties and the frequently disappointing harvests—notwithstanding the new machinery worth billions and billions of rubles that poured into the countryside—indicate that something was—and still is—wrong with Soviet agriculture. Yet, the village is one of the favorite fictional topics in Russia today.

How long will this trend last? Fond as I am of village literature, I venture to guess that it will run its course in the next few years. It has made its nostalgic point, rescued time-honored values, pointed out the limits to the exploitation of nature. The total number of people living in villages is decreasing; the most important and soon to be the most numerous group of people in the USSR are neither the villagers nor the factory workers but a middle layer of society that has already found one outstanding author, as will be suggested in the section "The Capital"; others of similar rank must follow sooner or later. On the basis of the most popular novels by our 24 writers, however, my impression is that many leading Russian fiction writers and their readers are more interested in the village than in the city, surprising as this may seem.

And Still the War

Only a minority of today's Russians have personal memories of the Second World War. The tremendous battle of Stalingrad that turned the tide in favor of the Soviet Union took place 40 years ago, and soon four decades will have passed since the war ended in Europe and in the Pacific. Yet the World War II novel still holds a surprisingly powerful attraction for Russian readers. This third surprise is especially striking in view of the rapid disappearance of this literary genre in the West.

Among the most popular Soviet authors, five have made their name with war stories (Bondarev, Bykau, Chakovsky, Simonov, and Vasilyev). Eight others gave the war much space in their works, some by describing its effects on the home front (Abramov, Aitmatov, Dumbadze, Ivanov, Pikul, Proskurin, Rasputin, and Semyonov).

Their interest in and near obsession with the war is understandable. These writers belong to the "war generation," except Abramov, Chakovsky, and Simonov, all were born after 1924. They experienced the war at their most impressionable age, either as young men at the front or as children and teenagers at the home front. Even Astafyev, whose main concern was with the problems of youth in Siberia, once called the war "the biggest event in the life of the people of my generation. . . . For me the war is a holy subject." It certainly is also a very patriotic subject and hence close to the heart of men who love their fatherland. For the authors, then, writing about the war is a natural outlet for their feelings and memories—mostly sad and horrible memories.

What is surprising is the extraordinary fascination war novels have for readers, including the young ones. Nobody forces people to read them; moreover, the books are very hard to find, and the endless repetition of the war theme in poetry, novels, and sketches published in the vast array of Soviet periodicals might have, one could think, rather the effect of overfeeding than of appetizing.

Before trying to understand this contradiction, we might remind ourselves what the war novels depict. In one way or other they cover the five different aspects the war had for the Russians. First, they recount the terrible defeats, retreats, and encirclements of 1941 and 1942 when the Germans moved to the gates of Leningrad, Moscow, and Stalingrad, and even to the summits of the Caucasus Mountains; it speaks well of the writers as well as of the readers of Russia that they do not close their eyes to these depressing events. Second, they portray the tragedy of the occupied areas including the guerrilla war behind the German lines, a dark and gruesome theme well suited for dramatic narration. Third, captivity in German camps is described, often in connection with attempted or successful escapes. Fourth, the main theme of course, they depict the powerful counteroffensive that led to final victory. And fifth, they describe the fate of people in the unoccupied territories.

The writers who worked as war correspondents at the front had some access to higher military echelons, but those who actually served in the armed forces were in junior positions. Hence in their books the emphasis is on soldiers and junior officers, on fighting and dying in the trenches and the mud. Contrary to novels appearing during the war and early postwar years, those most popular now are much more likely to reveal the sordid, the terrible, the painful side of the war. There is heroism, of course, for without it there can be no war, but more of the heartbreaking than of the grand opera type.

Nations have traditionally had "hurrah" war literature that described battles mainly as heroic and romantic encounters. But among the war novels singled out as their favorites by the Russians I talked to, not a single one shows war as pleasurably adventurous, not one could inspire a young man to wish for war. I would go so far as to say that the books summarized here are more antiwar books than war books; the horrors of war far outweigh the glamorous aspects.

The moment I discovered how amazingly popular war literature was even among women, I began asking everybody for the reason. Many at first seemed not to comprehend why this question was worth asking; their own fascination with this genre seemed so natural that they had apparently never examined it. After their initial surprise subsided, most people came up with autobiographic reasons ("My father was killed in action." "My husband has never been heard from again." . . .). Others explained that books about war were the most exciting kind of literature that, though a product of the author's imagination, was based on events that had actually occurred in one's own or one's parents' lifetime and that one should know something about this great episode in the country's history. The more sophisticated pointed out that war puts people in extreme situations and hence allows insight into a person's soul, be he a peasant in an occupied village, a guerrilla fighter, a prisoner of war, a soldier in a tank, or a nurse in a field hospital. Quite a few who were raised on Tolstoy's *War and Peace* mentioned that their love for this classic novel brought them closer to modern war literature. Some of my Russian friends also maintain that the readers' preoccupation with war novels is due to the clear and unambiguous ethical norms found there.

I accept all these explanations. Yet they are not sufficient, particularly if one compares the Russians with the other nations who participated in the war yet show scant interest in war stories. Not all of them, to be sure, were hit by the war in the same way. For the British and the Americans, World War II was an expeditionary and a naval war; their homelands and civilian populations remained unscathed save for the bombs on England and on Pearl Harbor. The nations allied with Germany—the Italians, Rumanians, Bulgarians, and Hungarians—fought only willy-nilly and suffered far fewer losses in a war that was not theirs. Sooner or later, they switched sides and ended up allied with the victors, blurring their image of the war. Finally, the countries overrun by the German blitzkrieg fought very briefly, a few weeks at the most, except in Tito's Yugoslavia; what followed was underground resistance or collaboration, not war. The neutrals were not touched directly at all, and the Chinese essentially fought a civil war.

Thus the Soviets, the Germans, and the Japanese fully battled and suffered through the Second World War, experiencing, though in different sequences, tremendous defeats and victories as well as terrible destruction; they form a group by themselves. Leaving aside Japan with whose literary scene I am insufficiently familiar, this leaves the USSR and Germany.

In complete contrast to the USSR, the Germans do not wish to be reminded of the war in their literature, not only because they lost it (defeat in World War I did not prevent them from producing a vast war literature during the twenties and thirties), but mainly because the Second World War has for them, in addition to its military side, a most horrible moral aspect. They have a dreadfully bad conscience, less because of the war as such, than because of the horrors committed by Germans at the behest of a German government. The discovery of these horrors at the end of the war overwhelmed them, and the majority have not been able to free themselves from this sense of moral revulsion to this day. German authors could not write about acts of heroism at the front—although there were sufficient examples—in the face of their knowledge that millions had been gassed at the same time. Apart from the early Böll, Grass, and lately Buchhein (*The Boat*), high-level German writers avoided the war, or, if they touched on it at all, then they did not deal with the fighting as such. This leaves only the Soviet Union.

Apart from the explanations already mentioned that the Russians gave me, there is, I believe, one more reason for the Russians' fascination with war literature. The victory over what had been the most formidable and efficient war machine is the Soviet Union's greatest success story in the eyes of its own people and—perhaps still more important—in the eyes of the world. The Russians are fully aware that whatever they themselves may think about other events in their country, such as the Revolution and Civil War, collectivization of agriculture and "purges," these experiences are judged rather negatively by vast majorities in the West, while Russia's industrialization, urbanization, space exploration, and other accomplishments are likely to be considered consequences of worldwide modernization rather than of the virtues peculiar to Soviet socialism.

That same West, however, was unanimous in acclaiming the tremendous success of the USSR, when, after initial disastrous defeats in World War II, the Russians rallied and, within a little more than two years, marched from Stalingrad to Berlin, won the greatest war in history, and secured an empire stretching almost to the gates of Vienna and Hamburg. That the United States and Great Britain contributed to this result had very little impact on the Russians. True, the Americans sent weapons and food, trucks and jeeps, but the Soviet people felt that this was the least they could do since they postponed their attack on the Germans month after month. In Russian eyes the victory over Hitler, like that over Napoleon, was a Russian victory, a victory in which all Russian virtues were tried and all Russians, including children, played a part, a victory that not even the most grudging Western critic disputes.

Naturally, Soviet literary critics maintain that the victory in the war was won not so much by *Russians* as by *communist* Russians, and nobody will blame them for adopting this line. As for me, after reading the war novels and conversing with Russians, I feel that the Russian soldier in World War II was primarily motivated by patriotism, by his determination to defend Mother Russia against the invaders, not by the desire to spread the glory of state-owned industries and collective farms to other parts of the world. After all, Napoleon led the most modern war machine of his time, yet he was beaten and chased out of Russia by feudal tsarist Russian armies.

True, between 1941 and 1945 many Russian soldiers went into battle with Stalin's name on their lips (not in the war novels singled out by the readers, however). But Stalin/Dzhugashvili, the non-Russian from the distant Caucasian Mountains, had by then become the personification of the Russian fatherland. Nor should it be forgotten that for the Russians this was a defensive war against an enemy who had only recently signed a friendship treaty with their government; who had been daily supplied from or through Soviet territory with many important raw materials; who had launched an unprovoked, treacherous attack and, in addition, soon proved merciless in the treatment of prisoners and occupied territories. It was far easier to whip up patriotic sentiments against Hitler's armies than it had been against Napoleon. In the 24 years between the Revolution and the war, the country had had many harrowing experiences that pitted one Russian against another. Therefore the feeling of unity in a war against a terrible *external* enemy was tremendously uplifting; it was especially so because it was crowned by victory. Hitler's war against the USSR generated among the Russian people a greater identification with the Soviet Union, perhaps also with the Soviet system, than had existed before.

At first, when one Russian after another included war novels among his favorites, I became apprehensive. But as I read them, my misgivings dissipated. These novels do not glorify Soviet intervention abroad, in Czechoslovakia or Afghanistan, for instance; they do not appeal to Russians to be fighters in support of communism in foreign lands. What they do instead is describe the Russians' participation in a war that was clearly defensive and encourage equal bravery in the event of another attack against Mother Russia.

In preparing the index, I was amazed to see how often the word "Germany" appeared compared to "America" or "France," for example. Prior to this study I had not quite realized that the Russian preoccupation with my country was extraordinary. But the reason is easy to understand: with three exceptions (Yefremov and the Brothers Strugatsky and Vainer), all our authors write about the Soviet period during which their land was far more affected by Germany than by any other nation.

As a German I might be permitted one final observation: no country suffered as much at the hands of the Germans as the USSR did in this war. Leading writers' keeping the war alive should, one would assume, contribute to the preservation of the violently anti-German sentiment that existed during the war and the early postwar years. Yet, Germans, the largest contingent of visitors from the West (tourists, businessmen, and students), rarely encounter any unfriendliness. One of the authors who speaks starkly about German atrocities, A. N. Rybakov, was rarely mentioned, the novels by A. M. Adamovich never. Thinking that this was perhaps due to politeness toward me, a German, I asked librarians who confirmed my impression. I am inclined to think that Russian war novels have contributed to calming rather than inflaming anti-German sentiments.

Were I to repeat this study in the 1990s, the result would probably be different; perhaps the war novel would have receded into the background by that time. Some Russians anticipate this, and there are, as the following chapter will show, some indications of a shift in emphasis.

The Capital

Before the Revolution, literature had essentially two locales—the city and the countryside. The latter was largely seen through the eyes of the landlord. Many of the writers were themselves part of the landed gentry, and the city was either the shining new capital in the north, St. Petersburg, or, in second place, its ancient predecessor, Moscow. But, except for Pikul's description of the end of the tsars and

Chakovsky's account of the city's blockade, none of the 111 novels in this book has its main theater of action in Leningrad. The city of Lenin, beloved though it is among Russians, has not taken the place of the city of Peter. Nor has Moscow, the Soviet capital, recovered the position it once held as the pre-Petrine city of the tsars. To be sure, some novels use Moscow as background, describing scenes after Stalin's death, for example. But that is not much.

Although Moscow is not the setting of many of our stories, it is a symbol, perhaps more than St. Petersburg was and even more than Paris is for the more sophisticated Frenchman. Moscow represents the Soviet empire and the communist world movement; it is the place where foreign statesmen arrive daily for talks with Soviet leaders. In the provinces people speak of their capital with awe, a *komandirovka,* an assigned trip to Moscow, is a great honor, a reason for rejoicing, and the walks there are almost pilgrimages. Hundreds of thousands take many unpleasantnesses upon themselves just to live in Moscow, and close to a million people, one is told, come to the city every day to buy what they cannot get in their hometowns or villages. Whenever I went by rail to the provinces, I found the train packed with people carrying two, three, or four bags filled with their purchases. (Russian train carriages are green, hence the joke: "It's green and smells of sausage—what is it?" The answer: "A train from Moscow." Last February it smelled of oranges, which were plentiful in Moscow—and in the trains I used—at that time. Moscow is the publishing center for numerous newspapers and reviews, and *Pravda* carries the capital's message to mountain towns and Pacific ports within hours. This list of reasons for Moscow's importance could easily be prolonged for another page or two. Thus there is a glaring contrast between its role in the life of the people and its role in our novels.

Before the First World War there were less than 2 million Muscovites; now there are officially 8.4 million, in reality close to 10 million if those living there without a permit are included. Thus the capital is largely a city of "immigrants" who are only beginning to acquire an intimate attachment to their place of residence. They are Muscovites all right, but with rather shallow roots in the capital's soil.

Being a *stary Moskvich* myself, an "old Muscovite" born in that city though of German ancestry, I can "smell" Moscow in the works of only 3 of the 24, Bondarev, Nagibin, and Trifonov, and it so happens that each one writes of some part of the city that is also dear to me. In his *Choice* Bondarev lovingly tells about *Zamoskvorechye,* the quarter "behind the Moskva River" where I spent my childhood. Nagibin, Moscow-born himself, has dozens of stories in which he draws on memories from his childhood around *Chistyye Prudy* (Clear Ponds) where I used to go skating with my parents and we used to visit their friends; to him these byways are not just a backdrop, a prop for his narratives; the backyards of this district and the stories he tells melt into one. And of course there is Trifonov. He too was born in Moscow, but the city he portrays is very different from the innocence and sparkle of the Clear Ponds. His novels are somber and tell of tragic events.

Trifonov's outstanding Moscow novel is *The House on the Embankment*. I have already pointed out the connection between this house and my own family's home and factory. But the main reason for the high value I attach to this novel is the masterly blending on its pages of decades of the city's dramatic and traumatic history. To a lesser degree, this can also be said of Trifonov's other books.

Moscow could have been praised as mankind's beacon toward a glorious future, the center of the world's proletariat, the capital of the great leaders Lenin, Stalin, and Brezhnev, the city with Red Square and the Lenin Mausoleum, the Mecca for all good Communists on earth, the home of Russia's largest library and greatest university. Trifonov, however, describes it quite differently, as the city of cold hearts (*Exchange*) and of a tired widow with her city-wise teenage daughter (*The Other Life*), as the home of a long-forgotten Civil War hero (*Starik*), as a painful abode for a frustrated and unsuccessful employee (*Preliminary Balance Sheet*), the sinister scene of humiliations and purges (*Embankment*).

And who are the people we meet in the streets of Moscow today? They mainly belong to one of two groups: the middle class, as I would call it, and the intelligentsia. The first group consists predominantly of the constantly growing army of employees, or rather civil servants since everything is of the state—trade, industry, administration, transportation, health, education, and so on. This section of the population is gingerly dealt with by sociologists because Karl Marx expected it to disappear soon. Marxist ideologues first denounced this group as having "small proprietary instincts" and as being "backward" and "petit bourgeois." In reality the middle class has become, next to the party, the leading element in the country. The intelligentsia, really a segment of the middle class, is mostly composed of professionals (such as teachers and physicians), scholars, students, and artists, including writers. True "workers from the workbench" rarely appear, as we have seen earlier. In other words, the few among our authors who write about Moscow describe the milieu they know best, and that is neither the proletariat nor the political leadership. Apparently their milieu is also the one the readers in Moscow might want to read more about because it is most familiar to them. This is fine as far as it goes. But the fact remains that the capital interests our Soviet writers only marginally.

The German nation today has no capital. Nevertheless we have novels about Berlin, and an Englishman even wrote a book about Bonn, the town the Germans call their federal village (Le Carré, *A Little Town in Germany*). American literati can choose between two capitals for their novels, Washington and New York, plus a number of regional centers such as San Francisco. And they avail themselves of this opportunity all the time. Moscow is a very important place, not only for those who were born there, but also for others who moved to the capital sometime during their life. For people in other parts of the country a visit to the metropolis is a tremendous event. Why then is Moscow, as rich in history and as picturesque as any large city, neglected by its country's top writers? Why do Russians not insist on reading about it? Here I am at a loss for an answer.

Certainly, old Muscovites grieve about the cruel architectural wounds that have changed their city. (One sure way to start a conversation in Moscow, I found, was to show some old photos taken by my grandfather around the turn of the century; they always elicited many "ahs" and "ohs" and "How beautiful that was!" as well as much eager discussion, surprisingly even with younger people, about what had replaced the buildings shown in the pictures.) But sorrow over the destruction of many beautiful sites cannot be the main explanation.

What amazes me is that the warmth I personally still feel towards the city of my childhood (I would surely choose it as the setting for a novel were I a writer of fiction) is absent in the Russians' most favorite contemporary literature. What a difference from the spirit demonstrated by Aleksandr Pushkin some 160 years ago in his epic *Eugene Onegin* when he described what his heroine Tatyana saw along Tverskaya (now Gorky) Street on her first ride into Moscow (trans. Oliver Elton [London, 1943]):

> Watchboxes, children at their play,
> Convent and palace, lamp and sleigh,
> Bukharian, merchant, Cossack, peasant;
> Huts, drugstores, boulevards, and towers,
> And gardens both for fruit and flowers;
> Shops, telling what's the mode at present;
> Balconies, lions topping gates;
> And dawns, on every cross, in spates.

Not one of the 24 authors, many of whom live in Moscow, has shown the love for that city once expressed by the gentleman from St. Petersburg in his *Onegin* lines:

> How oft in grief, from thee long parted
> Throughout my vagrant destiny,
> Moscow, what thoughts in each true-hearted
> Russian come flooding at that word!
> How deep an echo there is heard!

Most strangely the warmth withheld from the capital is lavishly accorded to a—for Western readers—most unlikely part of the country, to Siberia, of all places.

Siberia, Of All Places

Six of the 24 authors were born in Siberia or the Soviet Far East: Astafyev, Ivanov, Lipatov, Markov, Rasputin, and Shukshin. Abramov can be added, I think, as number seven because his life and work, especially the four-volume family chronicle, *The Pryaslins*, are intimately linked with the Russian Far North where the climate and the conditions of life and work are similar to those in Siberia. Of the *epopeya*s described in this book, five take place in Siberia, and one in the Far North, unless the scene shifts temporarily to the battlefront of World War II. Some of the finest of our 111 works are about Siberia—novellas by Rasputin and short stories by Astafyev and Shukshin. Lipatov, not my own favorite but very much read by the Russians, has set his major novels in Siberia. One might add that Proskurin, not a born Siberian, lived in the Soviet Far East at the start of his career as a writer and had his first book published in Khabarovsk.

So much for the amazing quantitative side. Certainly nobody could have predicted such an outpouring from Siberia a few decades ago. Now for the qualitative question: Is there anything Siberian in the work of these writers? My answer is a definite yes. Their books are as Siberian as Trifonov's are Muscovite. In the first place, the nature they describe is typically Siberian: the taiga, the endless primeval forest of Siberia with its giant trees in the south, the low-growing birches and bushes further north, the mossy tundra in the Arctic region with vast areas of permafrost that turn into swamps with myriads of mosquitoes in summer because the water cannot drain off through the frozen layers. The winters are inhospitably cold, down to 60 degrees below zero Fahrenheit or even lower. (I have personally experienced 55 degrees below zero.) The hardships and inconveniences this season entails around Moscow or Leningrad are child's play compared to a Siberian winter.

And now for the people, the *Sibiryaki*. As a result of the climatic conditions they are, on the whole, even tougher than the Russians in the European part of the country and also more independent-minded. History, in addition to nature, has shaped them, and Siberia's history has been a curious mixture of freedom and captivity. Ever since the first freedom-loving Cossack mercenaries moved across the Urals in 1581, Siberia has had the lure of a land of the free for many Russians, a place to which they could escape when their lives in European Russia, especially as serfs of the landed gentry, became unbearable.

But while serving as a place of refuge, Siberia was also one of exile for the disturbers of law and order, for the enemies of the tsars. These were by no means just the dregs of society; they often came from high nobility. Among the exiles were the men who, after returning from the wars against Napoleon with their minds full of the ideas of the French Revolution, tried to bring, in 1825, a constitution to Russia and a liberal monarch to her throne, as well as patriotic Poles who opposed Russian rule over their country in the rebellions of 1830 and 1863. Reliable statistics are unavailable, but estimates of the number exiled under the tsars run into the hundreds of thousands. Others, often those ill-adjusted at home, made the long trek into the wild and hostile land to find work in the gradually growing manufacturing industry or on the worlds' longest railway—75 hundred kilometers from the Urals to Vladivostok.

After the Revolution, four more waves of newcomers arrived: millions of kulaks with their families during the collectivization of agriculture in the early thirties, millions more during the purges a few years later in the same decade, still more millions in connection with the war (more than a million Germans from the Volga and from other parts of European Russia and all Crimean Tatars who were accused of having sided with the Germans), and finally countless mostly young people who followed the call of the Kremlin leaders, of Khrushchev especially, to go east in order to sow the southern Siberian prairies with grain, to build dams, and to mine the natural resources that are among the richest in the world. All in all, Siberia has been the land of the restless and the bold.

Because the language is the same, though with some local variations, I do not claim to be able to recognize a Siberian when I meet one, but a *Sibiryak* can often be distinguished by his ways; he is more easygoing, more self-reliant, prouder, and sometimes also somewhat taller. A certain Siberian clannishness can also be observed. Ivanov's *Eternal Call* is essentially an *epopeya* of Siberians. The soldiers whose exploits in the

Second World War he describes with such enthusiasm are all from one village in Siberia: one Siberian kills 100 Germans, two Siberians hold a hillock against masses of Germans, a single Soviet tank manned by an all-Siberian crew destroys twelve German tanks. In the Soviet army of fifteen million the men from this Siberian village run into each other even in the prison camps and, with the exception of one man who joins the enemy and one who collaborates while in German captivity, they perform miraculous feats of valor.

It is quite understandable that Siberians (like Texans or Berliners) love to tell tall tales about their native land. But whence their popularity with the readers from other parts of the Soviet Union? Why do some 235 million Soviet citizens who do not live in Siberia love to read about the roughly 35 million Siberians?

One explanation is probably quite similar to the reason why Russians love village literature: nostalgia for a hard and simple life. Other reasons are possible: Siberia's mineral wealth arouses the nation's imagination. Still largely an untapped treasure trove, its mighty rivers can produce fabulous amounts of power. In its southwestern region, it houses the center of the country's space program. For many Russians, Siberia is the Russia of tomorrow. Finally, one more explanation comes to my mind when I remember the fascination of hundreds of millions of Americans and non-Americans with stories of the Wild West. In Siberia the early Russian settlers also fought and decimated native tribes, but it would be very much against Soviet ideology to show Russians subduing and killing Siberian aborigines, quite apart from the fact that the Siberian Ostyaks or Yakuts, although distant relatives of the American Indians, were a sad sight compared to the proud and colorful Apaches or Navajos, and the Siberian taiga can offer no Grand Canyon and no Monument Valley. Therefore, the excitement of the Siberian conquest is not what attracts Russian readers, nor is it, so it seems to me, the adventure of building dams and railways. Instead the Russians are captivated by the "wide open spaces" of a continent bigger than the U.S. mainland, by the huge forests and the giant rivers, by the grandeur of nature believed to be still unspoiled—the antithesis to the soulless urban civilization. In the new novels about European Russia, the rivers— Neva, Dnepr, and Volga—play no role apart from presenting an obstacle to the enemy in the war, whereas three Siberian rivers are very much a part of several novels: with Lipatov and Markov the Ob, with Ivanov the Yenisey, and with Rasputin the Angara, which almost seems like a living beast as it devours the island of Matyora.

One facet of life in Siberia was never alluded to in the novels: China. Siberia shares a border of thousands of miles with that country, and during the sixties and seventies when so many of the novels were written, the "inscrutably dangerous Chinese" were often on the minds of the Russians. So why was China never mentioned? Was there a hint from above? But what would be the point of this? One might instead expect a hint to the contrary: write about the danger of the Chinese to make the Siberians, to make all Russians, aware of it! One can understand why non-Siberian writers in European Russia are silent about China, but why do Siberian authors avoid China, while the association between Siberia and China so readily comes up in Western minds?

I can only guess. Siberian authors may be so completely absorbed in their Siberian affairs that China never even enters their heads. In their novels they have not written about Siberia's international relations, not even about Siberian politics; their concern has been with Siberians, their lives, and their fates. China seems very far from Siberians' minds. This was confirmed by my visit to Siberia in 1981. The people I met were quite ready to discuss the affairs of the world with me (it was a few weeks after President Ronald Reagan's inauguration), and they were curious about the chancellor of my country at that time, Helmut Schmidt. But they never mentioned China. Siberia is a continent unto itself, though looking more westward to European Russia and Europe, a romantic wilderness busy with its own problems and fascinating to its inhabitants and to Russian readers all over the USSR.

A few words are sufficient for those theaters of action located neither in Siberia nor in European Russia; Dumbadze and Aitmatov have written about them. The local color and atmosphere of the Caucasus has been familiar to Russian readers for at least a century and a half, so Dumbadze has not opened any new vistas. Aitmatov, on the other hand, has done just that. More than any other Soviet writer he has put his native Kirgizia and neighboring Kazakhstan on the Russian literary map. But my impression is that the Russians accord him their high esteem not because he offers exotic tales about faraway countries but because he is a great and venerable writer.

Not many of our 24 authors have lived abroad for any length of time, and only a few use foreign countries as locales for their novels: Semyonov, the most traveled of them, does in his Stirlitz books, Chakovsky in his story of the Potsdam Conference, Bondarev in *Shore* and *Choice*, Pikul in his naval story about Japan. Obviously, our authors' primarily direct their attention toward their own country. Perhaps they feel that the readers' undoubted interest in other countries is satisfied by the many translations of foreign fiction.

Thus, among all the local centers of gravity in the 111 novels, Siberia clearly predominates.

Treating the Past

Repeatedly we have noticed Russian readers' growing interest in contemporary history, as demonstrated by the success Semyonov, Chakovsky, and Pikul enjoy. The Russians' fascination with *epopeya*s points in the same direction; these sagas cover decades of Russian history from the turn of the century to the present day. An unabating preoccupation with a war that ended some 40 years ago and the eagerness to read about recent history are quite understandable: they feel that they have been insufficiently informed and are very curious about what really happened. Hence they devour novels about contemporary history where they find hitherto unknown, exciting stories. For the same reason the memoirs of wartime leaders are eagerly consumed. In general, the Russians' appetite for all kinds of literature about their country's history—not only of the last decades—is remarkable. They seriously desire to know more about the past and thus about themselves, not wanting to be memory-deprived *mankurts* as in Aitmatov's great novel. However, one aspect of Russia's recent past is problematic for Soviet authors: Stalin. How should they treat the roughly three decades between Lenin's and Stalin's death? Here, as elsewhere, I give a strictly personal interpretation based on my discussions with Russians during the last quarter century.

Curiosity about the mysterious man in the Kremlin existed from the beginning. Working in the USSR as a foreign correspondent until early 1936, I could feel this avid interest everywhere, though it was rarely expressed in so many words. There was no news about Stalin's private life, his wife, or his children. Everything was hush-hush, and even speculation was considered inadvisable. The situation remained unchanged for the following twenty years. Even after his death nobody wanted to touch the dangerous topic at first. Khrushchev's courageous "secret speech" of 1956 changed the atmosphere, but a few more years had to pass before Stalin began to be discussed openly. Simonov in some of his war novels and Bondarev in *Silence* were among the pioneers. After that, others followed, and one Soviet critic in his book on the Soviet novel even speaks of a "fashion" (*moda*). "During the last few years more than one novelist tackled the portrayal of the complicated figure of the Supreme Commander. The reader flung himself (*kidalsya*) greedily on books of this kind." Together with some of the writers, the critic preferred to speak of the Supreme Commander (*verkhovny glavnokomanduyushchy*) rather than to use Stalin's name.

Except for Chakovsky's *Victory*, Stalin is never the central figure in our novels. However, in some of them, as we have noticed, two painful questions are touched upon: who was responsible for the complete lack of preparedness in June 1941 and the catastrophic defeats of 1941 and 1942 and who ordered the "liquidation" of the military leaders, including such brilliant men as Tukhachevsky, in the purges of the late thirties? The answer to both is undeniably Stalin—no matter what additional responsibility was born by the Yezhovs and Berias. But the novels that touch on these issues do so only briefly and focus on Stalin as the Supreme Commander and the great diplomat, roles where even foreign critics treat him with respect. This is especially true in Chakovsky's *Victory.* In a few places he mentions what he calls "Stalin's mistakes," but these are mistakes of the prewar period. He also shows him as depressed and even desperate on occasion, but always with the respect due to a great statesman. At Potsdam he stresses Stalin's brilliant maneuvering against Churchill and Truman. The reason for Stalin's success in Chakovsky's view is that "Stalin fought for a cause, the final outcome of which History itself had foreordained." (The author spells history with a capital *H* here.)

About the tragedy of the Warsaw uprising of 1944 that was crushed by German forces because the Soviet army did not support it, Chakovsky writes: "Churchill did not inform the Soviet side about the uprising until after it had started; he was willing to sacrifice thousands of Poles in the (vain) hope that the uprising would be successful and would enable him to form a pro-British government in Poland."

Alas, no Gallup polls in the USSR! This might be a suitable subheading for the following remarks about the Russian readers' reaction to Stalin and to the way he is represented by their most popular authors. I particularly regret the lack of polls in this case because whenever conversations turned to Stalin and the main events of his time, people became less communicative. How do they feel about them?

Industrialization and Five-Year Plans? I think it is safe to say that the vast majority agree that these were necessary and a smaller majority that they were only possible in a system where the government owns the means of production.

Collectivization of agriculture? Here I found far less consent. A majority might still agree that the government had to institute collective farming because it could not have become a world power with millions upon millions of poor peasant plots. (Russians do not deny that American farmers are far more productive than their kolkhozniks, but not much thought is wasted on the reason why on the same acreage one American farmer produces more grain than an entire kolkhoz.) Still, I would venture to guess that a considerable majority condemn the brutal methods used and the cruel treatment meted out to the kulaks, the peasants who were not quite so poor. Even a staunchly communist writer like Ivanov shows his criticism on that score. One must remember that more than half of the adult population has personally experienced the expulsion of the Kulaks in one way or another.

The purges? I never pushed this subject, but it has been raised by a number of the 24 writers. Whenever it did come up in conversations there was at first a painful silence. Everyone was conscious that in the midthirties, and to a far lesser degree in the midforties, something sinister, wicked, and bloody occurred that affected millions of families, including those of a number of the 24 authors, as we have seen. The dreadful consequences persisted until deep into the fifties when the surviving purge victims finally returned home. Not a single Russian ever tried to explain to me that the disappearance of millions of Communists and non-Communists into prisons and forced labor camps was due to a "personality cult," as the official version would have it; to say, "My father was shot because of the personality cult" would sound just plain foolish. If one must speak, it is better to refer to "Stalin's mistakes," as Chakovsky does. Authors who have more to say, mainly Aitmatov and Trifonov but also Bondarev, are respected for their courage. But in general: the less said the better.

The war? Here the attitude is quite different. Yes, Stalin, although he committed blunders and miscalculated, was a great leader of men and had a good deal to do with the final victory. "He licked you Germans, didn't he?" I sometimes heard this comment spoken in a defiant tone when the conversation turned to Stalin.

Sometimes Westerners say that men like Chakovsky propagandize the Russians into having a more positive view of Stalin than they had in the late fifties and early sixties after Stalin had been denounced by Khrushchev and removed from the mausoleum on Red Square.

Maybe this is true. But I feel certain that with time the image of Stalin would have become less tarnished than it appeared in those years in any case. The most enduring memory of the last decades is, after all, still the war. The fathers and husbands of millions of Russians dies in battle with Stalin's name on their lips. To think that he was a sinister tyrant, as Khrushchev described him in 1956, would be unbearable to most Russians. Hence the inclination is to see him in a more positive light. I even found this to hold true for people who themselves or whose fathers suffered in the purges.

While those people whom one might call liberals for want of a better word continue to react nervously to any signs of his revival, the majority of the "men and women in the street," if I am not very much mistaken, see him approximately as Chakovsky does. Stalin has been integrated into Russian history.

The People

Four hundred people in a single Soviet novel—this was one Soviet critic's final tabulation! None of the books discussed here has quite that many, but in all more than one thousand move through our 111 novels and stories; Proskurin's *Thy Name* alone has 126. This avalanche of characters in the most popular novels in itself proves that the Russians like reading about people. But then, who does not? One of the most popular magazines in the United States is *People*, and nobody understands the enormous significance of a human interest story better than authors and journalists in the West.

What stands out most clearly in one's mind as one thinks back on the thousands of pages written by our 24 authors? Obviously each reader will have a different answer. What I remember most vividly are some of the unforgettable characters who crowd the pages, probably because they are so different from what one would expect in communist litera-ture: Rasputin's dying old peasant woman, the deserter and his young wife, Maria's husband who is forced to borrow one thousand rubles; Semyonov's Stirlitz, of course, the intrepid, serious spy so unlike James Bond; Abramov's Pryaslins; Aitmatov's master of the fine horse Gulsary and the Kazakh railway worker, Yedigey; Nagibin's little girl collecting echoes; the cancer-ridden woman in Trifonov's *Exchange* with her son and daughter-in-law; Vasilyev's lover of swans; and many, many more.

The short stories alone, of which only a small, though representa-tive, fraction could be presented here, show the contemporary Russian in infinite generational, professional, and emotional attitudes. The vari-ety of people in these novels is extraordinary and especially striking if compared to the rather meager assortment of acceptable types in the novels written some 40 or 50 years ago. On the whole, however, I find them a somber lot. Because we in the West think that the Russians lead a hard life full of privations, we are inclined to assume that they would like to relax with novels filled with happy, smiling, confident people. The Russians find some of these characters in books of the Dumas type, but rarely in their favorite Soviet literature. Most of the ingredients in best-sellers the world over are missing in these 111 novels—carefree romances, exotic voyages, glamorous adventures, glorious sex, successful careers, and happy endings. Instead we find the opposite: the majority of the novels' personages lead difficult lives and fight nerve-racking battles within their own souls. Many Soviet novels have no happy ending; some do not even allow a glimpse of "the light at the end of the tunnel."

Thinking back to what Russians told me when I questioned them, I find that they were attracted less by the issues at stake, by the actual fighting in the war, for example, or by the functioning of the kolkhoz, than by the way the characters in the novels grapple and cope with these issues. They are not averse to reading about happy-go-lucky chaps like the three musketeers. But because of their own experiences in life, they feel drawn toward characters with problems even when reading for relaxation. The readiness to commiserate is an old tradition among Russians. The West, on the whole, tends to be more practical when it comes to dealing with suffering; take, for example, the countless excellent methods employed in the United States for helping the handicapped: ramps, special buses and parking areas, and even special toilets. I have seen nothing like this in the USSR.

The Russians, in turn, have something that is rare in the West; a sense that suffering has something mystical and even venerable connected with it, perhaps left over from the days when it was said that suffering came from God. The babushkas of today's readers were brought up on the stories of people who were holy because they were martyrs, and their grandchildren may have inherited their affinity with the *neschastnye,* the unfortunates, the insulted and the injured, as Dostoyevsky called them in one of his great novels. The unlucky ones, Trifonov said, are the ones who question the world and themselves more deeply. As one elderly Russian whom I met in Siberia told me: "I have had a hard life, and I enjoy reading about people who had it tough, too."

Russians in general have a harder life than we do. What do they find in their favorite literature when they look at it with the eyes of people who desire consolation that goes beyond what official materialist philosophy can give? They encounter a powerful stream of humanism in the works of their favorite writers, a word I am using here in its original sense of humane (as opposed to inhumane, not as opposed to religion), a humanism that expresses, as Aitmatov does, deep concern with the drift in the modern world toward an increasingly rootless and hence soulless civilization, a tendency that many of our writers try to divert by pointing to the intangible soul and by invoking the power of conscience that is far more than a function of political ideology, by appealing to morality, to history's lessons, and especially to the wisdom of their ancestors. This wisdom includes traces of Christian, pre-Christian, and even Moslem traditions; it includes quotations from the Old and New Testaments; saintly fools protected, as of yore, by some unseen force; visions of the

"Mother of God" who is said to have left a mark on an atheist soldier's tunic and even of Christ. None of this is emphasized; it is unobtrusive, and perhaps quite unintentional. But it is there.

The Authorities

This study deals with readers and authors. However, wherever I spoke on this subject, invariably the question was raised: "What about censorship?" So I shall say a few words on the relationship between authors and authorities—insofar as our 24 authors are concerned. They are, compared to the other ten thousand members of the Writers' Union, a tiny minority. What I say about them cannot be generalized and may even be not entirely accurate. For a person who, during more than half a century, has dealt only with noncommunist private publishers, it is quite difficult to understand the intricacies of publishing in a state economy. It seems to me that, for our 24, this is how it works. The first and unofficial censor the author faces is the editor of the review or publishing house where he submits his manuscript. He may accept recommendations for alterations right there. Then the manuscript is typeset. Once the galley proofs have been corrected by author and editor, they go to the official censor. He represents Glavlit, the Chief Administration for the Protection of State Secrets attached to the Council of Ministers of the USSR, and has, as far as I know, an office right in the publishing house. It is his job to ensure that the book does not divulge any state secrets and that it stays within accepted political limits. If serious disagreements arise between him and the editor or author, the case may go to higher levels, in some cases, as we have seen, to the Central Committee of the Communist Party. Once Glavlit has given its okay, the book or article goes through the last phases of the printing and publishing process.

I take it for granted that differences of opinion exist among those in authority; there must be personal sympathies for and antipathies against a given author as well as political disagreements. To be published a writer must not necessarily describe the Soviet Union in glowing colors (hardly one of the 24 does this); it is enough if they depict it as strongly established, as solid and powerful, as worth defending. This is what the authors of war novels do. Much of what they have written may not be to the liking of the authorities: they do not show all Soviet soldiers as paragons of military virtues free of all human weaknesses, nor the war as mainly glorious, nor the USSR as a wonderful place to live; the heroes in their novels shine less because of their newly acquired so-called socialist virtues than because of the sturdiness they displayed in many ancient battles against invaders from east and west. Critical writers are much forgiven and are even awarded State Prizes because they extol courage, discipline, the will to fight and, if necessary, to die, in short, because they are patriots.

The village writers too are forgiven much of their pessimism because they describe traditional Russian values and character traits, endurance and austerity among them, perhaps also because, by portraying the bucolic and pastoral side of country life, they counteract the continuing flight of the rural population to the overcrowded centers of population. Finally, writers of high literary quality with a strong following in the country and abroad can be valuable in themselves in the eyes of the authorities, even if they are, as Trifonov was, not optimistic in their portrayal of people and realities in the USSR.

"Okay," said one of the 24 writers to me, "you can speak of censorship in the USSR if you want to. But few of us are bothered by it. On the other hand, look at the Russian writers who emigrated to the West. They wrote far better books while they lived in the USSR although now they can write and publish whatever they please."

One way to examine the relationship between authorities and authors is to look at the literary prizes. There are many of them; the three especially prestigious ones are the Lenin Prize, the State Prize of the USSR, and the Gorky Prize. During the years from 1957 through 1978, 73 Lenin Prizes were awarded in literature, 7 percent of these went to some of the 24: Aitmatov, 1963; Bondarev, 1972; Simonov, 1974; Markov and Shukshin, 1976; Chakovsky, 1978. Ten of the State Prizes of the USSR were received by 9 of our authors: Aitmatov, 1968 and 1977; Bykau, 1974; Abramov and Vasilyev, 1975; Bondarev and Rasputin, 1977; Astafyev, 1978; Proskurin, 1979; Belov, 1981. The Gorky Prize was awarded to Proskurin in 1974, to Astafyev in 1975, and to Soloukhin in 1979. This means that a little over half of our authors received one or more of these three prizes. Aitmatov, a great but certainly critical writer, was awarded three; Trifonov, equally great and critical, none since his very first novel, *Students*. Other notable omissions include Nagibin, Pikul, and the two pairs of brothers, Strugatsky and Vainer. The amount of cash that accompanies a prize varies. For the Lenin Prize it was set at ten thousand rubles in 1966. More important for the bearer, however, is that being a recipient of an award increases his chances of obtaining the paper needed for large print runs.

As I mentioned earlier, I never inquired about authors whose works are not available in Soviet libraries. Such questions would have caused unnecessary embarrassment without helping me in my specific study.

Only one person, a journalist in his early fifties, volunteered the name of a writer living in the West today, Vasily Aksyonov. "It's a pity he left," the man said. "I liked reading his novels. We are about the same age, and I was quite taken with his *Zvyozdny bilet* (Ticket to the Stars) when it came out some twenty years ago. He should have stayed. I miss his youthful and cheeky slang."

Each reader of this book must judge the 24 authors and their works for himself. As for me, I do not believe that the only good Soviet writers are dissident writers. Obviously, writers in the USSR have to observe more rules than those in America or Germany. Most authors, and certainly our 24, have established a modus vivendi with the authorities. They know the rules of the game and the limits of the playing field. But unlike the limits in physics—the temperature at which water freezes and boils, for example—the outer limits in Soviet literature are not always the same. They may differ from year to year, from leader to leader, from editor to editor. Moreover, the nuances of party resolutions on literature may change.

One of the latest dicta, "On Creative Connections Between the Journals of Literature and the Arts and the Practice of Communist Construction," was issued by the Central Committee of the Communist Party last summer and reported in *Literaturnaya gazeta* on August 4, 1982. After praising the work of the journals and of the writers' organizations, the party admonished them both to pay more attention to portraying the "positive hero," which means a hero motivated by communist ideology, in order to "influence the behavior of the people." Some—unnamed—journals were reprimanded for publishing manuscripts in which "events in the history of the fatherland, of the socialist revolution, of collectivization are portrayed with serious deviations from the real truth." The resolution also attacks their occasional "confusion in matters of Weltanschauung (*mirovozreniye*)." Things must be seen "from clear class positions." Literature "should develop themes connected with the party's course . . . and consider the changes directed toward more intensive work in economy" and those "in the village's work and life," should "do away with an apolitical attitude and consumer psychology" and should "produce works with a patriotic resonance" that call "in poetic form for service to the fatherland and to the party, to the belief in the righteousness of our cause." What this involuted language demands from the writer is the education of the working people in a spirit of preparedness for the defense of the Soviet People's revolutionary achievements, as well as the struggle for the triumph of Marxism-Leninism and aggressive polemics directed against the ideological enemy.

Clearly these postulates are not being enforced at present; not many of the works discussed would fit into this rigid mold. But the resolution exists, as do many earlier ones of a similar nature. They have not been published for nothing. But they have not been invoked. Will they? Nobody knows, neither the writers, nor the authorities. This depends on many unforeseeable events.

The term *socialist realism* appears in one place in the party resolution. This is a loaded term. At the start of my investigation, I occasionally asked the people I interviewed whether they considered their favorite novels works of socialist realism. Their vague answers showed that they had not given much thought to this problem, that in fact they had not even perceived it to be an issue. This is quite a change in only a few decades.

In August 1934 in my capacity as a foreign correspondent, I attended the first Soviet Writers' Congress in Moscow. It was there that the term *socialist realism,* or *sotsrealizm* for short, was firmly established; it was approvingly mentioned by the meeting's grand old man, Maxim Gorky, and was also included in the first statute of the Writers' Union. "By concretely portraying reality in its revolutionary development" the Soviet writer serves "to transform and educate the toilers in the spirit of socialism."

What this awkward formula meant soon became clear: the author's duty was to describe as realistically as possible what did not exist, at least, not yet, namely a socialist society. Every novel, poem, or play written during the following twenty years was scrutinized from this one point of view: did it accord with the dogma of *sotsrealizm?* Even Aleksandr Fadeyev had to rewrite the novel *Molodaya gvardiya* (The Young Guard, 1945) for which he had already been awarded the Stalin Prize when the party found this book wanting.

Most Soviet novels of that period were insignificant as far as literature was concerned, even though impressive in their revolutionary fire, such as Nikolay Ostrovsky's *Kaz zakalyalas stal* (How the Steel Was Tempered). Its very title evokes images of furnaces, iron, and concrete. These novels were casually mentioned without much enthusiasm in response to my questions, perhaps as memories from school and Komsomol days. Even Semyon Babyevsky and Boris Polevoy, two authors belonging to the tradition of *sotsrealizm* whose works have recently, in 1976 and 1977, appeared in *Roman gazeta* with 1.6 million copies each, were not mentioned once. People apparently do not cherish this kind of novel anymore.

On the basis of my interpretation of *sotsrealizm*, only about half a dozen of our 111 works of fiction resemble the books praised under this heading in the thirties and forties. In the writings of Soviet critics I have lately found other terms such as *strogyi realizm* (severe realism) or *realisticheskaya obyektivnost* (realistic objectivity), the latter being used in connection with Rasputin's work for which it is not a bad description. Personally I prefer simply the word "realism" because it best encompasses what they have written and also because they all stress their debt to the great realist writers of the nineteenth century in Russia and the West. Most of these authors avoided discussing the political system of their day; they took it for granted and dealt primarily with human questions, observing and describing with a keen and critical eye. This is also what most of the 24 do. That they speak so much of life as it really is, of human weaknesses, of disillusionments, of harassments, of cooled feelings, of frustrations is in itself an expression of criticism. The term "critical realism" has been suggested; but does not any realistic writing imply some criticism?

The authorities can tolerate this implicit criticism because it is almost exclusively expressed in moral, humanitarian, compassionate terms and does not endanger the system. By speaking of people's individual concerns while taking the system for granted and leaving it alone, the writers do not encourage their readers to think about social change.

The prevalent Western belief that the USSR is a monolith, a rock without cracks, is incorrect, as is the notion that authors with large print runs, with television series made from their novels, secretarial positions in the Writers' Union, and literary prizes are necessarily all darlings of the authorities. Things are more complicated than that. Many differences of opinion prevail—from what to do about Poland to how many copies of which novels to publish.

There is one more question to be asked regarding the authorities: What is their role in our 111 novels?

Party authorities of all levels, from Stalin down to the local leaders, appear in these novels, but with few exceptions they come and go without holding the center of the stage. A reader without preconceptions, and I have tried to take the books at face value and to avoid reading into them, would rarely get the impression that he is reading about one of the most tightly controlled countries.

The many war novels describe hundreds of officers and soldiers, and the difference between those who are members of the party (or the Komsomol) and those who are not is hardly noticeable. Real party functionaries are few and far between. The role they play in the war novels is usually less significant than that of the officers; the exception is Sintsov in Simonov's *The Living and the Dead*. They are not superior to them, except perhaps in rank. In Bondarev's *Hot Snow*, the deputy commander for political affairs is more of a nuisance than a help to the military commander. During the war, the Russian writers—soldiers and young officers themselves—had to deal with other soldiers and officers more frequently than with *politruk*s. In these novels I did not find a single figure comparable to the heroine of V. Vishnevsky's *Optimisticheskaya tragediya* (Optimistic Tragedy, 1932), that iron bolshevik commissar in the Revolution's early stage, who molds a bunch of anarchistic sailors into a death-defying unit of the Red Army.

In most of the shorter stories describing civilian life, no party functionary makes an appearance; the party is not even mentioned as a rule, and when it is, the reference is casual. In the *epopeya*s there are, of course, party functionaries among the many people portrayed. In Ivanov's *Eternal Call* they play a more prominent role, partly because he starts with some prerevolutionary underground Bolsheviks whose lives he then follows through several decades, but even they supply only a fraction of the cast. Still, Ivanov, more than his colleagues, has a tendency to depict the party people as a special breed of heroes. In *Thy Name* Proskurin has a highly placed VIP, the head of a province, as one of the major figures, but he too is an ordinary human being and is even deserted by his wife. Ordinary humans with their virtues and failings are also the people in that other line of authority, the administration.

All in all, the leaders, the *nachalniki*, are just members of the cast, not an elite group off by themselves as they were in so many novels of the twenties and thirties. They are no longer placed on a pedestal as shining examples for all to see.

Of Love and Sex

Since the modern novel emerged, love has been its dominant feature. With some national and cultural variations, this is true almost everywhere. But in the novels described in the foregoing chapters, love, though important, is only one of various aspects of life, not the primary one.

After a brief postrevolutionary spell of "free love" as an expression of the libertarian streak in early communism, Soviet literature passed through a period when a man was expected to love his rifle or tractor more than his woman, and the woman to love her schoolchildren or the kolkhoz cows more than her man. This attitude, which to the West seemed very strange indeed, has ingrained itself to the extent that many of us are inclined to believe that love is still taboo in Soviet literature. But this is not true, as we have seen. Human love is back, though in a rather moderate way compared to the West. The grand, the irrational, the overwhelming passion is rarely shown, except in Nagibin's *Patience* and perhaps in Bondarev's *Shore*. Generally, love is temperate and soon leads to marriage and family. Marriages bring problems that are described; sometimes they also entail extramarital temptations, most of which, however, are overcome. No very big deal.

Most classic literature takes sex for granted but does not elaborate much less describe it. Even discussion of the female anatomy in literature was unusual until recently. Around the turn of the century, you could find practically nothing sexy in public libraries or on the bookstore's shelves and would have needed quite some time to locate the juicy passages in the ten volumes of Casanova's memoirs. If you wanted to simplify matters, you had to look for pornographic books, which, in those days, were as difficult to obtain as cocaine. The word *sex*, which indeed sounds like a pistol shot, was itself considered lewd, and its use was unknown in polite society. Its common use in public and the lurid descriptions of positions and sensations are phenomena of the last decades, of the period since World War II. I was a grown man before sex turned up in best-selling novels and at family dinner tables.

In the presentation of sex, Soviet literature is about where Western literature was in the years before World War II, perhaps I should say before World War I. That sex exists is not denied in the fiction presented here: children are conceived and born, some out of wedlock; spouses are deserted for others who are more attractive; young couples disappear into the hayloft; there are occasional grabs for a woman's breast. What we do not find is a description of the mechanics of sex.

The first sex manuals have made a hesitant appearance in the USSR (you will ask in vain in bookshops for them), and some stories in a few magazines are slightly explicit. But even these passages are primly innocent, I find, compared to what some Western best-selling writers offer their public to help them overcome their "fear of flying." Though now largely taken for granted in the West, what was classified as sexual perversion until some decades ago is never mentioned or even alluded to in the 111 novels.

It is difficult to determine whether the modest role of love and the practical absence of sex in Soviet literature is the result of directives from above or whether this delicacy reflects the natural character of the writers. Their attitude may be similar to that of serious Western authors prior to the sexual revolution: they lustily enjoyed sex for themselves but did not consider it necessary (or advisable) to describe it play-by-play in their novels.

But what about the readers? Prurient thoughts and the desire to see them expressed in writing or in pictures have existed in humans since time immemorial. There is no reason to assume that the Russians are different. In fact, I have observed Russian tourists abroad excitedly perusing sex magazines in the newsstands of Western cities. The difference between them and us is that such newsstands do not exist in the USSR and that such magazines or books are not available there, not even under the table. My impression, however, is that for most Russians their Victorian novels and monotone newsstands appear far more normal than our "adult shops," exciting though these may be.

With time, this too may change. Last year, *Literaturnaya gazeta* published the result of an opinion poll in Soviet Estonia (i.e., in a westernized part of the USSR where attitudes do not necessarily coincide with those of the Russians). This survey revealed a surprisingly permissive attitude toward sex between people who are not married; women were even more tolerant than men (see Table 6). To sum up: Whatever interest Russians may have in reading sexy stories remains unsatisfied by their native literature.

Love for people one cares about is as important for Russians as for anyone else. Yet not one of the people I questioned about their reading habits ever indicated that too little emphasis was given to love in their favorite novels. Human behavior and expectations are partly shaped by habit, and Russian readers have become accustomed to the low-key, even tepid, treatment of love their contemporary writers offer. Western readers on the other hand, brought up on a different fare, often find Soviet novels boring because of the absence of a powerful and intriguing love angle.

One consequence of the small role love plays in the contemporary Soviet novel is, I am convinced, the strong attraction Russians feel for their classics. Whatever may be lacking in romance on today's literary

Table 6

Opinion on Sex Between Unmarried People in Estonia (in percent)

	Women	*Men*
Quite natural	29	13
Permissible	43	48
Not very desirable	19	32
To be condemned	9	6

SOURCE: *Literaturnaya gazeta*, March 28, 1982.

menu can be found in abundance in the works of their beloved nine-teenth-century authors, who wrote some of the finest love stories in world literature.

On Women and Children

The readers of this book, especially the female readers among them, have certainly noticed that not one of the 24 authors has paid special attention to women or in any way catered to them as potential readers in the novels discussed. In view of repeated official and unofficial pronouncements on the equality of sexes, this may be less of a surprise than some others mentioned so far. Still it is worth a few minutes of thought.

Naturally, I tried to question men and women in about equal numbers. But I ended up interviewing a few more women, probably because they were more willing to be patient with me and to take the time to fill out my questionnaire and respond to my queries. This gave me a chance to ask about their views on women in fiction.

If we exclude war stories with their predominantly male casts, the remaining novels' characters are about evenly divided between the two sexes; the men have only a slight edge. Russian society, on the other hand, is still quite patriarchal, in the cities as well as in the villages. Any Soviet-watcher knows that many Soviet women have three jobs in addition to their profession: shopping (a most time-consuming and unpleasant chore), housekeeping, and child care. For obvious reasons, defenders of the Soviet system like to attribute Russian women's strength to their liberation by the Revolution. It would be ridiculous to dispute the influence the changes in society have had on women. It is impressive that a number of women, many of humble origins, hold leading positions, especially in the cultural sphere but also in economics (not at the top of the party, however). But the strong-willed and single-minded woman with a generous heart, an iron will, and courageous perseverance in the face of innumerable odds is not a new image. The young wife of the deserter in Rasputin's *Live and Remember* stands in the long line of heroines in Russian literature who are beloved by Russian women and men: Pushkin's Tatyana, Tolstoy's Anna, Turgenev's Asya, and Ostrovsky's Katerina (*The Storm*) are all cut from a harder metal than their male partners. And the old peasant woman in Rasputin's *Period of Grace*, who dies in simple but majestic dignity, towering high above her half-modern offspring, has her roots deep in prerevolutionary Russia.

Whether Russian women subconsciously crave novels written especially for them, I cannot tell. I found no indications of such a desire, but this could be due to my failing to ask the right questions. At any rate they can, on the whole, be quite satisfied with the way male authors portray them.

Though few of our stories are built around women (Belov's *My Life* and Trifonov's *Other Life* are exceptions), children are the heroes of many stories and novellas by Aitmatov, Astafyev, Dumbadze, and Nagibin. Two observations come to mind concerning their content. First, practically all these stories are autobiographical, even where this is not expressly stated. Second, the authors see childhood in a positive light although their own youth was a trying time for all of them. Growing up in the USSR in the twenties, thirties, and forties was not easy.

In my first book about the Soviet Union, *Youth in Soviet Russia* (1933), I described some of the stories about young Russians that were often read there at that time. One of the best known, N. Bogdanov's *The First Girl* (in the Komsomol) expressed what could be said of most of them: they were intensely political, full of childrens' and teenagers' heroic deeds during the Revolution, Civil War, collectivization, and First Five-Year Plan. What was destined to become the novel most widely read abroad appeared only some years later: Anton Makarenko's *Putyovka v zhizn* (Road to Life), published and filmed in the thirties (English edition, 1955). It is a book about the socialization of homeless and criminal children based on his own experience as their educator in a youth commune. The word *socialization* has a double meaning here: winning young people for society and for socialism. Makarenko's message was one of high hopes: the virtues of socialism can help turn young criminals into useful members of society.

Since then, the spirit of stories about children, educators, and parents has changed a great deal. None of the books written by the four authors mentioned above can be called propagandistic by any stretch of the imagination. Consider Astafyev's *Theft*; it tells of homeless children, including criminals, but his hero, a former tsarist officer as the reader may remember, tries to win the children's hearts through a maximum of personal love and a minimum of political indoctrination, although there is no denying that political slogans can be powerful didactic instruments. There is nothing didactic in Astafyev's other stories either; it is babushka's love that puts the young lover of gingerbread on the right road. The same can be said of numerous stories by Dumbadze; indeed babushka even appears in the title of his most beloved collection. And Nagibin's children are just that and certainly cannot be considered products of an ideology.

For the authors writing about youth and adolescence in the twenties and thirties, childhood was mainly a preparation for class struggle and socialist labor later on. But our authors describe childhood as a special phase of human development, they are inclined to show it not as something contaminated and in need of cleansing but rather as the bud of a flower that needs watching and tending, not bending and pulling by force. In the books of the twenties and thirties the family barely existed. The structure of the family was actually disintegrating and was, in addition, said to be backward, a danger to socialist progress and due to disappear, just like the private ownership of the means of production to which the family was supposedly closely tied.

This is no longer so. Instead of viewing the family as a barrier along the road to the glorious future society and as a remnant of prerevolutionary society just as prisons and taxes supposedly are, the family is now considered a blessing. Since the war, which tore apart and mutilated so many Soviet families, the complete family of three generations is believed to be the ideal social unit; children should have two parents and both pairs of grandparents. This perfect extended family cannot be found very often in real life, but this does not keep it from being the ideal.

A few words will suffice to explain why the Russians enjoy reading books about children. People everywhere have always liked children; they are some of the most charming and consistently heartwarming literary characters.

I did not inquire about books *for* children; this is certainly an important subject but quite different from the one I pursued. Nor did I question children about their favorite books. However, when I did talk to young Russians from about age seventeen onward, they did not add new names to my emerging list. Within that list, though, they professed a greater interest than their seniors in detective stories and science fiction, the two literary genres to be considered next.

Crime and Entertainment

During the first half of 1956 I worked for West German radio in Moscow. The great event then was, of course, Khrushchev's "secret speech" in which he denounced Stalin, but there were also many other newsworthy developments. For example, several times while buying papers at newsstands, I heard people ask for the latest issue of *Yunost* and saw their disappointed expressions when the saleswomen, whose faces were wrapped to protect them from the frosty air leaving only eyes and red nose visible, mumbled an irrefutable *nyet* through their shawls. Finally, I asked one, who was working in the newsstand of a hotel lobby and was therefore warmer in body and spirit, why people were so keen on that new issue.

"How come you don't know about it? They all want to read the latest installment of *Delo pyostrykh* (The Case of the Many-Colored [Gang]). I tell you, it's terrible exciting."

It took me quite some time to get a Russian friend to loan me his copies with all the installments. "Just for 24 hours—many are waiting for it." And many had read it before, to judge from the soiled look of the magazines. I found the story (by Arkady Adamov) only mildly exciting, but then it was the first Soviet detective novel published in this widely read journal for youth. Until the early fifties, detective stories were considered objectionable. They were "formed in the depth of bourgeois society with the detective serving as a defender of private property," according to the 1935 definition of the literary critic S. Dinamov. In 1952 the *Great Soviet Encyclopedia* still scorned the detectives' successes as "triumphs of bourgeois law." But in the encyclopedia's 1972 edition things looked different. Under the heading "Detective Literature" appears a rather neutral account. This genre deals "with the solution of enigmatic crimes, usually through a logical analysis of the facts." Le Carré and James Bond are even mentioned; the latter is characterized as "extolling toughness and sex," which is not far off the mark.

Now detective stories have a firm and popular place in Soviet literature. But they have had to undergo considerable changes from their Western counterparts. From the start their authors faced the problem of how crime can exist in the supposedly near-perfect Soviet society. In socialism there ought to be no crime at all since private property (apart from the proverbial toothbrush) has been abolished and with it supposedly the source of criminal activity. Crime still existed during the first years after the Revolution as a remnant of the capitalist bourgeois society, so it was said. But with capitalism gone for decades, there should be no basis left for evil doings. To be sure, there were imperialist spies and fascist agents who could be blamed, but they began to bore the audience. So the authors introduced other explanations, not without being criticized at first. They discovered that the children of the new leading bureaucrats, a kind of Red *jeunesse dorée*, were corrupted by their dolce vita; the formula was now frequently: "Dad is guilty, not society." Additional explanations were advanced and gradually accepted by the wary critics: love, envy, greed.

Foreign detective stories have been introduced in growing numbers; the yearbook *Zarubezhny detektiv* (Foreign Detective Stories) has a print run of 200 thousand copies. But, as the grand old man of Russian detective fiction, the author of *The Case of the Many-Colored*, recently complained, there is still no Soviet Sherlock Holmes or Maigret. He attributes this deplorable fact to the collective character of most detective work in the USSR where the idea of a star detective seems odd. But this thesis is unconvincing because he himself created Losev, and the Vainers invented Tikhonov.

As an occasional reader of Western and Russian detective stories I find that most of the popular authors in the West (with Chesterton and his smart but virtuous Father Brown as the most noticeable exception) write their stories without any pedagogical purpose apart from showing, by the detective's victory over the criminal, that "crime does not pay." Most of their fans (like myself) read these books for relaxation through enjoyable tension. Maybe the Soviet author would like to write in that vein, too, but his heroes must walk on educational cothurni, must explicitly contribute toward fighting crime. In itself I find this attitude good, even admirable; we could use some of this spirit in our Western whodunits that far too often follow the line: "perhaps crime doesn't pay but it's lots of fun." However, enjoyable tension for entertainment's sake does not combine well with educational moralizing. Arthur Conan Doyle's and Agatha Christie's stories were almost mathematical in character; from the start the reader knew that he could solve for the X in the mystery equation if he only followed the detective's logical reasoning. From the Soviet point of view this amoral attitude is quite irresponsible. But ever since I discussed *The Case of the Many-Colored* with Russian friends 27 years ago, my impression has been that Russian readers, just like those in the West, are more interested in the excitement of the story than in its moral message.

During a discussion of detective stories, one Soviet writer told me that he did not think much of the world-famous British variety—of Agatha Christie, for example—because they were just thrillers without any social message. I agreed that there is not much revolutionary zeal in the souls of the great British sleuths; their intent is not to change society but to fight crime, and they move quite happily among dukes and parsons, blue-blooded aunts and faithful butlers.

The moral rigor of detective fiction in the USSR has decreased, but it has not disappeared. Crimes are committed against society or against the state rather than against a British lord or a French storekeeper. As for spies (called "scouts" in the Soviet Union), they are courageous and devoted patriots, but then so are those in the West. Even 007, who usually does everything for the heck of it, appears as a patriot on occasion.

One cannot exclude the possibility that after reading about Stirlitz's exploits some young Russians will be still more confirmed in their patriotism and that others, under the spell of the Losevs and Tikhonovs, will leave the path of crime, which is not likely to happen to Western readers of Sherlock Holmes or Sam Spade, not to mention their sex-and-crime brethren. That the latters' lurid products are not printed in the USSR is, in my eyes, one of the rare advantages of a nonprofit, state-run publishing business.

Western mystery writers are not deadly serious from beginning to end. Part of Agatha Christie's charm is the delightful humor of her whimsical and lovable characters. Miss Marple and Hercule Poirot reveal their self-critical humility in almost every word they utter, in every gesture they make. And they like to laugh about themselves. No such frivolity pervades the Soviet detective world, nor is there any of the pleasant repartee between the simple but cunning country policemen and the much too sophisticated specialists from Scotland Yard.

It is quite true, however, that Russian writers do more. The Vainers bring in Ariadne's labyrinth and the ancient sixteenth-century physician Paracelsus, and Semyonov has an appealing way of humanizing his detectives by endowing them with families, children, and problems with their wives. Seven years is a critical time in marriage, muses one of Semyonov's detectives while on the criminal's trail. His has, as yet, only survived three, yet he is already asking, "What has happened? Why is she like this today?" While he is mulling over these thoughts, his wife is starching his shirt in the kitchen; she too is thinking: "He and I live together, yet I am a stranger to him. . . . Why live under the same roof then?" In the end, of course, their relationship gets straightened out, and the criminal and his gang are caught.

In the same novel, Semyonov brings up controversial subjects outside the purely criminal sphere. A seventeen-year-old schoolboy gets into trouble because he drinks, and he drinks because his parents hate each other. An old teacher has problems because his two sons, officers in the Soviet army, were shot for no apparent reason in connection with the Tukhachevsky purge in the thirties. Semyonov also uses his stories to speak out on sensitive issues. He knows, for example, that juvenile delinquency cannot be cured by prison terms only. One of his detectives has thoughts like these:

> Is a restaurant a Soviet institution or is it not? If you're going to regard a restaurant as a den of iniquity, wouldn't it be better in that case to get rid of them altogether? It's ridiculous. And there are lots of other ridiculous things here—trivial in themselves but extremely irritating. What can a young courting couple do on a Saturday? In summer it's all right. You can go to the park or

simply stroll about Moscow; . . . it brings you closer together. But what about winter? Why don't they build more dance halls and inexpensive cafes with small bands? Why not let cafes stay open at night not just till eleven but till one or two in the morning? If a chap's working on the second shift at a factory, why shouldn't he be allowed to take his girl to a cafe at eleven? . . . Young people in Poland or Czechoslovakia, for example, could dance gaily, sit in tiny cafes and drink wine or strong coffee and talk about what was dear and comprehensible to them. But what about our lads? They also wanted to spend their evenings the way people did in the Polish and Czech films. . . . Hypocrisy got into us. All we think about is whether this will distract our youth from what is most important. It won't distract them at all. [From Julian Semenov, *Petrovka 38* (London, 1965).]

One may safely venture the guess that the appeal of the mystery story has not yet reached its apex in the USSR. One can also assume that among those who have the last word about what will and what will not be published there must be some who think that reading such books is a terrible waste of time and that people should do some socially significant work instead. But so far they have been steadily retreating before the avalanche of detective novels. Others around their table probably soothe their apprehensions by saying: "The people must have some entertainment and recreation so let them read detective stories as long as these retain their law-and-order character. Watching football is a most horribly unproductive waste of time, too. But did I not see you, the other day, dear comrade, when Dynamo played Spartak?"

Adult Fairy Tales

There must be millions of science fiction fans around the world. I am not one of them, and it is highly unlikely that I would ever have read any Russian science fiction had not two authors appeared on my "most popular" list, Yefremov and the Strugatskys. I became aware of the existence of science fiction literature in the USSR years ago when one of my Russian friends married a girl named Aelita and informed me that this was the name of the heroine in Russia's first science fiction novel. Written in 1923 by Alexey Tolstoy (a relative of the great Tolstoy), *Aëlita* describes a revolution on the planet Mars. In the West at that time another Russian book became far more famous, Yevgeny Zamyatin's *My* (We, 1924). It was never published in the USSR, however, because this pre-Orwellian negative utopia was considered anti-Soviet.

The Russians' interest in science fiction received a powerful boost in the second half of the fifties in connection with the first Sputnik. Science fiction books and journals appeared in growing numbers, and two series were introduced specializing in science fiction. A yearbook called *Fantastika* began publication as well. Foreign authors were popular from the beginning.

Yefremov's *Andromeda Nebula* (1958) was the leader of this new wave. Published in countless editions, it is still very popular and probably the main reason why its author was invariably mentioned by the people I interviewed. The brightest name among present-day science fiction authors is that of the Brothers Strugatsky. Although their stories were published in relatively small editions, some in obscure literary reviews (such as *Baikal* and *Angara*), and one exclusively in the West (*The Ugly Swans*), they were mentioned as frequently as Yefremov. The English-language monthly *Soviet Literature*, published by the Writers' Union of the USSR, devoted an entire issue in January 1982 to Soviet science fiction; it includes nine brief stories, one by the Brothers Strugatsky, and a number of pertinent articles.

Interest in science fiction is universal today; in many bookshops in the United States, special shelves are marked SF. So there probably was no need to ask Russian enthusiasts why they like this genre. But I did, and the answers were more or less what they might have been in any country. Some said quite naively: "Because they are exciting." Others had more substantial reasons. One young man, a student of modern history, told me on a sunny bench near Moscow University: "We are all keen on technology and terribly curious about where it is taking us. New things are discovered and invented all the time. We know how rapidly everything is changing. Village literature is all very well, but soon there will be nothing left of this old-fashioned life-style. We want to look into the future. Some say science fiction consists of nothing but crazy guesses, of pure fantasy. But it is more than that, just look at Jules Verne: he wrote when science was still in its infancy, yet how much of what he described has come true! There is every reason to assume that what the Strugatskys write today will be reality before we know it. Some of it may be crazy, but much is based on solid facts. That's why we call this kind of literature *nauchnaya fantastika* (scientific fantasy)."

Although no one mentioned it, there might be another reason why Russians enjoy reading science fiction. The Brothers Strugatsky and some of their colleagues do more than just fantasize about the future of technology; they also contemplate the future of mankind in a sociological and even a philosophical sense as do indeed some of their Western colleagues. Take, for example, the Strugatsky's *More Than One Billion Years to the End of the World*. The book's literary value may not be very great (let others quarrel about that), and I did not find it very captivating because the characters and their dialogues sound artificial and the events seem all too improbable. But the problems raised and the very uncertainties of the ending stimulate the reader into thinking about our earth and its future.

One should assume that writers from a country that claims to be headed toward a happy and secure future would describe it so. But this is not what the brothers do. They see totalitarian dangers—and not just those of the fascist type—lurking innately within human nature and the nature of technology. Their utopias are on the whole pessimistic, and their inhabitants are skeptical, which explains the lack of official enthusiasm for their writings.

And yet, I do not believe that the Russians love this genre only for its probing and even critical sociological messages, but instead that they read science fiction books for more or less the same reasons people in the West do: they want to be carried into an exciting dream world of limitless dimensions where everything imaginable can happen. In a way, science fiction novels are fairy tales for adults in the technological age. Even Soviet critics write about "Old fairy tales and the most recent *fantastika*" (this is the title of an article in *Voprosy literatury* [Questions of Literature], 1977:1).

The Russians have a special term for this age of ours: *NTR,* from their words for scientific-technical revolution. For many years, NTR has been the constantly repeated slogan and the motivation for schools and colleges. It has no doubt contributed to the very advanced level of Soviet science. Why then does NTR play such a negligible role in the other fiction discussed? Apart from the two chemists in *Minotaur* and the two historians in Bondarev's *Relatives* (not summarized here), scientists rarely turn up as characters in the novels. They appear, for example, in Proskurin's two-volume novel, but only as peripheral personages, while artists hold the center of the stage in his *Black Birds* and in Bondarev's *Choice*. Certainly there is no "class reason" to avoid scientists in these novels. Since the witch-hunts of scientists suspected of all types of crimes, including hostility toward Stalin's favorite biologist, Lysenko, and of the Kremlin doctors who supposedly tried to poison Stalin, there have been no large-scale campaigns against scientists, at least not against scholars in the field of the natural sciences. On the contrary, scientists are the people most highly valued by the Kremlin and are among the best paid Soviet citizens. The narrow interpretation of *trud* (work, toil), originally used mainly to refer to manual labor, has long ago been extended to include any work considered valuable for the state and society. In *Sovietsky roman* (Soviet Novel, 1980), Mikhail M. Kuznetsov focuses on the role of *trud* in Soviet fiction; there is hardly anything he does not include under this heading, even counterintelligence is *trud*.

Writers are much more likely to rub shoulders with scientists, especially doctors, than with peasants or detectives. The infrequency of their appearance as heroes in Soviet fiction is even more surprising than the absence of factory workers. An entirely new genre in literature has developed. Why do we meet scientists working on distant stars in science fiction books yet rarely in their exciting modern laboratories in other novels? The science fiction fans had no explanation, and I cannot even hazard a guess at an answer.

15
Final Remarks

In these conclusions I have mentioned various surprises to be found in the literature the Russians like best. One might summarize them by saying: first compared to the revolutionary excitement and propagandistic zeal of Soviet writers during the twenties and thirties as well as to the vigorous and often wild experimentation of their modern Western colleagues, our 24 authors, excluding perhaps the Brothers Strugatsky, are conservative, so are their readers, and so was, under Brezhnev, the leadership in the Kremlin. Second, as a rule, with the exception, of course, of the Second World War, they do not treat political subjects in the proper sense of the word—neither U.S. imperialism (save for Semyonov's *TASS*), nor political problems at the top, nor meetings of the Council of Ministers, nor harvest emergencies and production quotas. To be sure, Western best-sellers usually do not do this either. But nobody expects it from them, while we still assume that the literature of the country that proclaims the world revolution must be revolutionary.

As far as our 24 are concerned, it is not. Sixty-five years after the Revolution, the fire of causes burns low. The world revolution that Lenin and his adherents hoped for and promoted so ardently is not even mentioned in the 111 novels and stories, nor do they advocate military expansion. What the leaders in the Kremlin think, I do not know, probably nobody does. I am speaking here about the content of novels that to the best of my knowledge are the most popular with the Russian readers.

Nor do these novels demand political changes within the USSR. Their authors may be critical of existing conditions, but they do not advocate reforms. On the basis of our 24 authors' writings, my personal conclusion is that no fundamental change in the USSR can be expected for quite some time. Those in the West who hope for change in Russia will not like my hypothesis, but they might still give it some thought as one of various probabilities. By disregarding political issues and concentrating on topics that are quite far removed from present-day realities (the old village, the war long over, historical events, mystery stories, and science fiction, for example), the writers teach their readers to accept the system or at least to live within it. People in the West can agree with quite a few of the virtues they stress, though they find them less often expressed in their own modern literature. If anything, the 111 novels may strike Western readers as too virtuous in their Victorian primness. At any rate, they are not likely to make them angry, rather perhaps slightly bored because of their long-windedness. In a number of cases, if the names of people and places were changed, an American reader might not even know that these books were written by members of the Communist Party of the USSR as he expects them to be.

The overwhelmingly strong sentiment among writers and their fans is patriotism. This is even true of many Russian expatriots. Some time ago I heard one of the most prominent of them tell an American audience with his voice raised when challenged to say where he stands: "My body is in America, my soul and mind in Russia." The patriotism of the Russians, who constitute one-half of the Soviet population, is in my mind a factor of world political significance that I take seriously; it is shared by the men in the Kremlin and the people of Russia alike.

In my view, some—not all—of our 24 have as much to say as leading writers in the West. To be sure, they are Soviet writers, but they are great writers and contribute their forceful voices to the chorus of today's world literature.

Appendixes

A
Russian Titles

No years of publication are given in this appendix because most titles are published in a multitude of editions. Very often, the copies I read were those of a later edition and did not mention the year of the first edition. In the text I provide the years of the copies I used. Titles listed in the Catalogue Database of the Research Libraries Information Service Network (RLIN) follow the Catalogue's system of transliteration; other titles follow the Library of Congress system (without diacritics). One hundred eleven books were summarized; the others were only referred to in passing.

Abramov, Fedor Aleksandrovich
 Priasliny (or *Brat'ia i sestry*)
  Brat'ia i sestry
  Dve zimy i tri leta
  Puti Pereput'ia
  Dom
 Sobranie sochinenii
 Vokrug da okolo

Aitmatov, Chingiz
 Belyi parakhod
 Dzhamilia
 I dol'she veka dlitsia den'
 Materinskoe pole
 Proshchai, Gul'sary
 Rannie zhuravli
 Sochineniia

 Soldatenok
 Vozkhozhdenie na Fudzhiyamu

Astaf'ev, Viktor Petrovich
 Karga
 Kon' s rozovoi grivoi
 Krazha
 Net mne otveta
 Pominki
 Poslednii poklon
 Sibirskii polones
 Sobranie sochinenii
 Starodub
 Tsar'-ryba

Belov, Vasilii Ivanovich
 Kanuny
 Lad

Manikiur
Moia zhizn'
Plotnitskie rasskazy
Privychnoe delo
Tseluiutsia zori

Bondarev, Iurii Vasil'evich
Batal'ony prosiat ognia
Bereg
Goriachii sneg
Iunost' komandirov
Poslednie zalpy
Rodstvenniki
Sobranie sochinenii
Tishina
Vybor

Bykau, Vasil Uladzimiravic
Alpiiskaia ballada
Ego batal'on
Obelisk
Sotnikov

Chakovskii, Aleksandr Borisovich
Blokada
Eto bylo v Leningrade
Mirnye dni
Pobeda
Sobranie sochinenii
Svet dalekoi zvezdy
U nas uzhe utro

Dumbadze, Nodar
Belye flagi
Ia, babushka, Illiko i Illarion
Ia vizhu solntse
Solnechnaia noch'
Zakon vechnosti

Efremov, Ivan Antonovich
Lezvie britvy
Sochineniia
Tais afinskaia
Tumannost' Andromedy
Velikaia duga

Ivanov, Anatolii Stepanovich
Alkiny pesni
Sobranie sochinenii
Vechnyi zov
Vrazhda

Lipatov, Vil' Vladimirovich
Derevenskii detektiv
I eto vse o nem
Igor Savvovich
Seraia mysh

Markov, Georgii Mokeevich
Sibir'
Sobranie sochinenii
Strogovy

Nagibin, Iurii Markovich
Chistye prudy
Ekho
Khazarskii ornament
Predsedatel'
Slezai, priekhali
Smert' na vokzale
Sobranie sochinenii
Srochno trebuiutsia sedye volosy
Svet v okne
Terpenie
Trubka

Pikul, Valentin Savvich
Bitva zheleznykh kantslerov
Mal'chiki s bantikami
Moonsund
Perom i shpagoi
Rekviem karavanu PQ 17;
  Dokumentarnaia tragedia
Tri vozrasta Okini-san
U poslednii cherty

Proskurin, Petr Lukich
Chernye ptitsy
Glubokie rany
Imia tvoe
Sud'ba
Taiga

Rasputin, Valentin Grigor'evich
Den'gi dlia Marii
Poslednii srok
Proshchanie s Materoi
Vasilii i Vasilisa
Vstrecha
Zhivi i pomni
Semenov, Iulian Semenovich
Al'ternativa
Bomba dlia predsedatel'ia
Brillianty dlya diktatury
proletariata
Dunechka i Nikita Maior Vikhr
Petrovka 38
Poisk 827
Prikazano vyzhit'
Semnadtsat' mgnovenii vesny
Tass upolnomochen zaiavit'
Tret'ia karta
Shukshin, Vasilii Makarovich
Energichnye liudi
Ia prishel dat' vam voliu
Izbrannye proizvedeniia
Kalina krasnaia
Klassnyi voditel'
Kliauza
Liubaviny
Mikroskop
Mil' pardon, madam
Na kladbishche
Obida
Oratorskii priem
Stepka
Srezal
Veruiu
Simonov, Konstantin Mikhailovich
Dni i nochi
My ne uvidemsia s toboi
Sobranie sochinenii

Tak nazyvaemaia lichnaia zhizn'.
Iz zapisok Lopatina
Zhivye i mertvye
Soloukhin, Vladimir Alekseevich
Aksakovskie mesta
Chernye doski
Izbrannye proizvedeniia
Kaplia rosy
Mat'-matchekha
Pis'ma iz russkogo muzeia
Slavianskaia tetrad'
Vladimirskie proselki
Vremia sobirat' kamni
Strugatskii, Arkadii and Boris
Natanovich
Dalekaia raduga
Piknik na obochine
Vtoroe nashestvie marsian
Za milliard let do kontsa sveta
Trifonov, Iurii Valentinovich
Dom na naberezhnoi
Drugaia zhizn'
Obmen
Otblesk kostra
Predvaritel'nye itogi
Starik
Studenty
Vremia i mesto
Vainer, Arkadii and Georgii
Aleksandrovich
Chasy dlia mistera Kelli
Ia sledovatel'
Lekarstvo dlia Nesmeiany
Oshchupiiu v polden
Vizit k Minotavru
Vasil'ev, Boris L'vovich
A zori zdes' tikhie
Ne streliaite v belykh lebedei
V spiskakh ne znachilsia

B
English-Language Editions

According to the Catalogue Database of the Research Libraries Information Service Network (RLIN) in October 1982 and the catalogues of the Green Library at Stanford University and the Main Library at the University of California, Berkeley, the following 66 titles by the 24 authors discussed in this book are available in English translations in 172 libraries of the United States, including the Library of Congress. Twenty-six of the English titles were published in Moscow, 40 in the United States or the United Kingdom; of the latter, 14 were authored by the Brothers Strugatskii. Apart from them, Aitmatov's books have been most frequently translated.

For further information, English readers should consult the forthcoming updated English version of the excellent encyclopedia of the 495 most important Russian and Soviet authors since 1917 written by my German colleague Wolfgang Kasack and published by Columbia University Press.

Abramov, Fedor Aleksandrovich
  The Dodgers, London, 1963.
  One Day in the "New Life", New York, 1963.
Aitmatov, Chingiz
  The Ascent of Mount Fuji, New York, 1975.
  Farewell Gul'sary!, London, 1970.
  Short Stories, Moscow, n.d.
  Tales of the Mountains and Steppes, Moscow, 1969.

The White Steamship, London, 1972.

Astaf'ev, Viktor Petrovich
  The Horse with the Pink Mane, Moscow, 1970.
  Siberian Polonaise, Moscow, 1970.

Belov, Vasilii Ivanovich
  —

Bondarev, Iurii Vasil'evich
  The Choice, New York, 1983.

The Hot Snow, Moscow, 1971.
The Last Shots, Moscow, 1973(?).
Silence, London, 1965.

Bykau, Vasil Uladzimiravic
The Ordeal, London, 1972.
The Third Flare: Three War Stories, Moscow, 1958(?).

Chakovskii, Aleksandr Borisovich
Light of a Distant Star, Moscow, 1965.
A Year of Life, Moscow, 1958.

Dumbadze, Nodar
A Sunny Night, New York, 1968.

Efremov, Ivan Antonovich
Andromeda, Moscow, 1959.
Land of Foam, Boston, 1959(?).
Stories, Moscow, 1954.

Ivanov, Anatolii Stepanovich
The Eternal Call, Moscow, 1979.

Lipatov, Vil' Vladimirovich
A Village Detective, Moscow, 1970.

Markov, Georgii Mokeevich
Siberia, Moscow, 1972.

Nagibin, Iurii Markovich
Dreams, Short Stories, Moscow, n.d.
Each for All, London, 1945.
Island of Love, Moscow, 1982.
The Peak of Success and Other Stories, Ann Arbor, Michigan, 1983.
The Pipe, Moscow, 1958(?).
Selected Short Stories, New York, 1963.

Pikul, Valentin Savvich
—

Proskurin, Petr Lukich
The Taiga and Other Stories, Moscow, 1974.

Rasputin, Valentin Grigor'evich
Farewell to Matyora, New York, 1979.
Money for Maria, St. Lucia, Qld., ca. 1981.
Live and Remember, New York, 1978.

Semenov, Iulian Semenovich
In the Performance of Duty, Moscow, 1963(?).
Petrovka 38, London, 1965.

Shukshin, Vasilii Makarovich
I Want to Live, Moscow, 1973(?).
Snowball Berry Red and Other Stories, Ann Arbor, Michigan, 1979(?).

Simonov, Konstantin Mikhailovich
Days and Nights, New York, 1945.
Friends and Foes, Moscow, 1951.
The Living and the Dead, Garden City, New York, 1962.
On the Petsamo Road, Moscow, 1942.
Stalingrad Fights On, Moscow, 1942.
Victims and Heroes, London, 1963.

Soloukhin, Vladimir Alekseevich
Searching for Icons in Russia, London, 1971.
Sentenced and Other Stories, Ann Arbor, Michigan, 1983.
A Walk in Rural Russia, New York, 1967.
White Grass, Moscow, 1971.

Strugatskii, Arkadii and Boris Natanovich
Beetle in the Anthill, New York, 1980.
Definitely Maybe, New York, 1978.
Escape Attempt, New York, 1982.
Far Rainbow: The Second Invasion From Mars, New York, 1979.

The Final Circle of Paradise, London, 1976.

Hard to Be a God, New York, 1973.

Monday Begins on Saturday, New York, 1977.

Noon, 22nd Century, New York, 1978.

Prisoners of Power, New York, 1977.

Roadside Picnic, New York, 1977.

Space Apprentice, New York, 1981.

Tale of the Troika, New York, 1977.

The Ugly Swans, New York, 1979.

Trifonov, Iurii Valentinovich

The Impatient Ones, Moscow, 1978.

The Long Goodbye, New York, 1978.

Students, Moscow, 1953.

Vainer, Arkadii and Georgii Aleksandrovich

—

Vasil'ev, Boris L'vovich

Dawns Are Quiet Here, Moscow, 1978.

His Name Was Not Listed, Moscow, 1978.

C
Editions and
Print Runs

In this study, I have repeatedly stressed that to determine the popularity of a Soviet writer it is necessary to question the readers, not the publishers, and to seek out the most wanted rather than the most printed books. If print runs reflected authors' popularity, the late Leonid Brezhnev would have been the readers' favorite by far. Roughly 17 million copies of his *Little Land*, *Rebirth*, and *Virgin Soil* (189 pages altogether in the Russian original) were published and distributed in 1978 and 1979. His work was awarded the Lenin Prize for Literature and, in the words of the Soviet press, was "read, reread, and diligently studied" in every workers' and peasants' collective, even in trawling vessels and mountain hamlets. Yet his name was never included among those of the most popular authors.

Nevertheless, print runs are not entirely without interest. To ascertain our authors', I consulted the best available source, the *Ezhegodnik knigi SSSR* (Yearbook of the Book of the USSR). Published every year in two volumes, this reference work purports to include all books and brochures that appeared during that particular year. The index gives the authors' names and the (scattered) current numbers under which their publications are listed. I cannot vouch for the completeness of the entries; in some volumes pages were misbound or numbers in the index inaccurate.

Not included in the following figures are the millions of copies printed by *Roman gazeta* (some indication of our authors' presence in that publication was given in Chapter 3, "The Road to the Top") or in literary reviews. If these had been added, the totals would be two or three times higher. For example, the total number of available copies of Iulian Semenov's nine most successful books is estimated at about 12.5

million; in the *Yearbook* the print runs of these novels total about 4.1 million copies.

I consulted the *Yearbook* for the years from 1967 to 1979. During these thirteen years, almost one thousand editions of the works of these 24 authors were printed; the combined print runs came to roughly 64 million copies. If the reader on his next trip to the USSR is willing to go to the trouble of visiting bookstores in several cities and trying to buy any of the 111 titles described in this study, he will find that, unless a new shipment has arrived the day before, not a single copy will be on sale except in the foreign-currency store (*Beriozka*). Part of these 64 million copies are in the country's libraries, a few are abroad, but most are on the shelves of private homes.

Here then are the total print runs for the 24 authors according to the *Yearbook*s for the years mentioned above. But let me remind the reader again of the caveat given in the first paragraph of this appendix.

Author	Total Copies Printed	Author	Total Copies Printed
Simonov, K.	7,203,970	Proskurin, P.	2,441,000
Markov, G.	5,162,060	Lipatov, V.	2,192,400
Semenov, I.	4,124,590	Bykau, V.	2,001,900
Aitmatov, C.	3,851,380	Dumbadze, N.	1,770,050
Astaf'ev, V.	3,608,400	Trifonov, Y.	1,747,500
Bondarev, Y.	3,419,700	Efremov, I.	1,695,440
Chakovskii, A.	3,349,000	Rasputin, V.	1,427,000
Soloukhin, V.	2,850,200	Vasil'ev, B.	1,367,300
Shukshin, V.	2,744,000	Ivanov, A.	1,230,700
Nagibin, Y.	2,636,770	Strugatskii, A. and B.	1,181,600
Abramov, F.	2,629,000	Pikul, V.	1,090,000
Belov, V.	2,598,210	Vainer, A. and G.	1,011,750

In the text, no attempt was made to rank the writers' popularity from 1 to 24; for this my sample was too incomplete. No such ranking will be made now; but perhaps a few comments are in order. Although place 3 for Semenov and place 4 for Aitmatov probably reflect their popularity, Rasputin's popularity with the readers is certainly much higher than his place 19 indicates. Similarly, Pikul and the Brothers Strugatskii and Vainer bring up the rear not because the readers lack interest in their work but because, compared to the other 21, they are outsiders in Soviet publishing.

D
An International Comparison of Paper and Book Production

How does Soviet paper and book production compare with that of other countries? The organization that consistently provides such information is UNESCO. The relevant data can be found in section 8 of its *Statistical Yearbook*; the data are supplied by the governments concerned, not by UNESCO. Though there is some disagreement among the governments about the terminology, the *Yearbook*'s figures do convey a general idea. Both tables are taken from the *Yearbook* for 1981.

The first table, taken from section 8.19, gives the consumption of all home-produced paper "for printing and writing," excluding paper for newsprint (and probably for some other uses as well).

1979 Per Capita Consumption of Paper for Printing and Writing (in kilograms)

Country	Paper Consumption
USA	65,603
Germany (West)	51,172
France	37,676
Japan	31,936
United Kingdom	31,794
USSR	5,117

The Soviet Union fares much better when it comes to publication of book titles. The figures are for works of literature only, which is one of 25 categories of books considered in section 8.4. Except for West Germany, "literature" also includes a relatively small percentage of books dealing with literary history and criticism. (See also the explanation preceding and following section 8.4.) It is not clear whether a Soviet title published in five Soviet languages is counted as one or as five.

Literary Works Published in 1978 and 1979

Country	Titles
Germany (West)	11,991
USSR	8,507
United Kingdom	8,474
Japan	7,392
USA	7,062
France	6,933

Index

About the Author

Klaus Mehnert was born in Moscow in 1906. His German family left Russia when the First World War broke out in 1914. His father was killed in action on the western front in 1917; his mother, born of German parents in Russia and deeply steeped in Russian culture, imbued her son with a love for Russian literature and kept alive his knowledge of the Russian language. Between 1929 and 1936 and again between 1955 and 1983, he visited the USSR frequently, sometimes once a year, spending a total of about six years there. As a German citizen, he travelled extensively between the Arctic Ocean and central Asia and traversed Siberia five times.

At the age of 26 he published his first book on Russia. It was based on his personal observations and was translated into a dozen languages, including English (*Youth in Soviet Russia* [New York and London, 1933]). Very early he considered literature a useful means of exploring the Russian mood. Since his first articles on Soviet literature appeared in 1931 and 1932 in the German monthly *Osteuropa* (Eastern Europe), which he edited, except for the Hitler years, from 1931 to 1975, he has frequently returned to this subject. His later publications on Russia have also been concerned with the human aspect and with Soviet literature.